The Disintegration of the Bible

Inkblotitis
Christianity's Dangerous Disease

Book 1:
The Disintegration of the Bible

Greg Fay, Ph.D.

Lighthouse Christian Publishing
Savage, Minnesota

The Disintegration of the Bible

© Greg Fay 2013

All rights reserved. Without limiting the rights under copyright reserved above, no part of this publication may be reproduced, stored in a retrieval system, or transmitted, in any form or by any means (electronic, mechanical, photocopying, recording or otherwise), without the prior written permission of the copyright owner of this book.

Published by
Lighthouse Christian Publishing
SAN 257-4330
5531 Dufferin Drive
Savage, Minnesota, 55378
United States of America

www.lighthousechristianpublishing.com

Contents

Introduction 1
    What Have We Done to the Bible?
    The Purpose of the Book

Claimers and Disclaimers 15
    What I'm Not Saying
    What I Am Saying

Orientation 29
    A Puzzling Predicament
    Context Rules
    Clues from the Past

1. Where'd We Get the Bible, Anyway? 39
    Treasure in the Trash
    A Collection of Inspired Books
    From Books to Book
        The First Testament as Books
        The First (Old) Testament as a Book
        The New Testament as Books
        The New Testament as a Book
    The Lost Books of the Bible
    What's In, What's Out: Who Made the Call?
    Ancient Copies and Versions of the Bible
        The Best Preserved Book in the World
        A Bridge to the West

2. The Bible Set Free 85
    A Dream Come True
    How Much for My Own Personal Version?
    Christianity's Dangerous Idea

3. Why It's Hard to Understand the Bible 119
    Is It Hard to Understand the Bible?

Reason #1: The Scope of the Bible
Reason #2: The Cultures of the Bible
Reason #3: The Genres of the Bible
Reason #4: The Content of the Bible
Reason #5: The Readers of the Bible
    The Personal: Individuality and Traditions of Interpretation
    The Personal: The Effects of Sin
        Self-Injury
        Deceived
        Still Injured and Deceived
Reason #6: The Ways We Read the Bible

4. **The Ways We Read the Bible** 159
What It Means To You
God's First Conversations
Why Do We Read the Bible?
Devotional Bible Reading
    Pietism
    When God Shows Up
    The Random-Point Method
Theological Bible Reading
Argumentative Bible Reading
Why Do *You* Read the Bible?

5. **Diagnosis: Inkblotitis** 203
"The Head of a Fox"
Random Access Bible Reading
What Is Inkblotitis?
    "Inkblot"
    "itis"
    "Inkblot-itis"
Does It Really Make a Difference?
History of an Illness
The Clinical Picture: Causes and Symptoms
    "Psychological Suppositionitis"
    How Can Something So Bad Come from Something So Good?
Wounds to the Church

  Wounds to the Person
    Missing God's Point
    Majoring in the Minors
    The Word of Me
    The Sword in a Stone
    Spiritual Narcissism
  Conclusion
    Diagnosis
    Prognosis

6. Classic Inkblots 253
  1 Corinthians 2:9: "Eye hath not seen, nor ear heard . . ."
  1 Corinthians 13:4-7: "Love is patient; love is kind. . . ."
  Psalm 2:8: "Ask . . . and I will give you the nations . . ."
  Ephesians 3:14-21: ". . . far more than we can ask or imagine . . ."
  Jeremiah 29:11: "I know the plans I have for you . . . ."
  Ecclesiastes 3:1-8: "For everything there is a season . . ."
    How Does It Fit?
    Parties and Puppies
    Life 101: Dust in the Wind
    Divine Barbed Wire
    The Gift of Joy
    Summit View
      The Picture on the Box
      The Question
  The Zoom-Out Challenge
    Matthew 5:5: "Blessed are the meek . . ."
    Romans 8:28: ". . . all things work together for good . . ."
  Conclusion

Appendix 1: Questions from Genesis 311

Preface

Many books are available on how to read the Bible—too many, actually. So why should there be another one, and why would you want to read it? The answer is because this study boils down the most important concepts of effective Bible reading to a single, usable principle and shows you how to apply it in your own Bible reading. Divided into a two-volume set, *Inkblotitis: Christianity's Dangerous Disease* exposes a "serious illness" in today's church, coming from the way we read and use the Bible, and presents a common-sense, contextual method as a return to the inherent nature of the Bible as a collection or library of the books of God.

Briefly introducing the content, nature, and history of the Bible, Book 1 (*The Disintegration of the Bible*) reveals what we've done to the Bible by breaking it up into thousands of small, disconnected pieces that often function more like spiritual or theological "inkblots" than objective revelation of the word of God. This is inkblotitis: when our own subjective thoughts and feelings become the primary lens through which we interpret verses of scripture. (Is there anything more potentially harmful than substituting "what I think" for "what God thinks"?) Replacing the books of God with (disconnected) verses from the Bible is Christianity's dangerous disease—and most of us have it!

Book 2 (*Rediscovering the Books of God*) presents the solution or "treatment." My goal is to help you rediscover the books of God by changing the way you read the Bible. Like putting together a jigsaw puzzle, reading the Bible in context means learning to see/hear each verse as it fits into the shape and purpose(s) of the document it's a part of—that is, the individual Bible book as a whole (Matthew, Mark, Romans, etc.). Having a book-level perspective gives readers a Spirit-authored vantage point to understand the individual verses as part of their inspired picture, as they were originally intended.

At the risk of giving away the secret at the very beginning, the most important principle for understanding the words of scripture as they were originally intended (and thus for treating the serious, hidden illness of inkblotitis) is simply this: *Zoom Out!* Learning to zoom out to the book-level context of each Bible book is the key that opens the door to God's inspired library. I invite you to turn the key and enter his presence.

Numerous people played important roles in helping me with this book. Without going too far into the annals of my personal history, I'd like to express gratitude to the key women in my life, starting with my grandmother, Mavine Snyder, and my mother, Rachel Wallis. Like Lois and Eunice in the life of Timothy (2 Timothy 1:5), the faith that undergirds my work in the Bible first existed in these two strong women of faith in our family. I'm reminded at times that what they passed on to us spiritually came over years of tenacious and practical dedication to us. To illustrate, my mom went to work in a convenience store while I was in college so she could send me money—money used to a large extent to buy books on the Bible that became the building blocks of my personal library. Real faith and love express themselves in the daily grind of life on planet earth. Without the faith and love of my mother and grandmother, my pursuit of scripture would not have been possible.

I'd also like to thank my wife, Cheryl. In more ways than I can express, she has been with me through thick and thin, working hard—with this same sort of enduring, practical faith and love—in order to allow me to pursue God in his word. "Thank you" is infinitely insufficient.

A very special word of appreciation goes to Dr. Carroll D. Osburn, who was a professor of New Testament at Harding School of Theology in Memphis when I attended there. (Most recently, he was the Carmichael-Walling Distinguished Professor of New Testament Language and Literature at Abilene Christian University, from which he retired in 2004.) Dr. Osburn changed my life with the idea of learning to read the Bible in context. If there is anything good in this book, much of the credit goes to him. The bad—I'm sure there are things he would not like or agree with—belongs to me. Dr. Osburn rocked my world with his scholarly and persistent insistence that we learn to ask the right questions of the text, and in particular with the concept of how a verse or passage of scripture functions in the book as a whole. In the course of our studies—on the other hand—he also urged us not to "preach the method." I believe I understand what he meant and hope that the pages of this book do not violate that admonition, but simply elucidate a key idea of Bible reading as a means of pointing to *the Word* of God who gives life.

Several friends have been a great blessing in proofing and editing various versions of the manuscripts. In particular, I appreciate the consistent and thoughtful observations, both conceptual and stylistic, of Dr. Brian Casey and Norbert Herman. Their suggestions impacted and improved many portions of the text (Brian's keen eye for details of English writing has been invaluable throughout the process). Perhaps most valuable of all has been their encouraging interaction as friends.

Reading about God and experiencing him in the books of God (which is the Bible) is a gift beyond price tag. I pray that something in this book will encourage you to keep pulling the ribbon off the package and opening the gift of the words of life.

Introduction

What Have We Done to the Bible?

What if I told you we were in danger of losing one of the most valuable gifts of history? . . . a priceless treasure beyond all wealth and imagination? What if I told you that in many cases we already have?

Most people don't know the Bible as it really is, even those of us who are personally familiar with the Bible. The Bible is a collection of the books of God. In a sense, it's the library of God. Each book contains a unique set of teachings from and about God. Most of us, however, only know the Bible as verses—a verse or a short set of verses that we've heard or memorized or are reading. This switch from *books* to *verses* is not a small change. In fact, it actually redefines the Bible and has real potential to hide and distort the word of God. What message has God revealed to us through the book of Genesis? What about Exodus? What message does God give through the book of Ruth or Isaiah? What primary truths are disclosed in the book of Matthew? Mark? Romans? Revelation? The extent to which we can't answer these questions is the extent to which we have lost the books of God.

Deep within the culture and habits of Christians today a practice thrives—a practice so potentially destructive that it could go down as one of Satan's greatest victories, so cunningly hidden as to be modeled and passed on by the best of church leaders among us, and so subtly subversive that it infects us with the terrifying tendency of turning the "word of God" into the "word of me." From Sunday sermons to small group Bible studies to individual devotions, from classrooms to books to electronic media of all sorts, from our churches to our living rooms, Christians and non-Christians alike have become infected with a disease—a serious and debilitating disease. And what if I told you the illness is hidden, that it doesn't show

Introduction

up on typical scans and masquerades even as something good for us? In other words, it's a silent killer—a sly and cunning virus that cloaks itself in spirituality and even orthodoxy. An ancient evil has awakened and is spreading with new virulence and aggression in our day. Though seemingly innocuous and passive, it attacks all of us as human beings and especially those who would come to know God through his word, the Bible. Promising wisdom, strength, and peaceful clarity, this dangerous disease delivers, in actuality, a deceptive form of ignorance and insecurity, opening its victims to distortions, weakness, and sanitized self-absorption—the opposite of the message of God in Christ revealed to us in the Bible. What is this spiritual, aggressive, modern, serious illness? I call it "inkblot-itis."

I went to church this morning. As I entered the auditorium, an usher handed me a program—a "bulletin"—filled with information about the church and the events of the morning. On the backside of the sermon outline was a list of daily Bible readings for the "Weekly Bible Studies" series. Each day had various, isolated scriptures, grouped by a given topic, and a paragraph of questions and thoughts on that topic. Shortly after finding our seats, we stood and began a period of worship music. The songs often have pieces of verses from the Bible woven into the fabric of the lyric: "Blessed be Your name . . .", "Oh, Lord my shepherd be . . .", "Our Father who art in heaven . . ." Some—both traditional hymns and contemporary worship songs—are mostly scriptures.

At our church, the pastor begins every sermon with a scripture reading—he asks us to stand to honor God's word—of a single passage or sometimes two (Matthew 12:22-28 and 2 Corinthians 10:3-5 this week), from which he highlights the topic of his sermon for the day. He refers to the text from time to time in the course of the message, though I don't know I've ever heard him explain how it contributes to the message of the biblical book as a whole. During a recent sermon, the speaker made the comment, "As you read the Bible, you know how a verse or section will often just sort of jump off the page at you and really connect with what's going on in your life? That's God's way of trying to get your attention and speak to you," he suggested. (The pastors at our church are not unique or

Introduction

exceptionally egregious in this regard. In fact, one of the reasons we attend this church is because of the desire of the senior pastor to be biblical in his teaching.)

While I was thinking about this on my way home from a recent road trip, I looked up and saw a billboard on the side of the road. In big, bold words, it read, "Jesus said, 'It is finished.' John 19:30," followed by a website address. That's all it said. Knowing the context of the reference, I thought that was kind of cool. I'm sure you've seen similar signs with brief passages of scripture. Not just on the side of the road or when we go to church, verses of scripture cited in sermons or scrolled on the screen during worship videos or songs, or John 3:16 posted behind the end zones at football games or pasted on the fronts of t-shirts; but all over the place, we bump into phrases and verses from the Bible.

A few weeks ago, my daughter got an invitation to a friend's high school graduation. It had a picture of a butterfly at the top, followed by the well-known verses, "For everything there is a season, a time to laugh, a time to cry . . ."

Everywhere we look, the Bible is presented to us in pieces—small, colorful pieces—kind of like Legos. These pieces are both the cause and the symptom of the infectious condition threatening the Bible and the church today.

The church has an illness—a serious and systemic illness. It started a long time ago, has grown and spread through the centuries, and is now contracted weekly in our pulpits and reinforced daily in our homes. It fills our publications, clings magnetically to our refrigerators, and is even taught explicitly as the proper way to study the Bible in many "How to Read the Bible" books. Symptoms of the illness affect the whole world—our churches, our schools, our hearts—weakening us as followers of Christ and producing in effect a new form of spiritual captivity. *The church has an illness*—and remember the church is the people—*caused by the way we read and use the Bible.*

"God loves you." That's a clear and simple statement. Clear and simple enough that most everyone reading it will understand it similarly, right? What if, however, I told you it was actually a quotation from the following?

Introduction

"Religion is the opiate of the people"—one of Karl Marx's most frequently quoted statements—does not go far enough. Not just salve for suffering humanity, but—as Sigmund Freud would have it—immature and fearful people create God to give us hope and plans for a brighter future in the face of myriad social, political, and economic ills. "God" is nothing more than a human construct, a symbol that insecure and ambitious people use to gain confidence, and to acquire power and influence over other people. Is there a greater ego trip than to imagine that you speak for God? Is anything more reassuring than to trust that you are living on the basis of his divine will? Priests, ministers, and politicians alike thus evoke divine concert and authority, all the while asserting— whenever the deepest outcries of the human spirit need a little anesthesia—"God loves you."

Knowing that the phrase "God loves you" is a brief citation from the previous paragraph changes everything, doesn't it? It's not hard to recognize that we read it in the first place in a way entirely different from what the writer intended. In fact, we pretty much inverted its meaning.

Let's take another example. Suppose I were to quote, "God hates fags. . . . and so should you." Immediately—if you've been exposed to American television in recent years—the words evoke stark images of angry faced protesters, signs in hand, picketing on street corners at weddings or funerals of homosexuals and soldiers. We all get it, right? But what if the words were really just a small snippet from a young lady's web blog?

"God hates fags." Can you believe someone would actually say that? I saw a strange group of angry-looking people with signs like that outside of a church while driving home from work today. They were yelling and seemed so hateful. I heard on the news that this is some church group that always protests against homosexuals at weddings and stuff. They were protesting at a funeral of a soldier who had died fighting for

Introduction

our country. Can you believe that? This guy gave his life to defend the freedoms that give these people the right to wave such signs! And they do it in the name of God! Could anything be further from the heart of God? That kind of obvious hatred is totally unlike the God of love I read about in the Bible. And it's so counter-productive. Jesus taught us to love our enemies, didn't he? And wouldn't that include those we disagree with? As a Christian, I want to always reflect the heart and life of Jesus and so should you, and so should anyone who claims to be a Christian. At least, that's what I think.

I'm obviously using extreme examples. If, however, we were attempting to understand what someone meant by "God fates fags. . . . and so should you," the first thing we would notice after reading the entire paragraph is that the quotation is obviously taken out of context. It radically distorts the writer's intended meaning by taking very small pieces of a larger context and putting them together in a way that's clearly inconsistent with the intent and purpose of the original.

Reading and understanding a small portion of something in isolation from its context is what I mean by "inkblot-itis" (I'll shorten this to "inkblotitis" from now on). Inkblotitis is a condition where meaning is potentially distorted by the way we read or use a text—all the more so when the things we're reading or talking about are important to us, such as when we read the Bible. For example, the ideas of God and his will for us, issues of right and wrong, images of love, violence and protest as depicted in the previous, made-up citations come with a lot of baggage. I don't mean "baggage" in a negative sense. I just mean that they come with a lot of pre-existing ideas and values that necessarily color the way we think when these ideas are brought up. Our experiences, desires, and resulting thought-life

Introduction

erect thick and dynamic interpretive filters. Allowing these filters to become the primary influence over how we take a word or sentence opens wide, doors of opportunity for individual, subjective readings—readings that will naturally differ from person to person and often distort the intended meaning.

One more example: "For God so loved the world that He gave His only Son that whoever believes in Him might not perish but have everlasting life." Is it possible that we read and quote the Bible—even beloved portions of it like John 3:16—in ways that predispose us to miss or distort the intended meaning? The scary answer, and a main point of this book, is yes.

Introduction

The Purpose of the Book

I'm writing this book to change the way you read the Bible. That's not to say you're doing something bad or harmful when you read the Bible. On the contrary, almost any Bible reading is better than not reading. I'm not trying to be discouraging in any way about reading the Bible. I believe the Bible is the inspired word of God and our most concrete source for coming to know God in Jesus Christ, and nothing matters more than knowing and loving God in Christ. For this reason, not only do I want to encourage Bible reading, I want to promote and foster it. I want to help you see God clearer as you pick up the book of books and turn its pages. With all my heart, I pray that this book will contribute to a renewed passion for knowing and understanding scripture in the churches and in our lives. And we need it! We need it because we've all been infected with inkblotitis.

Let me say off the bat that this is not a technically accurate use of the Latin suffix *itis*. I know. The Latin word *itis* refers to an inflammation or swelling. We thus speak of infections causing inflammation of various organs in our bodies, like tonsillitis or bronchitis, arthritis or appendicitis. When I use the word "inkblotitis," I'm not talking about an inflaming or enlarging of an inkblot, though that's what the word would mean literally. I am, however, talking about a spreading of a particular approach to Bible reading that treats scriptures as small pieces of self-contained communications, almost oracle-like—"inkblots," if you will—and a type of *swelling* that occurs as we read scripture that way.

Obviously, I'm taking the image of an inkblot from Rorschach. You've heard of the Rorschach Inkblot Test—a psychological test used by psychiatrists and psychologists to probe the personalities and psychological health of their patients? The inkblot isn't anything of itself—just a blot of ink (sometimes multi-colored). What individuals see in it, however, is thought to tell us something about the mental and emotional makeup of the person interpreting, that is, "reading" the blot. The test is projective by design. The shapes don't represent anything in particular (*objectively*), but evoke *subjective* responses in the viewers. The test itself doesn't say anything *to* the

Introduction

person, but rather tells us something *about* the person. The test-takers project meaning and thereby reveal things about themselves. So the theory goes.

The vast majority of all modern Bible reading is infected with Rorschach-like inkblotitis. (You may want to put the book down at this point, this is such a potentially alarming statement. But hang in there; there's light at the end of the tunnel.) Be sure you don't misunderstand. I'm not saying that most Bible reading is a misreading or misunderstanding of what we're reading. I'm not saying that at all. "Inkblotitis," as I'm defining it, is not necessarily a misunderstanding or distortion of the meaning of a verse or set of verses. It is, however, the increased potential for such because of the way we are reading it—usually in rather small pieces, separated from their original contexts. The isolated verses (as short as a single phrase or verse, or as long as several chapters) are the inkblots. Removing them from intimate connection with their contexts is the "itis," which, as I'm using it here, amounts to a swelling of our subjective, projective potential (seeing things the way we are inclined or would like to). That doesn't equate to misunderstanding or distortion, but it greatly increases the chances for such. (Let me anticipate a principle: the greater the distance from the controls of the original context, the greater the chance for misinterpretation.) From this perspective, not only would I have to say yes, we are guilty, but would go so far as to say that a large percentage of the way we read and use the Bible today is infected with at least a degree of inkblotitis—reading and using scriptures in isolation from their original contexts to the extent that what we see in them often tells us more about the reader than the (intent of the) writer. In other words, we turn verses of scripture into Rorschach inkblots by the way we read and use them. And almost everyone does it.

Sadly, this is the state of affairs in the church today and consequently the world in general when it comes to the Bible. It is no less than a modern plague upon the churches, and I believe it has serious consequences. That's why we need a new passion and a new sense of purpose for Bible reading. If we believe that God himself (through inspiration) is the ultimate author of what we are reading,

Introduction

and our purpose for reading the Bible is to hear from God and be changed by what we hear, then "Houston"—or maybe I should say "Heaven"—"we have a problem"—a serious problem. "Inkblotitis" is dangerously increased potential for *projecting meaning onto biblical texts* by isolating them into small, disconnected entities—and the scary fact that we do it all the time.

What if when we go to read our Bibles or when we hear verses of scripture quoted or read, we actually reveal more about ourselves than we learn about God? What if we turn inspiration into self-reflection? . . . a little navel-gazing, to use a common expression? Do we ever do that? What if we do it even a little? Is that a problem? When I gaze into the looking glass of scripture to see a reflection of the Creator himself so I can learn about him, to become more and more like him, to hear an objective word of God, but instead, like Narcissus in the ancient Greek myth, I see and fall more and more in love with myself; that is the subtle but tragic potential of inkblotitis: spiritual narcissism! Biblical writers refer to it as having a hard heart—eyes that don't see; ears that don't hear. It's what full-blown inkblotitis looks like. It's the opposite of why we read the Bible, and sadly, it's all over the place. (Of course, those of us who use the Bible frequently would rarely if ever suspect such a condition could apply to us, would we? Have you ever noticed how folks seem to use the Bible to support whatever they believe, and sometimes conversation seems futile?)

When I was in graduate school, I had a Hebrew professor, Dr. Jack P. Lewis, who used to make us sing children's songs in Hebrew (Dr. Lewis has two earned doctorates, a Ph.D. in Old Testament from Hebrew Union and a Ph.D. in New Testament from Harvard). Here we are a group of mostly twenty-something-year-old geeky guys and one very intelligent and serious young lady (you'd have to be, to be in with that group), aspiring to be scholarly preachers/teachers of the Bible, assembling for our very stressful session on the fundamentals of Hebrew grammar. Dr. Lewis was known for his no-nonsense approach to the classroom and demand for excellence from his students. To put it bluntly: he scared us to death! On several mornings, however, while we were all still half-asleep but already

Introduction

beginning to sweat over our turns at the exercises, Dr. Lewis would start the class by singing to us in Hebrew (not very pleasantly, I might add, but he didn't care; that was beside the point). He sang to us in Hebrew—elementary school, children's songs (that's all we could handle). Then he'd have us join in: *Sha-na To-va Sha-na ya-fa bru . . .* I'm a visual person with a bad short-term memory, so I never could remember the words and felt rather stupid as I stumbled along. It was funny and seemed rather silly to us at the time. But Dr. Lewis was simply exposing us to one of the best ways to learn new words and ideas, putting them to music. Simple repetition set to music has been used throughout history to instruct children and adults.

After we butchered the songs, on one occasion Dr. Lewis made another point—a point that has since become more profound to me. He said that most people in churches learn more of what they know about God and the Bible ("doctrine," we sometimes call it) from the songs that they sing (traditionally church songs and hymns and now praise and worship songs) than they do from the Bible itself. Sobering thought, isn't it? Nothing inherently wrong with it ("Jesus love me . . ."),[1] unless it really is where our Bible learning stops. Putting scriptures into songs is another way we separate them from their Bible contexts. It's great for learning, teaching children basic tenets of the faith, reminding us of the things we hold sacred. On the other hand, if our understanding of some aspect of God and the Bible comes primarily from what we've heard in a song, it's another clear example of how we often experience the Bible in pieces. By its very nature, it's subject to inkblotitis.

The purpose of this book is not only to point out the pervasive problem of how we often "break-up" the Bible, but also to offer a common-sense basis for how to put it back together—to teach and demonstrate principles of good Bible reading as a solution, a treatment, if you will, for the serious illness of inkblotitis. Inkblotitis is how to read the Bible to *miss* God's point;[2] I want to show you, or remind you, how to read the Bible to *get* God's point. The treatment is found in learning to see/hear Bible verses within the framework of their original contexts.[3] ("Duh!" might be an appropriate response at this point, since this is something we've been told all our lives, but

Introduction

keep reading.) By "context," I'm referring to the environment or setting of the individual Bible books—66 of them in the standard Protestant Old and New Testaments, 13 or 17 more if you're reading a Catholic or Greek Orthodox Bible.

The Bible was not written at one time as a single volume. On the contrary, the individual "books" of the Bible were written during a 1,500 year span by as many as 40 different authors. The Bible is, therefore, actually a collection of books that reflect specific historical and literary settings. A miracle of inspiration is that the combination of all the books produces a unified, albeit multi-dimensional (colorful), picture of God and his interactions in human history. Ultimately, good Bible reading will frame and condition its understanding of biblical writings within the overall picture or "context" of the Bible as a whole (I'll call this the "Bible-level" context). But because the individual books were written by different authors . . . at different times . . . in different circumstances, each individual book provides the most basic and direct set of controls over the meaning of passages (verses) from that book. This is the "book-level" context.

Like a mountainside panorama, each Bible book projects its own individual snapshot of some awesome aspect of God and his kingdom, and, like the outside wrapper or plastic "skin" of a liquid-filled container, each book gives shape to the meaning of the contents of that book. When we take small pieces of the books out of the control of the confines of those books—their defining contexts—like cutting out a small section of a picture from a magazine, taking an individual stone from a mosaic, or, even better, like removing a single piece of a put-together puzzle, we turn those snapshots into inkblots. In many ways in today's religious world, the Bible is not a collection of divinely inspired books that fit nicely together to create God's revealed word to us, but is more like a great big pile of inkblots (or Legos, to retrieve the earlier reference). We pick up verses or sections of verses from time to time, hold them up, use them as we like, and then thrown them back into the pile.

As I suggested earlier (with the "Duh!" comment), the idea that we should understand a Bible text within its own context—its literary and historical contexts to be more specific (I'll explain these

Introduction

below)—is not a new idea. It's really just common sense. It's been around for about as long as reading and writing, and is always "taught" as a fundamental tenet of good Bible study. We've heard it all our lives. Problem is . . . we just don't do it. It's like one of those common-sense things we all know we ought to do, but somehow never get around to doing. You know, like losing weight and exercising, or flossing our teeth after every meal. It's bricks and mortar, bread and butter. (That's part of the reason this is such a serious issue.) We all ought to do it, yet very few do. Most of us don't even know how; our leaders never taught us. Critical for the treatment of the modern plague of inkblotitis, then, is a renewed sense of purpose to read/hear scriptures within their own literary and historical contexts. And it's not as hard as you might think, just different.

In summary, then, the purpose of this book is twofold: (1) I want to alert you to the problem of reading and using the Bible in small, disconnected pieces—thus exposing the hidden illness of inkblotitis. And (2) I want to propose a common-sense, purpose-filled method of reading the Bible to treat the illness. Learning to read/use the Bible in context, as simple as that sounds, is no less than the rediscovery of a doorway to a treasure-store of God's life-giving revelation of himself to us in his written word. It is, in essence, a rediscovery of the books of God.

Introduction

Chapter Resources

Osborne, Grant R. *The Hermeneutical Spiral.* Downers Grove, IL: InterVarsity, 1991.

Notes

1. Putting spiritual concepts into songs is actually very biblical and goes way back, as, for example, when God instructed Moses to use a song to remind the Israelites of critically important ideas and values (Deuteronomy 31:16-22).
2. Or perhaps more accurately "how to read the Bible *and* miss God's point," since no one would intentionally miss the point.
3. What I'm proposing in this book is really one particular piece of a comprehensive biblical hermeneutic (see, e.g., Osborne, *The Hermeneutical Spiral*). The concept of interpreting biblical verses within their own literary context is by no means everything, but I believe it is the most fundamental aspect of a successful hermeneutic, seriously under-valued and -achieved both in scholarly exegesis and everyday Bible reading today.

Claimers and Disclaimers

What I'm Not Saying

Never Use a Single Verse by Itself—Not!

Before diving in to the ins and outs of inkblotitis, I'd like to be clear about a few things that I'm not saying in this book. First, I'm not saying that a verse or short set of verses can never be self-contained and communicate truth by itself. Depending on the type of literature you're reading (the genre), some verses may in fact be intended as self-contained—picture-in-a-picture—ideas, axioms, or what I call "faith summaries." Obviously, psalms and proverbs come to mind (though the question of whether there is a bigger-picture structure or thematic flow is always a legitimate question). The parables of Jesus are another example of relatively small pieces of communication that tell a "complete" story as isolated units.[1] Their role in the bigger-picture of the book as a whole is an essential question, nonetheless.

Thinking about content and meaning raises the rather complex philosophical and linguistic question of how much context (common ground) is necessary for objective communication to take place? The answer depends on numerous factors, including the genre and the ideas being communicated, among other things. I'm not trying to say that objective truth can never be communicated briefly or through short expressions. If there's enough common ground, something as small as a glance or a single word can produce shared meaning. If you're in a building, smell smoke, and someone yells "Fire!", then just one word can do the trick. In a different context (say you are blindfolded in front of an old-fashioned *firing* squad), it could mean something entirely different. What this really shows is that even if a piece of communication is brief or apparently "contextless," we will wrap it with enough of a surrounding to make it comprehensible (if possible). There's really no such thing, then, as contextless communication or understanding, and the smaller the written or spoken context, the more it will come from somewhere else, supplied by one's own values and thought-world. So, I'm not saying that no sentence, verse or set of verses is self-contained. What I am saying, however, is that the more context, the more the chances for a meeting of the minds. I am saying that the context is determinative for shaping and grasping the meaning, and that whatever context exists should always be taken into consideration when trying to understand the meaning of something.

A unit of thought may stand on its own, but it may not; and if it's a part of a larger context, then *The Question* (more on this below) should be asked about its potential relation to the bigger (in this case, book-level) picture. Take the Parable of the Good Samaritan, for example. What purpose does it serve in Luke's unfolding story about Jesus? Is it just a wonderful, picture-in-a-picture that we can take out of Luke and use as a message about equality and compassion for all? Is it "printable" as an individual snapshot? Perhaps. But is there a deeper, more God-shaped meaning because it is somehow organically connected to the fabric of Luke's inspired bigger picture? How does it fit and help create Luke's book-level story about Jesus? Would I be wrong to say that I bet most of us have no idea?

Isolating Verses Always Leads to Misunderstanding—Not!

I said this earlier, but let me say it again here: I'm also not intending to say that whenever we take a verse or set of verses out of context—like the Parable of the Good Samaritan or of the Sower, for example—and use it as a self-contained unit, we are necessarily misreading or distorting it; or that we can't receive inspired truth from such a passage. In short, not every disconnected reading is a misreading. Neither is every de-contextualized ("undressed") reading destructive and void of inspiration. Often we get it right because of the history of Bible reading and interpretation, and our own (church) contexts; and sometimes, there are multiple levels of legitimate meaning. I'm not saying that sections of scripture don't communicate spiritual points that can be pulled out (abstracted) and taught or applied (in many cases, preached) to a modern audience or used to teach elementary and foundational tenets of our faith. In fact, I think that's what we're supposed to do. To understand what *I am* saying in this book, however, you need to understand, or come to understand, the difference between *sharing* or *professing* our faith and *reading* the Bible *in order to* hear from God and thus *acquire* our faith. There is a fundamental difference between reading to acquire understanding and reciting to share it. Does that make sense? And I ask the question, do we still have things to learn from the books of God?

The question is whether we've first understood a verse or section in its original context. If not, how do we know that we're getting and abstracting the right point(s), and using the right verses? Our goal is to become so familiar with the big-picture contexts of Bible books that even when we use single verses or snippets of scripture, we interpret them in light of their book-level contexts. We remember the overall picture; we take the context with us, so to speak. This is, in my opinion, an important responsibility of a pastor, speaker or writer when using quotations of scripture in sermons or other public forums. The point is not to condemn every shortened or isolated use of the Bible as inherently evil, but—in all seriousness—to alert us to the real, insidious potential of treating all scripture as disconnected units (like oracles or proverbs), disregarding the bigger-picture contexts in which God saw fit to speak and preserve for us in writing. I am deeply concerned about turning kingdom snapshots into religious inkblots that in many cases come from and go toward supporting what we already believe or our personal agendas; and in some cases that function more like compact mirrors (recalling the analogy of Narcissus) than windows to God.

Introduction

We'll All Agree and Get Along—Not!

Though I think there is potential for increased dialogue and possibly even greater unity in the church from paying closer and consistent attention to the book-level contexts of the Bible, I do not want to give the impression that I believe in a sort of utopian, we-will-all-agree-and-get-along-fine community if we just read the Bible this way. There will always be differences of opinion and different interpretations of biblical texts. There were dramatic disagreements about who Jesus was and the meaning of his teachings even while he was here and then in the early church. I'm not intending to say that we will always agree if we just read everything in context. Of course, there are other powerful, spiritual variables at play that keep us from getting along and being Christ-like in all situations than just how we read the Bible.

I'm also not trying to say that we can suspend subjectivity when we read the Bible. To see and interpret things according to our own unique—always distorted to some extent—perspective is an inherent characteristic of the human condition. Some things are difficult to understand, moreover, and we certainly will not see everything alike. Be careful not to take this to the other extreme, though. It doesn't mean that we can't see *anything* alike. We communicate constantly, agree on many things, and live on the basis of belief in objective truth every minute of every day. I do believe that learning to do this with scripture—learning to read and hear the words of scripture with an eye on their original contexts—is an essential part of the remedy for inkblotitis. And in the end, it may help us get along better.

You Need to Be a Bible Scholar—Not!

Here's something else I'm not saying: I'm not saying that the message and messages of the Bible are esoteric and difficult to understand, and that you have to become some kind of Bible scholar or a member of our club to hear the voice of God.[2] Clearly, some things in the Bible are hard to understand. The authors often wrote about the most complex topics in life, issues about life and death that thinking people have debated since time began. Certainly, distances of time and culture create gaps of meaning that sometimes make it difficult for us to understand the writings of scripture as they were originally intended. (We'll explore the issue of why the Bible is hard to understand in Chapter 3.) But please don't mistake the messenger for the message. Messages of faith, hope, and love come shining through the pages and stories of the Bible to inspire us to a higher vision of life and encourage us in our struggles.

I'm not trying to make this more complicated than it needs to be. The simplest things are often the most profound, for the very reason that they are "simple" and therefore most basic. "But what you are saying sounds complicated at times. Can't I just read it?" The answer is yes—just read it. But read it like a book, each book as its own individual and complete book, not like a reference book. And know that the message of God's saving love for us in Christ is simple and clear enough that anyone can hear and receive it, and that often happens by a simple telling of those truths from one person to another. When a young man tells a high school friend how his life can be made better because God really does love him no matter what he's done, the truth of God is effectively communicated, and you don't have to know a thing about literary contexts.

The Holy Spirit Is Gone or Silent—Not!

Finally, let me say as loudly and strongly as I possibly can that God is God and in no way do I ever intend to suggest that God can't communicate his inspired word through the Holy Spirit whenever and however he likes, to anyone, by whatever means he chooses—inkblot . . . sunspot . . . or whatever. I never intend anything I say to suggest otherwise. The Spirit of God is not subject to our weaknesses, notions, or methods—or lack thereof. He is the God of the moment just as much as the God of history. But he is also as much the God of history as of the moment. The present alone is not God. The past by itself is not God. God is the sum of the past, the present,

Introduction

and the future. Anything less limits our perspective and approach to God.

I pray that you will never think I am somehow intending to put God in a box by the way I present the ideas and principles of this book. I couldn't if I wanted to. On the contrary, what I want to offer is a reminder, a renewed call to appreciate and make our best use, of an invaluable work of the Holy Spirit—the very words of the book he inspired. That's part of the reason I'm writing this book and what *I am* saying.

What I Am Saying

I am saying that we read the Bible much more *out* of context than we do *in* context. In fact, it's normal to have very little idea how a passage fits within the bigger picture of the book from which we take it. Even when we are reading through the Bible, we start and stop and forget what we read and don't really connect what we are reading with the rest of the book (at least not very carefully). Though almost any Bible reading is better than no reading, I believe out-of-context Bible reading—inkblotitis—is a serious problem. God saw fit to reveal essential teachings of Jesus, the Word of God, in the form we have them. Ignoring and/or abusing those contexts would seem to suggest a disregard for the very work of God and for those who literally gave themselves to make it available to us (more on this later).

If our own subjective impressions, opinions, or internal voices are really all we need to draw close to God, then what do we need with the Bible in the first place? The fact that God spoke to us through his son Jesus, revealed through the writings of scripture, suggests that we need to hear something that comes from outside of us. *We need the Word of God.* The Word that comes from God is ultimately the only cure for all forms of spiritual illness, including inkblotitis. On the other hand, the more we read and hear Bible passages in isolation from their original contexts, the more we remove the God-given controls over their meanings. The more we remove the God-given control over the meaning of a text, the more we hear what we already think and interpret things the way we are accustomed to or want to, and thereby invite ("inflame" or "swell"—remember the *itis* part of "inkblotitis") our subjective, sinful potential to speak from ourselves to ourselves. Like pricking a water-balloon with a sharp pin, our subjective ideas come gushing out and soak (= control) the meaning. If, moreover, the diction of our inner voice springs in any way from the misleadings of the deceiver,[3] whose original temptation was, not coincidentally, for us to put ourselves in the place of God, how destructive is the potential of inkblotitis? Ultimately, it can result in or at least contribute to a sort of lordship or tyranny of the subjective, a condition that I believe has replaced other forms of political and spiritual suppression that have arisen throughout the course of history.[4]

This book thus speaks to the indiscriminate mysticism of our day, which is a part of the generalized disintegration of the Bible, of community, and ultimately of the self. For what I hope are the majority of the readers of this book, forgive me for having said that, that way. What it means is that far too often, too many people today listen to God only from within themselves. We use the Bible merely as a stimulant, not as the objective, eternal word of God. Like spiritual incense we light to put us in the mood, we use the Bible to evoke what's already in us, to bring it to the surface, so to speak. We hear the voice of God from within, but rarely, if ever, from without. This is, I believe, one of the greatest tragedies and threats of our day. We believe the voice we hear when we use the Bible to be the voice of God, and in many cases it probably is. But how do we know? How do you know? A mystic knows because she knows. But so do many of the most stubborn, unchristlike characters around. They are what they are. They know what they know. Just because—because they know it or feel it. God told them.

The supreme value of the word of God revealed to us in the Bible is, however, that its messages come to us from outside of us—beyond our inclinations, our thoughts and feelings, beyond our imaginations. This is why it *is the word of God* that can lead us to salvation. David Daniell captures a vital piece of this idea in his book on the history of the English Bible:

> God's Word, while so often balm to the bruised spirit, is not intended, in the modern shallow phrase, "to make me feel good about myself": a second's thought should show that by his very nature God is different from humanity, and his expressed word is usually unexpected.[5]

Without the "unexpected" voice of God outside of us, we can't be saved. Without the voice of God outside of us, we don't need to be saved—and I know that's not true.

Each perspective—the Bible as brief, isolated calls to the subjective (which we know as verses) and the Bible as interconnected revelation from outside of us (the books of God)—produces a radically different paradigm or model for how we approach and use the Bible. This is the underlying premise of this book. One approach results in inkblotitis; the other, the word of God.

So . . . what is the Bible? A pile of verses. It's a pile of disconnected verses. Or perhaps a small set of verses—memorized, framed, or refrigerator-posted. What is the Bible? It's a collection of sound bites, played—sometimes looped—by preachers, evangelists, Christians, and within our own heads. A string of proof-texts, punctuating a sermon. What is the Bible? An assortment of puzzle pieces—a great big box full of disconnected pieces, from different puzzles no less, mixed together for maximum accessibility (and confusion). What is the Bible? It's a set of inkblots—spiritual inkblots of oddly shaped snippets of inspired speech that instead of illuminating us with God's word evoke the best of interpretations—or the worst—from each of us. "What do *you* see?" "What does this mean *to you?*" This is the Bible, at least for many people. Verses. For the most part, our culture, both inside and outside the churches, has come to know and identify the Bible as verses from above or long ago—short sayings or sections of scripture that may or may not be divinely inspired.

The problem is . . . that's not what the Bible is or ever was. It's not thousands of isolated verses or sets of verses, given as self-contained aphorisms, proverbs, or oracles from God. It's not a collection of sound bites from heaven. It's not self-adhesive, punch-out confirmations of what we already think or preach. It's not thousands of spiritual inkblots to be held up so that our divine sides might be summoned to speak. On the contrary, the Bible is a library of Holy Spirit-inspired books—communications from God—revealing the mind, heart, desires, and plan of God for humanity. It is God's revelation of himself to us. And he gave it to us as historically inspired writings (of various types) that we've collected together into a book we call "the Bible"—the book (though the Latin word *biblia* was actually plural—the books). The Bible is really the books of God. *I believe*

Introduction

the disintegration of the books of God into verses from the Bible—randomly sorted, subjectively used—to be one of the greatest dangers within Christianity today. It is, in fact, Christianity's dangerous disease. On the other hand, the books of God are the key to spiritual health and freedom, releasing us to a lifelong journey of knowing and loving God in Christ.

In addition to the dilution of the word of God caused by inkblotitis, along with the moral and spiritual consequences (we'll explore these as we go), a troubling footprint of inkblotitis is the distorted views of God and the Bible that come from using verses in isolation from their contexts. How many people are pushed away from Christianity by destructive images of God and his nature, and distorted teachings about Christ and the church given to them by folks—often well-intentioned folks—using snippets of scripture to present caricature-like portraits of God and "biblical" ideas. To be more personal, what if what you've been told is not really what the Bible says? What if what you've been taught about God came from someone who was using verses out of context? On the other side of the coin, think of the potentially life-changing, renewing release becoming aware of the dangers of inkblotitis offers as an incentive for rediscovering the books of God. An early reader of this material called my attention to an aspect of this potentially liberating benefit. In effect, he said, "It's exciting to think that some of the deeply embedded (negative) images and ideas I have about God and guilt and sin may very well not be from the Bible at all." How freeing it is for many of us to learn that what we were told about God or Jesus or Christianity simply isn't true, that it didn't come from God or from the Bible, but from somewhere else. Then imagine the exciting adventure ahead of rediscovering the real God in his real word for the rest of your life.

In the following chapters, we'll explore some basic ideas relating to the challenge of putting together the picture of a Bible book and then reading/hearing each section of the book as part of that overall picture. In the first part—Book 1—we look at the problem (the illness), which amounts to how to read the Bible to *miss* God's point. In the second half—Book 2—we'll explore the treatment: how to read the Bible to *get* God's point. If you don't see how a verse or set of verses fits within its wider, book-level context, you can't know if you know what it means. If you aren't seeing it in close connection with its surrounding picture, you have removed the divinely inspired controls God placed around how the verse is to be understood. This is inkblotitis, and I suspect you have it. But don't feel alone, we all have it. It is no less than an epidemic in the modern church and consequently the world.

To put it bluntly: the way we read and use the Bible is making us sick. The remedy is a renewed passion and purpose for hearing the Word of God through the words of his books. The problem is what we've done with God's revealed word: we've blown it into pieces (or verses, as we call them). The solution is to dump out the pieces we've accumulated in our theological closets (for some that's a little, for others it's a lot) and rediscover (= reassemble) the books of God. The solution is to start over and replace Bible verses with the books of God.

Introduction

Chapter Resources

Daniell, David. *The Bible in English: Its History and Influence.* London: Yale University, 2003.

Thompson, Mark D. "Biblical Interpretation in the Works of Martin Luther." In *A History of Biblical Interpretation: The Medieval through the Reformation Periods*, pp. 299-318. Edited by Alan J. Hauser and Duane F. Watson. Grand Rapids: Eerdmans, 2009.

Notes

1. It is believed that in the earliest period of church history, the stories and sayings of Jesus circulated as more isolated, individual items that were told and retold by the early Christian communities, as they recalled and relived the events and teachings of Jesus' life. As the passion narrative of Mark and the Gospels as a whole illustrate, however, they were soon organized into more thorough-going, event- and theologically driven accounts.
2. This is sometimes referred to as the "clarity" or "perspicuity of scripture," that core teachings are clear and can be ascertained by ordinary Christians and that difficult parts can be understood in light of clearer passages. Martin Luther (cited in Thompson, "Biblical Interpretation," 303) provided one of its classic statements:
    > "Or tell me, if you can, who finally decides when two statements of the fathers contradict themselves? Scripture ought to provide the judgement, which cannot be delivered unless we give to Scripture the chief place in everything, that which was acknowledged by the fathers: that is, that it is in and of itself the most certain, the most accessible, the most clear thing of all, interpreting itself, approving, judging and illuminating all things. (WA 7.97.19-24)"
3. Compare Romans 8, in the context of Romans, of course.
4. If, moreover, much of what we get out of the Bible comes from what we bring to it as individuals, this raises the important question of who is shaping what we as individuals think and know. Who is providing the education that feeds our interpretive framework in today's world? American pop-culture, transfused through the media, public education,

and the internet, now plays a major role in what most of us bring to the table. If political and religious institutions of the past controlled what people were to believe and think through overt methods of power and suppression, a potential, new form of tyranny arises from who controls and proliferates information today (which is an essential part of any form of tyranny).
5. Daniell, *The Bible in English*, 14.

Orientation

A Puzzling Predicament

Most school have some sort of "orientation" to help young people with the transition when they go off to college, leaving behind the familiarity and protections of home. As we enter "the brave new world" of considering how we read the Bible and of learning to read verses as part of their book-level contexts, a little orientation is in order. To that end, I'd like to introduce some key concepts that I'll use throughout the book, starting with a puzzle.

As a single piece of a puzzle looks much like a Rorschach inkblot, putting together and taking apart a puzzle provides a rich image for learning to read/hear the Bible within its own book-level contexts. A biblical book is like a puzzle—not in the sense that it's mysterious and we need some kind of secret code or hidden key to unlock its meaning. I don't mean "puzzle" that way. I mean it in the sense of a single, multi-colored picture that has been separated ("cut") into smaller parts. Bible books become like puzzles when we demarcate verses or sections and then attempt—for whatever reason—to understand them in those isolated units. Learning to read and hear verses within their own contexts is, in theory, no more complicated than putting together the picture of an individual Bible book and then interpreting each individual verse or section as it relates to the picture as a whole.

Like putting together a puzzle, if you see the big picture, it's much easier to understand the individual parts (that's why the picture on the box helps so much). You can point to any piece of a puzzle while it's put together and see clearly what that individual piece is and how it relates to the whole. This is the common-sense, "picture-point" method of Bible reading that I want to promote here. If you "see the *picture*," you can easily "get the *point*." See the picture, get the point. Take the puzzle apart, on the other hand, and you have a pile

Introduction

of inkblots (unless, of course, you remember the big picture). Hold up one of those blots (a "verse-blot" or "versing," I call it), the way we often use scripture, and the meaning becomes "to each his own." (I'll use another way of envisioning this "picture-point" method in the Conclusion as the solution for every potential Bible-verse inkblot.)

Biblical passages (as with any sort of written communication) live in reciprocal, essentially organic, relationship to the words and ideas surrounding them. Similar to the image of a puzzle and perhaps even more telling is to compare the parts of scripture to a living creature. The parts of our bodies, for example, only have meaning in relation to our bodies as wholes. As vital as a heart is, take it out, place it by itself on the floor, and what happens? It might beat for a minute or two (how fascinating, even if a little disgusting), but in the end both the heart and the patient die. A heart by itself has no meaning. That's not completely true. It does have meaning. It's just not what it's supposed to be; it's no longer a functioning "heart." It's a gross distortion of its meaning and purpose, to say the least. The same with every part of our bodies, and we understand those parts in relation to the whole.

Now, an alarming affirmation. This is perhaps the most important assertion and principle of this book ("If you take anything home with you . . ."). If you don't know how a verse or set of verses fits in the overall picture of the book as a whole, you don't know if you know what it means. Put another way: if you can't see how a verse functions in relation to the verses around it and to the book as a whole, if you don't see how the part contributes to the whole (even if you can't articulate it like a scholar or a grammarian—if you are not reading it *as* it fits, in other words), you can't know if you are understanding it properly. Notice that I didn't say you are misunderstanding it; I said you *don't know* if you understand it, because, in essence, what you have is an inkblot, a single piece of a disassembled puzzle. Even if it's a rather small, self-contained unit of thought, simple and easy to understand—at least at first glance ("God loves you")—words and sentences carry all sorts of color and shades of meaning that are significantly if not distortingly altered when taken out of their contexts. No matter how short or important or seemingly self-contained an isolated passage is (John 3:16, for example), it's like a heart beating on the floor. It might be interesting and even amazing in its own right, but ultimately distorted and potentially worthless for the purpose for which it was designed.

How does John 3:16 fit within the overall setting and purposes of John's Gospel? What function or role does it play in communicating John's primary message(s)? What *are* John's primary messages? What about 1 Corinthians 13—the love chapter? What blood does it pump through the veins of Paul's message to the church at Corinth? (That one's pretty easy to see, isn't it? once you start thinking like this.) What about Acts 2:38 or Romans 3:23 or 12:1-2 or Hebrews 11 or Revelation 13 or . . .? (If those verses don't mean anything to you, that's okay. In some ways you have an advantage when it comes to reading them in context over those of us who "know" them inside and out—less "theological" baggage).

Bottom line: If you don't know verses of scripture within the contexts of the books of the Bible, then you have lost the divine Spirit of control God placed around the meaning of those verses. Ultimately what we have lost, then, is the God-given control over the meaning of the words of the Bible.

Indulge me one last time for now: if you don't know how a verse or set of verses fits into its own book-level picture, if you don't see how that verse helps to accomplish the picture and purposes of that book, if you don't see it as a piece of a bigger whole, *you have inkblotitis*. Inkblotitis is a loss of control over what voices you are hearing; and that's scary, especially when it comes to questions of love and war, life and death, heaven and hell. See why I say this is a serious problem? Do you think it might have anything to do with division, hypocrisy, impotence, and various other evils in the church?

Introduction

Context Rules

Another way of saying the same thing—and this is the oft-vocalized-but-seldom-implemented rule—is that the specific meaning of a word or phrase, a verse or a chapter depends on the context. Generally speaking, "context" is everything that surrounds and gives place and meaning to something else. It's used for words and sentences in literature and for facts and circumstances in events (you've heard of "circumstantial evidence"). One is the *literary* context; the other, the *historical* context. The historical context, as I'm using it, has two levels. In a general sense, it refers to the culture and influences of the times. In a more specific sense, it refers to the particular set of circumstances that produced the writing. Both the literary and the historical contexts are important when reading books of the Bible—that's why I talk about reading a Bible book within its own literary and historical contexts. Throughout this book, I often bundle these ideas into the phrase "book-level context." The book-level context is, first of all, the words, phrases, sentences, and paragraphs of a particular book and only that book (this is the literary context); and, second, everything in the surrounding circumstances—the general culture and the specific situation—that went into producing that book (this is the historical context). Like a balloon to the air inside it, the book-level context gives shape to the meaning of the individual items within that book.

I know this begins to sound a little technical at this point. So don't worry too much about it for now, especially the historical context. There is a sense in which our ability to see and reconstruct the details of the historical context depends on the literary context. In other words, we wouldn't know anything about what was going on unless we read about it in the book (sort of like hearing one side of a telephone conversation). We get our most concrete ideas about the situation, therefore, from the book itself. In this sense, the literary—all the words of a given book—is primary. Fundamentally, we have to start with the text. So focus on that. *Focus on reading the book.* When it comes to context, remember that the book is best: history is good, books and commentaries can be better because they focus on the issues at hand, but the book is best. The picture that emerges from the text comes from the words, the events that produced those words (often implied to us as readers rather than stated explicitly), and how the writer hopes they are to impact the situation. When we read the book as a whole, we begin to get the picture these contexts produce.

From where and how do words get their meaning? One way to answer the question is with the idea or analogy of focus. All sight—or actually the objects of sight ("sights," you might say)—must be brought into focus in order to see clearly. The light from the objects converges onto a screen through some sort of lens, which *focuses* the image. Similarly, words and ideas get their specific color and shape, focused as meaning on the screens of our minds, by other ideas that surround and connect to them. This is the context. Some of it comes from what we already know (our assumptions, thoughts, and values); the specifics come from the sentences and paragraphs we're reading.

When we take a passage of scripture outside of its book-level context, we remove the inspired lens of focus and replace it with our own set of mental and emotional glasses. Our own knowledge and perspectives will always be involved (we couldn't think or read the words without them), but removing the biblical context removes the more specific, author-supplied control over the meaning. Small wonder that we often take away only what we bring to the table. Instead of being overwhelmed by the presence of a Holy God who seeks to change us into his image, we tend to see only what we already see. We think the way we see/hear it (= interpret) is the right and maybe only way to see it, while often knowing very little about the bigger picture of God's focusing context, maybe even missing the main point altogether. This is the highly subjective perspective that inkblotitis creates. (After all, "It's *my* faith and *my* life and *my* world." But how much is it really like God or a part of *his* kingdom?) In other cases, we don't understand the Bible at all and quit trying, maybe quit reading altogether. This, too, can be the result of the way we've been taught to read it. I don't know about you, but when I read the Bible, I want to hear from God, even if (like Isaiah in the presence of a Holy God) I am for a time undone, only to be put back together by the loving and artistic hands of the Creator himself. When we read the Bible with book-level focus, we are attempting to allow the literary and historical contexts of that book—a divine moment in time—to serve as the primary lens of focus for understanding what we read. We are, in essence, yielding to the Spirit of God.

Is a particular topic—say love, for example—an important theme of the text I'm reading? Or is it more my question than a concern of the writer? What's he trying to accomplish? How do I know what ideas or exhortations are most important? When we pull a verse or set of verses out of context, we have no real way to know the relative value of what we're reading: Is verse 1 as important as verse 32? Should I underline verse 15—put it on a billboard or postcard, perhaps—or maybe verse 20 instead? That's not intended to say that some verses are unimportant or less inspired; it just means that they function differently. For example, when Paul says, "Grace and peace to you from our Lord Jesus Christ" in almost all of his letters, do we take that to be the main point of the letter? Or, to put it another way, if we can't see the forest, our attention may be on the individual trees to such an extent that we miss the writer's perspective and primary purpose. Inkblotitis sets us up for potentially majoring in the minors (I seem to recall Jesus saying something to the Pharisees about that) or the proverbial "miss-the-forest-for-the-trees" syndrome, and we just might miss God's point in favor of our own interests.

It doesn't have to be that way, though. Many facets of understanding a piece of written communication (no matter what type or "genre") are basic, common-sense concepts and are for the most part—if the author has any degree of skill—inherent in the text. Others are more stylistically and culturally based. Either way, a common-sense, picture-point (see the picture, get the point) approach to Bible reading begins to notice such things as the place and repetition of words, word groups, transitions, summaries, and various other (literary) devices that help to weave a tapestry of meaning out of the individual threads of words and sentences.

Just as a puzzle has a built-in design that causes the pieces to fit together and create a unified whole, so also structure plays a vital role in the literary context of a Bible book. Sentences have structure;

so do stories and letters and poetry. Even words have a basic structure through the order of the letters. Structure is, therefore, a fundamental characteristic of communication at all levels. You don't read a book backwards, for example. You can't end with the beginning or randomly pull a section out of the middle and expect it to retain its meaning. A common-sense reading of a biblical text will, therefore, be aware of the structure to a certain extent, even if it's just an intuitive, perhaps subconscious awareness that comes from the natural design and effectiveness of the text itself. And don't let the word "structure" throw you. It's really just another way of talking about how the parts fit together. Like looking for a particular section or shape when putting together a puzzle, paying attention to the design of a document—where and how a verse or set of verses fits—increases the likelihood that we will understand the intended role or function. "How does it fit?" is really a question of structure, and "structure" in a literary sense has to do with the shape of the text or story.

Introduction

Clues from the Past

Though much of this is common sense and applies to almost any kind of document, because the Bible was written a long time ago, in a faraway land, some of the practices of writing and structuring texts are different from today. For example, the Bible was written in an oral culture, way before the invention of the printing press. Oral or spoken forms of communication thus shape the style and design, as texts were typically written to be heard (being read to an audience, like a speech or sermon). Stories or units of thought often unfold in more circular or concentric patterns, as opposed to linear, outlining arrangements of printed text. In addition, ancient schools of rhetoric taught formal methods of how to put together a speech for various persuasive purposes. Scholarly research and archeological discoveries reveal some of the standard practices of writing letters and other types of documents during Bible times.

Though you don't have to become a scholar to begin reading the Bible with an awareness of the book-level context, a little knowledge about some of the conventions of the times will sharpen your vision for reading the Bible within its own contexts. Like looking for the straight-edges when you begin to put together a puzzle, a little information about "how they did it back then"—the broader historical context—can give us some important "aha" moments as we seek to untangle the layers of a text. To help us do that, then—to help us construct the big picture within which we are to see the little pictures—I'll include some information on structural clues from ancient letters, ancient speeches, from narratives, and from the oral culture in general. The clearest form of picture-point reading will thus combine a wide-angle, common-sense perspective with insights ("clues") from the cultural habits of the time for a more focused understanding within the confines of the original, book-level context. Before launching into modern applications (which are important, but should be based on the originally intended meaning) or assigning divine authority to our own inkblot-like opinions, we want to read the Bible *to get God's point.*

Orientation

What I'm proposing is not a new way to read the Bible, but it may seem that way. What's unique is the uncompromising consistency in which we apply the principle of using the context of a particular book (seeing the big picture) to help us understand the individual parts (the little pictures) of the book. Every verse or set of verses should be seen as part of its larger whole. To some extent, it's possible to boil down the main point of this book to this single principle or question: How does it fit? Or even better, how does it function or contribute? How does a verse or set of verses function within its book? What is Mark 4:1-34—the parable chapter—doing in Mark? for example. What role does it play in communicating the message of that book? This is the question that forces us to see the picture and consequently get the point. This is the "function-" or "role-rule." I'll call it "The Question" for short (and for emphasis). To understand a biblical text, answer The Question. And remember, if you can't answer The Question, you can't know for sure if you understand the verse as it was intended. How does this verse or set of verses function within its own book-level context should always be asked of every verse or set of verses to prevent and treat the condition of ink-blotitis.

Consistently applying this principle (until it becomes habit and second nature) will be, for many of us, essentially a new way of reading the Bible. So, naturally, we'll need some examples as to how it works when applied to Bible passages. I'll do this as we go and include a "How To" section in the latter part of our study. Using some of the cultural clues of how ancient documents were put together and shaped, we'll take an extensive look at consistently applying this principle by means of a picture-point, book-level analysis of Paul's letter to Philemon. I've found this short letter to be a great, hands-on model, primarily because it is so short (like a beginner's puzzle with only a few pieces) and because it incorporates several of the clues from ancient letters and speeches regarding the structuring (= shape) of Paul's letters. Shifting gears to a story or narrative text, we'll then use the Gospel of Mark to begin to apply the principles to a larger Bible book.

Introduction

So where do we start? To understand the nature of the Bible as a collection of the books of God, we should probably start at the beginning: where in the world did we get the Bible, anyway?

Chapter 1

Where'd We Get the Bible, Anyway?

Warning: The following chapter is boring . . ., unless you like history. And this isn't just history. It's sacred, providential, world-altering history—history unfolding from some of the greatest moments of all time, revealing the most exciting discoveries, motivated by the hottest passions and deepest pursuits, culminating in the most monumental decisions.

There. I warned you.

If you find yourself having little or no interest in the details of the historical process of how we got the Bible, read the first ("Treasure in the Trash") and the last ("A Bridge to the West") sections and then go on to the next chapter. Even if history is not your favorite subject, consider sticking with it so that you'll have a basic knowledge of how we got the Bible.

Chapter 1

Treasure in the Trash

> It was in April, 1844 . . . The desire which I felt to discover some precious remains of any manuscripts . . . of a date which would carry us back to the early times of Christianity, was realized beyond my expectations. It was at the foot of Mount Sinai, in the Convent of St. Catherine, that I discovered the pearl of all my researches. . . .[1]

These are the words of Dr. Constantin von Tischendorf (1815-74), as he begins to describe one of the most exciting moments of his life. Dr. Tischendorf was a biblical scholar who devoted himself to finding, studying, collating, and preserving ancient copies of the Bible from all over the world. At a time when the known copies were scattered and relatively recent, he traveled the world in search of ancient manuscripts, wanting to ensure that we have the oldest, most accurate copies of the Bible.

While visiting the monastery of St. Catherine, in the middle of a great hall, Tischendorf saw "a large and wide basket full of old parchments" that the monks were using to feed the fires of their ovens. To his surprise, Tischendorf noticed in the heap of papers what looked to him like pages of a copy of the Old Testament in Greek, older than any he had ever seen. Since they were "destined for the fire," the leaders of the convent allowed him to take about a third—43 sheets—of the parchments; but because Tischendorf got so excited, the monks became suspicious and wouldn't let him have the rest. Dr. Tischendorf eagerly copied a page from Isaiah and Jeremiah and told the monks that they should take "religious care" of such remains, which they obviously hadn't been doing. When he first noticed the pages about to be burned, the librarian told him that "two heaps of papers like these, molded by time, had been already committed to the flames."

Though Tischendorf produced many influential volumes of the Greek New Testament and discovered hundreds of Bible manuscripts in the course of his life, none were like the pages he had saved from the fires at St. Catherine's. He longed to find where they came from and in fact made two trips back to the monastery "to discovery any further traces of the treasure of 1844," but with no luck—the other pages had vanished and their parent seemed not to exist. On his second visit to the monastery, he found even more rare biblical manuscripts than he had on the first trip; but he also found a small fragment of 11 short lines of Genesis that convinced him that the manuscript he was looking for originally contained the entire Old Testament! So he went a third time, but again, came up empty.

Just before he was about to leave, having given up the search, on the last night of his third visit to the monastery, 15 years after discovering the treasure in the trash, Tischendorf had an extraordinary evening. Returning from an afternoon walk with the steward of the convent, just before sunset, the steward "begged" Dr. Tischendorf to have refreshments with him in his cell (a small, simple room in a monastery). Resuming their former conversation about the Greek Bible called the Septuagint, the steward said, "And I, too, have read a Septuagint." Then . . . from the corner of the room, he took down a big book wrapped in a red cloth and laid it before Dr. Tischendorf. In Tischendorf's own words:

> I unrolled the cover, and discovered, to my great surprise, not only those very fragments which, fifteen years before, I had taken out of the basket, but also other parts of the Old Testament, the New Testament complete, and, in addition, the Epistle of Barnabas and a part of the Pastor of Hermas. Full of joy, which this time I had the self-command to conceal from the steward and the rest of the community, I asked . . . for permission to take the manuscript into my sleeping chamber to look over it more at leisure. There by myself I could give way to the transport of joy which I [felt]. I knew that I held in my hand the most precious Biblical treasure in existence—a document whose age and importance exceeded that of all the manuscripts which I had ever examined during twenty years' study of the subject. I cannot now, I confess, recall all the emotions which I felt in that exciting moment

with such a diamond in my possession. Though my lamp was dim, and the night cold, I sat down at once to transcribe . . .

The "pearl of the Convent of St. Catherine" had been found. "It really seemed a sacrilege to sleep," Dr. Tischendorf wrote in his diary, describing the night and the joy he felt at the discovery of the fourth century manuscript copy of the Bible now known as codex Sinaiticus, one of our oldest and most complete ancient copies of the Bible. When he first laid eyes on the pages of "this priceless treasure"—to repeat the point—they were in the trash and the monks were using them to stoke the fires of the monastery.[2] Though it took tremendous political and practical effort, 15 years of searching, and even longer to acquire for the world, this ancient manuscript copy is now an important part of our collective witness to the text of the Bible.

A Collection of Inspired Books

Where'd we get the Bible, anyway? Seems like a really important question, doesn't it? And it is. Dr. Tischendorf's work helped, but there's much more to it. The short answer is "from God." The long answer goes beyond the scope of this book. So let's see if I can give you something between the two.

The word "Bible" comes from the Greek word *biblos*, which referred to the papyrus plant used by ancient Egyptians to make paper and eventually to the writing products made from the plant. Our word "Bible" actually comes from the plural form of the word (*biblia*) and thus means "little books" or "scrolls."[3] The word *biblia* was taken over into Latin and passed on to western languages as a single noun, which is how the Bible came to be known as "the Book" instead of "the books."

Rather than a single book, the Bible is actually a collection of individual writings—some, as long as typical books; others, as short as a single page. Religious Jews (regarding the First/Old Testament) and Christians (both Old and New Testaments) believe this collection of books documents God's direct interactions with humans throughout the course of history. We believe the books are "inspired" by God. The word "inspired" comes from the Greek word that literally means "God-breathed" (*theopneustos*). The idea is that God supervised the writing of the Bible; more poetically, that he streamed or "breathed" his word (= what he wanted to say) through the writers of the Bible and thus speaks to us through its pages. The classic text is 2 Timothy 3:16-17, which refers to the Old Testament scriptures and functions as part of the overall training of Timothy to be an effective evangelist:

> All scripture is inspired by God and is useful for teaching, for reproof, for correction, and for training in righteousness, so that everyone who belongs to God may be proficient, equipped for every good work.[4]

Chapter 1

The individual books of the Bible were written by as many as 40 different authors during a 1,500-year span. Some—like Moses and Paul—wrote several books; others wrote just one. The Bible is divided historically and theologically into two major parts, with a third grouping of books called the "Apocrypha" (which means hidden or disputed; more on this below) sometimes included between them. The "First" or "Old" Testament ("testament" is an old word for an agreement or contract) covers the history of the nation of Israel from the creation of the world through the writings of the Jewish prophets (roughly to about 500-400 BC). The contract or agreement signified by the word "testament" was that between God and the people based on the Law of Moses. The New Testament starts with the birth of Jesus and takes us through the beginning, life, spread, and persecution of the early church. The testament or contract between God and humanity revealed in the New Testament is that of a restored relationship between humans and God through Jesus Christ in the Church. The Bible is, therefore, a collection of books—a library in a sense—that reflects God's interactions with people at critical times during the course of human history and his words to us in the midst of those world-altering events. These writings were collected at various points along the way into what we now know as the Bible.

Why were the books that are in the Bible accepted or recognized as being "inspired" by God? This too is a very important, though somewhat complex, question. There are several reasons, along with considerable historical journeys, unfolding and supporting those reasons. Before taking you through a little of that history, I'll summarize briefly the primary reasons the books included in the Bible came to be regarded over time as truly containing the revelation of God to his people.

The first has to do with who wrote them. The books that came to be accepted as having come from God were believed to have been written by individuals directly, or in some cases indirectly, involved in the events and times of which they speak. In the case of the New Testament, this meant that they were written by one of the original disciples or "apostles" (followers sent on a mission) of Jesus or by someone closely connected to an apostle—"authentic apostolic connection," Jeffery Sheler calls it.[5] In conjunction with this inherent credibility and authority of the writers, other reasons books in the Bible came to be accepted as inspired by God came from the consensus use (in the churches and by the early church leaders), and consistent and life-altering content of the books themselves. In other words, they passed the tests of time and scrutiny of real life, emerging as having God's own stamp of approval:

> Without question the books which are Scripture and which are truly the word of God have about them a self-evidencing quality. They carry their uniqueness on their face. To read them is to be conscious of being brought into the presence of God and truth and Jesus Christ in a unique way. They have always exercised, and still exercise, a quite unparalleled power upon the lives of men.[6]

The writings included in the Bible thus became accepted as part of the official "canon" of scripture (a "canon" is a rule or standard by which something else is measured or judged, in this case the list of accepted books).

The history of the collection of God's books into a single book (the Bible) is detailed and extraordinarily meaningful.[7] In retrospect, it is a testament to the genuine faith and faithfulness of those who were involved in the process at each step and, most importantly, to the presence and providence of God. The purposes of this book prevent us from going into the nooks and crannies of that history, though I encourage you to study it in depth, if this is of interest to you. Like most historically significant developments, it's an amazing story of faith, dedication, loyalty, and good ol'-fashioned hard work. Painting with very broad strokes, let's overview that journey under four headings: (1) From Books to Book, (2) The Lost Books of the Bible, (3) What's In, What's Out: Who Made the Call?, and (4) Ancient Copies and Versions of the Bible.

Chapter 1

From Books to Book

The First Testament as Books

The first thing we know of the writings of the Bible is of Moses (around 1500 BC), the great spiritual and literary leader of the nation of Israel, as the "children of Israel" emerge from slavery in Egypt to a new existence as a nation under God. Leading them to an encounter with God on Mt. Sinai, Moses receives the Ten Commandments—written on tablets of stone with the finger of God—and goes on to author the first five books of the Bible called the Pentateuch (Genesis, Exodus, Leviticus, Numbers, and Deuteronomy). This becomes the "Law of Moses" for the Jewish people. Though the story begins with Moses from a literary perspective, some of the material contained in the Old Testament, like, for example, the story of creation and the fall of man, Noah and the ark, the Nephilim/giants, the tower of Babel, and perhaps the book of Job, likely predate Moses by hundreds of years. We don't know what ancient stories or sources Moses might have used as he tells the prehistory of Israel back to its beginnings with Abraham (roughly 2000 BC), all the way back to the creation of the universe itself. According to the Bible, God communicated with humanity orally prior to Moses. Sometimes called the "Patriarchal Age," the pre-Moses era portrays God as speaking directly to such men as Adam, Noah, Abraham, and Jacob.

After Moses, other writings of the interactions of God with people were created by the leaders and holy men of the nation, like Joshua (who took over after Moses), Samuel and the times of the great kings (Saul, David, Solomon), and Ezra and Nehemiah, who led the rebuilding of Jerusalem (starting in 536 BC) after its destruction by the Babylonians in the sixth century. As is the tendency with peoples and nations throughout history, the important spiritual, literary, and historical documents began to be collected and respected as instructional and authoritative at various levels. This tendency is reflected early (Deuteronomy 31:24-25) with the charge to keep the book of the Law beside the Ark of the Covenant—yes, the Indiana

Jones Ark of the Covenant—which held the tables of stone containing the Ten Commandments, Aaron's (Moses' brother) rod that had budded, and a bowl of manna (food God provided in the desert). Another good example comes from 1 Samuel: "Samuel told the people the rights and duties of the kingship; and he wrote them in a book and laid it up before the Lord" (10:25).[8] Over time—from Moses to Malachi (the last book of the Old Testament) was roughly a period of about 1,000 years—these authoritative books of Judaism were collected into three categories, comprising the Hebrew Bible: the Law, the Prophets, and the Writings. Most of the Old Testament was written in Hebrew, with a spattering of Aramaic, and each of the books reflects and addresses the particular times, events, and circumstances in which it was written.

The First (Old) Testament as a Book

Starting with books of the Law and then the Prophets, the First Testament grew gradually and was assembled into an accepted collection of sacred scriptures about the time of Ezra (400 BC).[9] The Prologue to Ecclesiasticus (about 131 BC) speaks of "the great things handed down—the writings of the Law and the prophets and of others who have followed in their steps," referring to all three: the Law, the Prophets, and "the rest of the books."[10] Jesus himself appears to have known the Jewish Bible as a collection of writings in this format, speaking of "the Law, the Prophets and the Psalms" (Luke 24:44; 11:51). The apocryphal work of 2 Esdras (also known as 4 Ezra), written in the first century AD, also gives clear evidence of a 24-book collection of Hebrew scripture.[11] Writing about 100 AD, the Jewish historian Josephus says that no book was added to the Hebrew Scriptures after the time of Ezra, Nehemiah, and Malachi.[12] Though the purposes of the meeting are debated by scholars today, many have suggested that this collection was finalized as the canon of authoritative scriptures at the close of the first century by a group of Jewish leaders at the council of Jamnia about 90 AD.[13] Over the next few centuries, Origin, Eusebius, and Jerome affirm this same collection.

At critical moments and through various stages, the writings of the First/Old Testament were thus preserved and collected for use as reverenced spiritual guidebooks[14]—holy books or "books of God," we might call them. Some of the most important work of this kind (collecting and caring for the texts of scripture) was done over a period of several hundred years by a group of ancient Hebrew scribes known as the Masoretes (about 500 AD), though concern for the care of scripture obviously predates their work. The Masoretes added a system of vowels and accents (for pronunciation purposes) to the consonant-only original Hebrew and developed intricate methods for guarding against scribal errors when copying the sacred documents,[15] examining and appraising all the textual materials they had received from at least several centuries before their time. Their work was so careful and successful that today scholars/students often refer to our Hebrew text as "the Masoretic text."[16]

The result of this historical process is a Hebrew Bible consisting of 24 books (= 39 books in English Bibles), divided into three sections:

The Law (*Torah* in Hebrew)
Genesis, Exodus, Leviticus, Numbers, Deuteronomy

The Prophets (*Nevi'im*)
Former: Joshua, Judges, Samuel (1 and 2), Kings (1 and 2)
Latter: Isaiah, Jeremiah, Ezekiel, and the Book of the Twelve (Hosea, Joel, Amos, Obadiah, Jonah, Micah, Nahum, Habakkuk, Zephaniah, Haggai, Zachariah, Malachi)

The Writings (*Kethuvim*)
Psalms, Proverbs, Job, Song of Songs, Ruth, Lamentations, Ecclesiastes, Esther, Daniel, Ezra-Nehemiah, Chronicles (1 and 2)

Though arranged and divided differently in our English Bibles, the books of the Hebrew Bible are exactly the same.[17]

Another assembling of the First Testament books into a single book is found in the then-common-language, Greek translation of the Hebrew Scriptures known as the Septuagint (LXX). The name comes from a tradition that 70 (or 72) scholars participated in the translation of the Pentateuch (the first 5 books of the Old Testament), having been summoned to Alexandria by the king of Egypt at the request of the librarian of the famed library of Alexandria, no less.[18] Whatever the primary motivation, it's believed that the first part of the Hebrew Bible was completed in Alexandria around 250 BC. Translations of the additional books of the Old Testament were added later before the time of Christ (thus from 250-100 BC), as were the apocryphal books. The Septuagint translation was extremely important and influential because it became the Bible of the early church and is the text most quoted when New Testament writers made reference to the Old Testament (as opposed to the Hebrew text). It was highly respected in ancient times and served as the basis for a number of ancient translations of the Jewish scriptures. The Septuagint appears never to have had a closed list of books[19] and often included additional writings from the apocrypha like Tobit, Judith, and Baruch (see "The Lost Books of the Bible" below for more on these), thus influencing the inclusion of these books in Catholic and other Bibles today.

The New Testament as Books

The New Testament begins with the good news of the birth, life, death, and resurrection of Jesus, the Christ, in the books we call "Gospels" ("gospel" means good news). We have no documents written by Jesus himself. In fact, as far as we know, it took a while for the earliest Christians to narrate at length the things they had seen and heard of Jesus; not because they didn't think it was important, but because they were still living it.[20] Oral accounts by eyewitnesses were highly valued, as one would expect. An early Christian leader named Papias, bishop of Hierapolis, around 130-140 AD (or earlier) said he was not so interested in what he could learn from books, finding greater value in "the utterances of a living and abiding voice."

> . . . if a person came my way who had been a companion of the elders, I would inquire about the sayings of the elders—what was said by Andrew, or by Peter, or by Philip, or by Thomas or James, or by John or Matthew or any other of the Lord's disciples.[21]

We don't know how much of Jesus' teaching the first disciples might have memorized—a common practice of students in those days[22]—or when the stories and sayings of Jesus were first written down.[23] We do know, however, that at some point while the earliest disciples and many eye-witnesses were still living, the apostles and other original followers of Jesus began to recall, collect, and record the details of the life and teachings of Jesus, whom they believed was the Messiah, the son of God. The result was the first four books of the New Testament—the Gospels: Matthew, Mark, Luke, and John. Luke included a history of the early church (Acts) as a second volume to his story of Jesus, as Christianity spread from Jerusalem to Samaria and beyond.

Before the Gospels were completed, the apostle Paul had begun planting churches in Asia Minor (comprising most of modern Turkey) and into Eastern Europe, traveling as far west as Rome to evangelize and encourage young Christians. The earliest writings in the New Testament are, therefore, letters of Paul sent to churches in prominent cities like Corinth, Thessalonica, Ephesus, Colossae, Philippi, and Rome. Paul visited and wrote to these cities somewhere between 40 and 65 AD. Each of his letters reflects and addresses issues of faith and morality in the churches, as the earliest Christians grew—and struggled—in the meaning of their faith. In addition to the letters of Paul, several other letters and documents witnessing to the presence of God in early Christian communities were written by apostles and key Christian leaders (like James, Peter, John).

The books of the New Testament thus sprang from the cutting edge of faith in practice, not as arm-chair theology or sterile systems of academic thought. They embody the faith and practices of the earliest Christians. Each of the Gospels has a particular thrust and point of view on Jesus as the Christ. Paul's letters, as Barclay puts it, "were meant to deal with an immediate situation in a definite community at a particular time."[24] The book of Hebrews, as another example, portrays the supremacy of Christ in a highly Jewish setting and style, in a context of criticism and even persecution. The last book of the New Testament, the Revelation of John, is a fantastic narrative of "apocalyptic"—meaning revelatory and thus prophetic, larger-than-life—symbolism, aimed at encouraging first century Christians who were having to give up their lives to hold on to their faith against intense persecution by Rome and the Roman emperors of the time.

The New Testament as a Book

Though written in a relatively short span of time (50-100 AD and possibly shorter), the New Testament as we know it today came into existence gradually.[25] Treated with respect and authority, the letters of Paul began to be read in public worship assemblies and shared among the churches almost immediately (1 Thessalonians 5:27; Colossians 4:16; 2 Peter 3:15-16), circulating in collected form by the end of the first century. Clement of Rome, writing to the Corinthians about AD 96 in a letter called 1 Clement, includes references to Paul's letters and clear citations from Hebrews.[26] In addition to Clement, Ignatius (35-110 AD), bishop of Antioch, and Polycarp (69-155 AD), bishop of Smyrna (writing around 115 AD), appear to be acquainted with a collection of Paul's letters.[27] Put succinctly by William Barclay (1907-78: Scottish minister and scholar, dedicated to making biblical scholarship available to the average reader): "It is clear that by A.D. 100 Paul's letters had been collected and were widely known and widely accepted."[28] (The first efforts among the Christians to define a clear list of sacred books may have come in response to perceived threats of misguided or heretical teaching, like that of Marcion [110-160 AD], who eliminated all the books that were to him too Jewish and unlike "the best of" Paul.[29]) Though we don't know the exact details, we do know that the collection of Paul's letters came to be designated by the word "Apostle" ("To the Romans," "To the Corinthians," etc.), being widely read in public meetings sometime before the middle of the second century.[30] To this collection, Acts, Hebrews, and other writings of the New Testament were later added.

The four Gospels appear to have been united into a single collection at an early date as well, the collection being known as "The Gospel" ("according to Matthew," "according to Mark," and so on) rather than the "Gospels." Luke tells at the beginning of his "good news" about Jesus (Luke 1:1) that many had begun to create narratives of the things that had happened about Jesus as told by eyewitnesses. The *Didache*, a manual of church discipline written toward the end of the first century, introduces the Lord's Prayer with an encouragement not to pray as the hypocrites, "but as the Lord commanded in his Gospel."[31] About AD 115 Ignatius may have been referring to the four-Gospel collection when he speaks of "The Gospel" as an authoritative writing.[32] Polycarp writes of "the apostles who brought us the Gospel."[33] Writing in the middle of the second century, Justin Martyr (110-165 AD) was acquainted with several Gospels and stated that in the worship assemblies, Christians read together the "memoirs of the apostles" with "the writings of the prophets."[34] Around 170 AD, an Assyrian Christian named Tatian created from the fourfold Gospel a "Harmony of the Gospels" called the *Diatessaron*, which became the "Authorized Version" for Assyrian Christians until the fifth century.[35] By 180 AD the idea of a fourfold Gospel had become established in the church at large to the extent that Irenaeus (around 125-200 AD), bishop of Lyons in Gaul, compares it to the four winds or points of a compass, arguing for the fundamental nature of the fourfold Gospel: "It is not possible that the Gospels can be either more or fewer in number than they are."[36] Again, Barclay offers a telling summary:

> It may be said that our four Gospels held undisputed sway long before A.D. 200. Very occasionally we come across

quotations from or references to other Gospels, but, as far back as we can go, our four Gospels are the fundamental documents of the Christian Church.[37]

As a continuation of Luke's story of Jesus, Acts may have circulated with the Gospels in the earliest collections[38] and was unanimously received by the early church as belonging in the Bible.[39]

By the end of the second century, substantial lists of New Testament books began to appear.[40] Because the collections were made in different places, the contents sometimes varied. The Muratorian Fragment (or Canon, it's sometimes called) is likely the oldest known list of New Testament books (about AD 170).[41] Part of the list of New Testament books is missing, being a mutilated or "fragmentary" copy; nevertheless, the only books not included are Hebrews, James, 1 and 2 Peter, and 3 John.[42] Irenaeus put together a list of books that he believed were authoritative, which, along with those of his contemporary Tertullian (155-222 AD) and student Hippolytus (170-236 AD), helped to create a core list of New Testament documents.[43] The existence of such lists at that time implies that the process of collection began much earlier and demonstrates that—though some debate existed in the early church—the major writings were accepted by most Christians by the middle of the second century. The disputed books—a small part that we might call the "fringe" of the canon—would be worked out in the third and fourth centuries. Text scholar Bruce Metzger puts it this way:

> By the close of the second century . . ., we can see the outline of what may be described as the nucleus of the New Testament. Although the fringes of the emerging canon remained unsettled for generations, a high degree of unanimity concerning the greater part of the New Testament was attained . . .[44]

In the third century, Origen (185-254 AD)—"the greatest scripture scholar of the ancient church"[45]—names all the New Testament books, but says that Hebrews, James, 2 and 3 John, and Jude were questioned by some.⁴⁶ Early in the fourth century, the church historian Eusebius of Caesarea (265-340 AD) likewise names all the books, dividing the most widely circulated books into three categories: "recognized," "disputed," and "heretical."⁴⁷ Eusebius included James, 2 Peter, 2 and 3 John, and Jude as "disputed" or suspect, but adds that they were accepted by the majority.⁴⁸ "Thus, all twenty-seven books of what would become the canonical New Testament were listed favorably by Eusebius."⁴⁹ In his 39th Easter letter of 367 AD to the church of Alexandria, Athanasius (293-373), bishop of Alexandria, published a list of 27 books of the New Testament that were recognized at his time as the only accepted books of the New Testament, exactly the same as in our Bibles today.⁵⁰ Jerome (347-420 AD) and Augustine (354-430 AD) followed suit in the West, and under Augustine's influence, this general practice of the churches was officially recognized by church councils held in North Africa at Hippo Regius in 393 (the Synod of Hippo) and in Carthage in 397 and 419 (Council/Synod of Carthage),⁵¹ the first to classify the canonical books of the New Testament.⁵² By the end of the fourth century in the West and the fifth century in the East, with a few exceptions, there was unanimity on the matter of the New Testament canon.⁵³

As Sheler concludes, "By the end of the fourth century, then, the New Testament canon for the church in the West was virtually set."⁵⁴ Neil Lightfoot draws this conclusion: "The Bible had grown in relative proportion to its divine revelation—gradually—and its books likewise had gradually assumed the roles which their inherent authority demanded."⁵⁵

Similar to the fourfold arrangement of the English Old Testament (Law, History, Poetry, and Prophecy), the books of the New Testament are sometimes categorized as Gospels, History, Letters, and Prophecy and are arranged as follows (Paul's letters and the General Epistles being ordered by length):

Gospels
Matthew, Mark, Luke (the Synoptic Gospels)
John (the Fourth Gospel)

History
    Acts (of the Apostles)

Letters/Epistles
    13 Attributed to Paul   To Christian communities:
    Romans, 1 and 2 Corinthians, Galatians, Ephesians, Philippians, Colossians, 1 and 2 Thessalonians

    To individual church leaders:
    1 and 2 Timothy, Titus, Philemon

    Hebrews (sermon)

    7 General Letters
    James, 1 and 2 Peter, 1, 2, and 3 John, Jude

Prophecy/Apocalypse
    Revelation

These are the books of the New Testament as a book. Though they are collected into a single volume—the second half of the Bible—they each have a unique history and message that, taken together, gives us an authentic and powerful mosaic of the life, teachings, and impact of Jesus and his followers.

Chapter 1

The Lost Books of the Bible

Both the Old and New Testaments have a group of "other" books called apocryphal books or the "Apocrypha,"[56] written for the most part after the times of the accepted books. The word "apocrypha" means hidden or concealed, but came to be used for books whose origin and/or authenticity was doubtful or unknown, thus referring to any text or group of texts that was not a part of the accepted books.[57] Though "the apocrypha" could apply to either, since both the Old and New Testaments have books that didn't make the cut, it usually refers to the set of Jewish books not found in the Hebrew Bible.[58] These are the books written after the ending of the Hebrew Old Testament in the period from 400 BC to 100 AD, sometimes called the "intertestamental" literature—coming between the Old and New Testaments. These 14 or 15 books (depending on the method of counting) include

Tobit
Judith
Additions to Esther
Wisdom of Solomon
Ecclesiasticus (or the Wisdom of Jesus Son of Sirach)
Additions to the Book of Daniel:
    Baruch, including the Letter/Epistle of Jeremiah (= Baruch
      chapter 6)
    The Prayer of Azariah and the Song of the Three Young Men
    Susanna
Bel and the Dragon
1 and 2 Maccabees

Books in the Greek Orthodox and Slavonic Bible,
not in the Roman Catholic Canon

1 and 2 Esdras (3 Esdras in Slavonic and 4 Esdras in Vulgate Appendix)
The Prayer of Manasseh
Psalm 151

3 Maccabees
4 Maccabees[59]

    Due primarily to the influence of the Septuagint (the Greek translation of the Old Testament)[60] and some Old Latin translations, 12 of these books (excluding 1 and 2 Esdras, The Prayer of Manasseh, 3 and 4 Maccabees) are considered canonical (= belonging in the Bible) by the Roman Catholic Church, the list or canon of Augustine having been reconfirmed by the Council of Trent in 1546. After the destruction of Jerusalem in 70 AD and the rise of Christianity, the apocrypha fell into disuse among Jews, surviving primarily because of their inclusion in the Septuagint and the resulting interest of Christians.[61] Based on the Hebrew Bible, statements of Jesus, Josephus, Origin, Jerome, and other sources, most Protestants do not accept these other writings as a part of inspired scripture. Some take a moderating position (the Church of England, for example) and use or include these works only on a secondary level for reading or moral exhortation, which is why they are included in some Bibles as a separate section or appendix.[62] Thus, the Old Testament apocrypha are taken in three ways: not included, included, or included at a secondary level. Whatever position one takes on the Old Testament apocrypha, the question of the canon has been answered or "closed"—that is, the standard 39 books of the Old Testament (24 in Hebrew) are accepted by all, the apocrypha viewed at various levels, and other books are excluded.[63]

    Like the Old Testament, there is an assortment of works completed after the basic time frame of the New Testament (the second century AD and later), referred to loosely as New Testament apocrypha.[64] These writings include different types (genre) of works (gospel, acts, epistle, apocalypse), such as The Gospel of Philip, The Gospel of the Egyptians, . . . of Peter, . . . of Thomas, The Acts of Peter and the Twelve Apostles, The Acts of Paul, . . . of Peter, . . . of Andrew, . . . of Pilate, The Apocalypse of Paul, . . . of Peter, etc. Unlike the Old Testament apocrypha, there is no real debate about these books: the New Testament apocrypha are rejected by nearly all branches of the church and are not included in modern versions of the Bible.[65] These books are often sensationalized, however, as "the lost books of the Bible," though they're not lost and—as we have seen—are not in the Bible.

The real lost books of the Bible are not the Old Testament or New Testament apocrypha. The real "lost books of the Bible"—and this is what I'm affirming in this book—are the books of the Bible themselves, like Matthew, Mark, Luke, John, Acts, Romans, etc. They are lost to the extent that we don't know them as separate literary, historical, and spiritual works. As independent theological works, emerging from unique real-life situations, they have distinct literary and historical contexts. We often blur their meanings, however, into the overall, general scope of the Bible as a book—which would be fine, if we understood them first on their own terms. Of course, their messages should be interpreted in light of the context of the Bible as a whole, but not until they've been seen in their unique literary and historical contexts; otherwise—and this is in effect the cause of ink-blotitis—we read them without any real defining context at all, except our own generalized set of religious and theological presuppositions.

To oversimplify the point: reading the Bible *as a book* is for most people the same as reading the Bible *as verses*. Does that make sense? Unless you have a strong knowledge of the history and content of the books of the Bible, it's really not possible to read the books in the context of the Bible as a whole, without slipping into a sort of momentary, verse-by-verse understanding. The Bible is simply too big and diverse and covers too much ground, unless you know it quite well—and that's a big unless. In this way, we lose the targeted messages of the books themselves, and this has been going on for a long time.

Sort of like Tischendorf's treasure in the trash, the books of the Bible have become lost in a great big pile of disconnected verses. They really are treasure! Filled with the inspired, life-changing thoughts and desires of God. But, like yellowed sheets of moldy parchment, stuck together by years of non-use, for many their power has faded, as we use them for purposes other than those intended by the original authors, "destined for the fire" of our own subjective passions and prejudices. Not intentionally, but because of the way we read and use pieces of them in separation from their book-level contexts and—I would add—their Bible-level context. Let me overuse the metaphor one more time: they've become "committed to the flames" of inkblotitis, which is to say to subjectivism. Like Tischendorf, how exciting would it be to pull them from the trash, light our lamps, and read them again—perhaps for the first time!

Chapter 1

What's In, What's Out: Who Made the Call?

Who made the decision as to which books belong in the Bible, and how did they decide?[66] Obviously, this is a crucial question for those of us interested in the Bible, and many books have been written on the subject of "the canon of scripture." The word "canon" means cane or reed and was used as a rule or standard for measuring things. As a standard, it came to be used with reference to the books accepted as a part of the officially recognized books of the Bible.[67] But who made the call? Who determined which books were in and which were out?

Again, the short answer is God, as the books of the Bible came to be recognized by the early church as having the character of divine inspiration. Remember, the books were not written in one place at one time, but scattered, if you will, in the grips of real-life, albeit amazing historical moments when God interacted directly with the new-born church through the risen Christ (in the case of the New Testament). That's why the collection of the books among the churches was such an important and natural process. The early Christians and their leaders thus began "choosing" the books by a natural process that we believe was also providentially supernatural. As F. F. Bruce puts it: "The historic Christian belief is that the Holy Spirit, who controlled the writing of the individual books, also controlled their selection and collection, thus continuing to fulfill our Lord's promise that He would guide His disciples into all the truth."[68]

The historical process of determining which books belonged in the Bible was a nuanced and sometimes lengthy process. Though, as far as we know, the books of the New Testament were not put into an accepted list until much later, I am intrigued by some of the early evidence for the popularity and acceptance of New Testament books.[69] For example, in three early Christian works written around AD 100 (the Epistle of Barnabas: perhaps from Alexandria; *Didache* or Teaching of the Twelve Apostles: Syria or Palestine; 1 Clement: to Corinth from Rome), there are references to the common Gospel tradition (Matthew, Mark, Luke), Acts, Romans, 1 Corinthians, Ephesians, Titus, Hebrews, 1 Peter, and possibly others. Letters of

Ignatius (bishop of Antioch) written on his way to martyrdom in AD 115 appear to quote from Matthew, John, Romans, 1 and 2 Corinthians, Timothy, Titus, with possible allusions to Mark, Luke, Acts, Colossians, 2 Thessalonians, Philemon, Hebrews, and 1 Peter. Polycarp's letter to the Philippians (about 120 AD) quotes from the common Gospel tradition, from Acts, Romans, 1 and 2 Corinthians, Galatians, Ephesians, Philippians, 2 Thessalonians, 1 and 2 Timothy, Hebrews, 1 Peter, and 1 John. Other writers did the same, giving the clear impression that books of the New Testament were precious and authoritative to early Christians, as—with no printing press!—they spread quickly and were quoted and used widely.

As time passed, with the inevitable capturing in writing of the footprints and heartbeats of history, it was only natural that at some point a definitive list of "sacred" books would need to be made. In summary, it seems that the books of the New Testament were circulating and beginning to be collected by the end of the first century. By the end of the second century, the core of the New Testament was in place, but with a significant number of additional documents being written and read. By the end of the third and fourth centuries, the collections as we know them today had been established.

Supported by divine guidance, early Christians used common sense, thoughtful evaluation, community and personal impact in coming to recognize the books of the Bible.[70] Without going into the details of the process, let me outline some of the basic criteria that were used.[71] First, however, I'd like to underscore the point that the widespread use of New Testament writings and the collections themselves initiated the process of selection.[72] See what I mean? They only collected the works that had great significance for some reason, and those reasons included the most basic criteria, starting with the use of books in public worship: "Once a book began to be so read, it had acquired a status which lifted it out of the ruck of ordinary literature."[73]

The first and most important criteria used by early Christians to determine if a book belonged in the Bible was whether the book was believed to have been written by one of the original apostles of

Chapter 1

Christ or someone having close connection to an apostle (for example, Mark was the "interpreter" of Peter, Papias says).[74] This is often called "apostolic origin" or "authenticity" and was sometimes supplemented by the idea of an unbroken succession of authorized church leaders or "bishops."[75] Naturally, eye-witness testimony was paramount. Over time other important criteria, such as the age or antiquity of a book (from the right time period), the content (theological orthodoxy: whether it agrees with the basic teachings of Christianity), and usage of a book (read in the churches and cited by early Church Fathers) grew in significance. In the third and fourth centuries, Christian leaders looked back to how a book was used in earlier periods by church leaders and theologians.[76] Widespread church usage and acceptance, or lack thereof, supported by the way the books were treated by the Church Fathers thus became the dominant criteria.[77] Historians sometimes refer to this criterion as "universal acceptance."

Though others are sometimes included,[78] four "criteria for canonicity" are often recited as summarizing the strongest reasons why some books were selected and others not:

1. **Apostolic Origin**: Was it attributed to the teaching/preaching of an original apostle of Jesus (directly) or someone close to an apostle (indirectly)?

2. **Liturgical Use**: Was it read publicly when Christians gathered for their weekly worship assemblies?

3. **Universal Acceptance**: Was it acknowledged and accepted by the early Church Fathers and the major Christian communities of the time (up through the third and fourth centuries)?

4. **Consistent or Orthodox Message**: Does it contain theological teaching and outlook compatible with the accepted Christian writings?

It's not easy to apply all of these criteria in the same way to each book, but these were the types of considerations used in the selection process, resulting in the view that each book was believed to be inspired by God and should, therefore, be accepted into the New Testament canon.

Even though there has been and continues to be some disagreement over whether the Old Testament apocrypha should be included, there is strong consensus regarding the remainder of the Old and New Testament books. The self-evidencing power of these books in the lives of people gives final witness to their divine character:

> Here is the unique effect of the Bible. Its power is self-evidencing. When Coleridge was asked what he meant by the inspiration of the Bible, he said that he could give no other answer than to say: "It finds me." It is the simple truth to say that the New Testament books became canonical because no one could stop them doing so. There were other books circulating; and there were even other books which in certain Churches enjoyed for a brief time a position in which they might possibly have entered in canon. Many of these books we still possess; and we can say that to read them and then to read the New Testament is to enter into a different world.[79]

Chapter 1

Ancient Copies and Versions of the Bible

The Best Preserved Book in the World

Though not as impressive as the stack of ancient manuscripts and sources for the New Testament, our sources for the Old Testament still vastly outnumber the evidence for non-biblical, ancient historical documents. Before the discovery of the Dead Sea Scrolls, the oldest surviving piece of the Old Testament was the Nash Papyrus from the first or second century BC, containing the Ten Commandments and the *Shema* (Deuteronomy 6:4-5: "Hear O Israel, the Lord are God is one . . .").[80] The oldest manuscript of the entire Old Testament is the Aleppo Codex from around 930 AD. Several of the oldest and most important manuscripts of the Hebrew Bible are (1) the Cairo Codex of the Prophets, containing the Former and the Latter Prophets (895 AD), (2) the Aleppo Codex of the entire Old Testament (about 930 AD), (3) the Leningrad Codex of the entire Old Testament (about 1008 AD), (4) the Codex of the Pentateuch (about 950 AD), (5) the Leningrad Codex of the Prophets (916 AD), and (6) the Reuchlin Codex of the Prophets (about 1105 AD).[81] We also have fragments in Greek from about the same time as the Nash Papyrus and copies of the Greek Old Testament (the Septuagint) as part of the Christian Bible dating from as early as the fourth century AD.

For a time, legitimate questions could be raised about the potential corruption of the Old Testament text because of the recent nature of our sources, after all, the oldest surviving Hebrew manuscripts were from the ninth and tenth centuries AD. Knowing something of the exacting carefulness of ancient Jewish scribes reduced the concern,[82] but the reliability of the Hebrew scriptures received resounding confirmation when in 1947 a young Bedouin goat- or sheep-herder threw a rock into a cave to drive out a missing animal near the ruins of the ancient settlement of Qumran, on the northwest shore of the Dead Sea in the West Bank. The sound of shattering pottery drew him into the cave, where began the discovery of the now famous Dead Sea Scrolls. In the caves of Qumran, excavators found texts of the Hebrew Scriptures (and other ancient writings)—get this—that predated (to 150 BC) our oldest copies by 1000 years![83]

What did the discovery reveal about the transmission and reliability of the Jewish scriptures? When the texts were compared with those we had from a thousand years later, they were amazingly similar, attesting to the remarkable accuracy of the copying of the Hebrew Bible.[84] After reviewing the history of the text of the Hebrew Bible, Ewert draws this conclusion:

> It is hard for anyone to comprehend fully the vast amount of labor that has gone into the preservation of the biblical text of the OT. After giving full credit to the thousands of faithful scribes and printers who played a part in giving us a trustworthy OT, we are reminded of God's promise to Jeremiah, "I am watching to see that my word is fulfilled" (Jeremiah 1:12).[85]

Evidence for the reliability of the text of the New Testament is extraordinary.[86] Not only is the Bible the best-selling book of all time, it is by far the best preserved book of antiquity. There are more than 24,000 partial and complete copies of New Testament manuscripts, more than 5,000 in Greek, and many of these are quite ancient.[87] Though new discoveries are still being made and analyzed,[88] for some years, it's been thought that our oldest, small piece of a manuscript, known as p^{52} (for papyrus number 52), contains portions of John 18:31-33 and 37-38. It dates back to around 125 AD and possibly as early as the late first century, showing that the Gospel of John was circulating in Egypt within a few decades of its composition.[89] That's really quite amazing. A papyrus copy of Paul's letters (p^{46}) is dated about 200 A.D.[90] One of the oldest copies of a significant portion of the Greek New Testament is a papyrus (p^{66}) codex (bound as a book) of the Gospel of John, from about 200 AD or earlier.[91] The earliest known copy of Luke and one of the earliest of John (p^{75}) is dated between 175 and 225 AD.[92] There are many others, and some of the dates are being challenged by scholars suggesting even older dates. Our oldest (relatively) complete copies of the

Bible are codex Sinaiticus (300s), codex Vaticanus (300s), and codex Alexandrinus (400s).[93]

Our oldest copies of New Testament books thus date to within 200-250 years from the originals, with pieces and partial copies as close as 100 years or less. Compared to other historical literature, this is remarkable. For example, we have 8 copies of Herodotus's historical works (1,350 years removed from the original), 7 copies of Plato (1,300 years removed), 5 copies of Aristotle (1,000 years removed), 9-10 copies of Julius Caesar's *Gallic War* (900 years removed), 35 copies of Livy's Roman History (300-400 years removed), 20 copies of the historian Tacitus (1,000 years removed), 7 from Pliny (750 years removed), 8 from Thucydides (1,300 years removed) . . .[94] You get the idea: there's no comparison! There are many more copies of biblical manuscripts than any secular classic from antiquity.[95]

In addition to the manuscripts themselves, early Church Fathers, writing from between the first and fifth centuries, provide many allusions to and quotations from New Testament books. In the words of renowned textual scholar Bruce Metzger: "Indeed, so extensive are these citations that if all other sources for our knowledge of the text of the New Testament were destroyed, they would be sufficient alone for the reconstruction of practically the entire New Testament."[96] Thousands of worship books called Lectionaries also contain quotations of scripture. If that weren't enough, the books of the New Testament began to be translated into other languages at a very early date, and we have ancient copies of many of these other-language versions. The documentary evidence (thousands of ancient copies, quotations, and translations) thus insures the reliability of the New Testament scriptures and thereby reassures us that the accuracy of the New Testament is not in doubt.

A Bridge to the West

Not long after the books of the Bible were written and circulated, they began to be translated into other languages. These are the first "versions" of the Bible.[97] The Samaritan Pentateuch, Aramaic Targums, and the Septuagint are examples of ancient translations of the Old Testament. As one would guess, the earliest versions of the New Testament were prepared primarily to help missionaries spread the Christian faith to people who didn't speak Greek. We have whole or partial copies of ancient translations in Old Syriac, Old Latin, and Coptic dating from as early as the third and fourth centuries, reflecting much earlier traditions.[98] And there are many other ancient translations of the Bible like Gothic, Armenian, and Ethiopic, for example.

As Latin began to replace Greek as the common language of the western part of the Roman Empire, various Latin translations of the Bible were made.[99] Jumping ahead a little, because of the number and imperfections of the many Old Latin versions circulating at the time, one of the most important ancient translations of the Bible was made in the late fourth century.[100] In 382 Pope Damascus I commissioned Eusebius Sophronius Hieronymus (347-420 AD)—Jerome in English—the leading Bible scholar of the day, to make a revision of the Old Latin versions. Though Jerome himself apparently didn't translate all the books (he mainly worked on the Old Testament),[101] the final product—a result of several revisions assembled over a period of time—was called the Latin Vulgate, or just the Vulgate. As is often the case with new versions, it took a while to catch on, but Jerome's version eventually won the day to such an extent that the Latin Vulgate became the Bible of Western Europe for the next thousand years (c. AD 400–1530).[102] It became so esteemed that at later church councils, the Vulgate was carried in triumph in a golden reliquary—a repository for relics.[103] Ewert says, "In the history of Bible translation no version, other than the Septuagint, has had such a profound influence on Christianity."[104]

I mention the Latin Vulgate as an example of an ancient version of the Bible, but also as bridge to the next chapter. It has an important and elongated history. Just as the Old Latin versions had become corrupt over time through repeated copying, so copies of the Vulgate began to deteriorate through the years as well.[105] In order to purify scribal errors, a number of revisions were made during the

Chapter 1

Middle Ages, but each attempt resulted in additional textual corruption and mixture of text types—to which the 8,000 Vulgate manuscripts available today attest.[106] This is an interesting point because as time passed and the church spread westward, Latin—the language of the Vulgate—eventually became a relic of the past, as Greek had before it. Instead of replacing it with new translations in the common languages of the people,[107] however, the Bible became more and more the property of the educated theologians and politicians of the day, since the people didn't have access to copies of the Bible and couldn't read them if they had (many not being able to read and certainly not Latin). Instead of a book that produced life and freedom, the Bible began to be used as a tool to control and exploit the religious experiences of the people.[108]

Here's the point: what was once an amazing achievement—one of the greatest versions of all time—had become something else, something it wasn't intended, not quite so amazing, to say the least.[109] Isn't it ironic that things good at one time in their original purposes can at another time become or be used for things not so good? The best version of its day, used and honored for years to come, Jerome's Vulgate, ultimately led to or at least supported the very lack of religious freedom. It led to the Roman, that is, Latin captivity of the Bible.[110]

Before we move on to that theme, let's conclude the current one. Where did we get the Bible, anyway? I hope you've seen that we didn't get it from church councils[111] or the Roman emperor Constantine. We got the Bible from a very naturally developing, carefully researched, and faithfully executed historical process, controlled by supernatural forces and divine selectivity. We got the Bible from the Church of Jesus Christ through the providence of God. I personally am persuaded and reassured by the history of where and how we got the Bible.

In addition to the process, multiple factors help me believe in the inspiration of the books of the Bible, not least of which is their ability to make sense of deeply confusing and even conflicting things about myself and about life. Through the years and in comparison to everything else I've ever read or been exposed to, the Bible shines a soft yet brilliant light on things in this world that otherwise make absolutely no sense at all, on people, on what's really valuable, on what works—and what doesn't. My darkest demons are exposed by a picture of a God so holy and transcendent that a whisper of his presence instantly explodes my right to be here, and yet so loving that he somehow draws near enough to catch my tears on his outstretched, wounded hands, as he gently lifts my sagging soul to a new hope . . . of life in the constant joy of his eternal presence. When you read the Bible, you come to see this for yourself. William Barclay always had a way with words:

> The story of the making of the Bible is a story which enables us to see the supreme value of the books of the Bible as nothing else can or does. It enables us to see that these books did not become Scripture by the decision of any Church or any man; they became Scripture because out of them men in their sorrow found comfort, in their despair hope, in their weakness strength, in their temptations power, in their darkness light, in their uncertainty faith, and in their sin a Saviour. That is why the Bible is the word of God. When the Church did make its canonical list, it was not choosing and selecting these books; it was only affirming and attesting that these already were the books on which men had stayed their hearts and fed their souls. And that is why there never can be a time when the Church or the Christian can do without this Bible which has always been the word of God to His people, and the place where men find Jesus Christ.[112]

Chapter 1: Where'd We Get the Bible, Anyway?

Chapter Resources

Aland, Kurt, and Aland, Barbara. *The Text of the New Testament: An Introduction to the Critical Editions and to the Theory and Practice of Modern Textual Criticism*. Translated by Erroll F. Rhodes. Grand Rapids: Eerdmans, 1987.

Barclay, William. *The Making of the Bible*. New York: Abingdon, 1961.

Barton, John. *Holy Writings, Sacred Text: The Canon in Early Christianity*. Louisville: Westminster John Knox, 1997.

Bruce, F. F. *The Canon of Scripture*. Downers Grove, IL: Intervarsity, 1988.

The New Testament Documents: Are They Reliable. 5th ed., rev. Grand Rapids: Eerdmans, 1960.

Keating, Corey. "The Criteria Used for Developing the New Testament Canon in the First Four Centuries of the Christian Church." Fuller Theological Seminary Paper (2000) 1-15. Published online at http://www.coreykeating.com/SeminaryPapers/SeminaryPapers.html.

Charlesworth, James H. ed. *The Old Testament Pseudepigrapha*. 2 vols. Garden City, NY: Doubleday & Company, 1983, 1985.

Childers, J.W. and Parker, D.C., eds. *Transmission and Reception: New Testament Text-critical and Exegetical Studies* [in Honor of Carroll D. Osburn]. Texts and studies. Third series 4 (Piscataway, NJ: Gorgias 2006).

Daniell, David. *The Bible in English: Its History and Influence*. London: Yale University, 2003.

Dungan, David L. *Constantine's Bible: Politics and the Making of the New Testament*. Minneapolis: Fortress, 2007.

Elliott, J. Keith. "The Text of the New Testament." In *A History of Biblical Interpretation: The Medieval through the Reformation Periods*, pp. 227-53.

Edited by Alan J. Hauser and Duane F. Watson. Grand Rapids: Eerdmans, 2009.

Evans, Craig A. *Ancient Texts for New Testament Studies: A Guide to the Background Literature*. Peabody, MA: Hendrickson, 2005.

Ewert, David. *A General Introduction to the Bible: From Ancient Tables to Modern Translations*. Grand Rapids: Zondervan, 1983.

Gamble, Harry Y. *The New Testament Canon: Its Making and Meaning*. Eugene, OR: Wipf and Stock, 2002 (previously Philadelphia: Fortress, 1985).

Lewis, Jack P. "Jamnia Revisited." In *The Canon Debate*, pp. 146-62. Edited by Lee M. McDonald and James A. Sanders. Peabody, MA: Hendrickson, 2002.

Lightfoot, Neil R. *How We Got the Bible*. Grand Rapids: Baker, 1963.

McDonald, Lee M. *The Biblical Canon: Its Origin, Transmission, and Authority*. Peabody, MA: Hendrickson, 2007.

McDonald, Lee M., and Sanders, James A., ed. *The Canon Debate*. Peabody, MA: Hendrickson, 2002.

McDonald, Lee M., and Sanders, James A. "Introduction." In *The Canon Debate*, pp. 3-17. Edited by Lee M. McDonald and James A. Sanders. Peabody, MA: Hendrickson, 2002.

Metzger, Bruce M. *The Text of the New Testament: Its Transmission, Corruption, and Restoration*. 2nd ed. New York: Oxford University, 1968.

Nickelsburg, George W. E. *Jewish Literature between the Bible and the Mishnah: A Historical and Literary Introduction*. Philadelphia: Fortress, 1981.

Rummel, Erika. "The Renaissance Humanists." In *A History of Biblical Interpretation: The Medieval through the Reformation Period*, pp. 280-98. Edited by Alan J. Hauser and Duane F. Watson. Grand Rapids: Eerdmans, 2009.

Chapter 1

Schneemelcher, Wilhelm, ed. *New Testament Apocrypha*. 2 vols. Translated by R. McL. Wilson. Westminster: John Knox, 1991, 1992.

Sheler, Jeffery L.. *Is the Bible True?: How Modern Debates and Discoveries Affirm the Essence of the Scriptures*. New York: HarperCollins, 1999.

Notes

1. Constantin von Tischendorf, "The Discovery of the Sinaitic Manuscript," in *When Were Our Gospels Written? An Argument by Constantine Tischendorf. With a Narrative of the Discovery of the Sinaitic Manuscript* (New York: American Tract Society, 1866). I found a copy of this extract from Tischendorf's book online at http://rosetta.reltech.org/TC/extras/tischendorf-sinaiticus.html.
2. See Metzger, *Text*, 42-46 for details of Tischendorf's discovery; also Lightfoot, *How*, 32-35; cf. also Aland and Aland, *Text*, 11-14.
3. The earliest Christian use of the word *biblia* with the sense of "the books" of scripture appears to be around AD 150 in 2 Clement 14:2: "the books and the apostles declare that the church . . . has existed from the beginning" (cf. Daniel 9:2) (F. F. Bruce, "Bible," in *New Bible Dictionary*, pp. 137-40 [2nd ed., ed. J. D. Douglas, et al., Wheaton, IL: Tyndale House, 1982] 137). See Daniell, *The Bible in English*, 1-3 for a nice, brief summary of the contents and purpose of the Bible, under the heading "What the Bible Is."
4. 2 Peter 1:20 is also often cited: "First of all you must understand this, that no prophecy of scripture is a matter of one's own interpretation, because no prophecy every came by human will, but men and women moved by the Holy Spirit spoke from God."
5. Sheler, *Is the Bible True?*, 19-20. Consequently, as Sheler points out, some otherwise highly regarded writings like 1 Clement and the Shepherd of Hermas were excluded from the Bible.
6. Barclay, *Making*, 77.
7. A classic presentation of this material, created originally as a series of lessons for adult Bible classes is the book by Neil R. Lightfoot, *How We Got the Bible*.
8. 2 Maccabees describes Nehemiah (around 400 BC) as having "founded a library and collected books":

> "The same things are reported in the records and in the memoirs of Nehemiah, and also that he founded a library and collected the books about the kings and prophets, and the writings of David, and letters of kings about votive offerings. In the same way Judas also collected all the books that had been lost on account of the war that had come upon us, and they are in our possession" (2:13-15).

Judas Maccabeus (around 167 BC) likewise collected sacred books (1 Maccabees 3:48-49, 2 Maccabees 2:13-15; 15:6-9).

9. A common position is that the Old Testament canon took shape in three stages, corresponding to the three divisions of the Hebrew Bible: the Law/Torah was canonized around 400 BC, the Prophets around 200 BC, and the Writings in the neighborhood of AD 100 (see McDonald and Sanders, "Introduction," 4; Lewis, "Jamnia," 148-49; Bruce, *Canon*, 36). Bruce says that although this is not an unreasonable and even attractive account, it's completely hypothetical with no evidence for it in the Old Testament itself or elsewhere. As Ewert (*Introduction*, 69-70) suggests, moreover, from the fourth century BC, it was a common view among Jews that God had ceased to speak directly to or through the prophets, reflected, for example, in Zechariah 13:3: "And if anyone still prophesies, his father and mother, to whom he was born, will say to him, 'You must die, because you have told lies in the Lord's name.'" Intertestamental books expressed a similar view (1 Maccabees 14:41, 2 Baruch 85:3).

10. Ewert, *Introduction*, 70; Barclay, *Making*, 11-12, 34. Ewert concludes that the tripartite division of the biblical books into the Law, Prophets, and Writings was by then established. Barclay says that the threefold division goes back at least as far as 180 BC.

11. Barclay, *Making*, 13; Ewert, *Introduction*, 70.

12. Josephus, *Against Apion* I.8; cited in Lightfoot, *How*, 20; Ewert, *Introduction*, 70-71, and others. Most scholars believe Josephus is combining Ruth and Judges, and Jeremiah and Lamentations to get his list of 22 books (instead of 24). His statement is forceful and informative:

> "We have not 10,000 books among us, disagreeing with and contradicting one another, but only twenty-two books which contain the records of all time, and are justly believed to be divine. Five of these are by Moses, and contain his laws and traditions of the origin of mankind until his death. . . . From

the death of Moses till the reign of Artaxerxes, king of Persia, who reigned after Xerxes, the prophets who succeeded Moses wrote down what happened in their times in thirteen books; and the remaining four books contain hymns to God and precepts for the conduct of human life" (*Against Apion* I.8; Lightfoot, *How*, 82-83).

13. Barclay, *Making*, 36; Lightfoot, *How*, 82-83; Ewert, *Introduction*, 71. Due largely to the work of Jack P. Lewis, most modern scholars do not believe that the "assembly" or "court" of Jamnia functioned in the sense of Christian councils to officially pronounce or close the canon of Jewish scriptures; see, e.g., Lewis, "Jamnia Revisited," 146-62.
14. See, for example, Deuteronomy 31:9, 24; Joshua 24:26; 1 Samuel 10:25; Jeremiah 36:2; Daniel 9:2; Nehemiah 8:1-8 (cf. Lightfoot, *How*, 20).
15. Here's how Lightfoot (*How*, 71) describes the process the Masoretes developed for checking against scribal errors:

    "More than this, they sought ways and methods by which they could eliminate scribal slips of addition or omission. This they achieved through intricate procedures of counting. They numbered the verses, words and letters of each book. They counted the number of times each letter was used in each book. They noted verses which contained all the letters of the alphabet, or a certain number of them, etc. They calculated the middle verse, the middle word, and the middle letter of each book. (The middle verse of the Pentateuch is Leviticus 8:7, while the middle verse of the Hebrew Bible is Jeremiah 6:7). Some of these notations can still be found in our printed Hebrew Bibles. With these safeguards, and others, when a scribe finished making a copy of a book he could then check the accuracy of his work before using it."

    On the pre-Masoretic and Masoretic contributions and practices, see also Ewert, *Introduction*, 87-91; see p. 87 for the careful rules of copying scriptures in Talmudic times.
16. Lightfoot, *How*, 71-72.
17. The collection is referred to in Hebrew communities by the acronym Tanakh (**TaNaKh**), which comes from the initial letters of the names of the three traditional divisions.
18. The primary source of the tradition is the *Letter of Aristeas* (Lightfoot, *How*, 73).

19. Lightfoot, *How*, 93: The Septuagint did not appear to have a fixed or closed canon of books, however, as no "two early Greek manuscripts agree as to which books are to be included in the Septuagint." In spite of the appearance of a less restrictive canon, some of the early users of the Septuagint, like Philo of Alexandria (20 BC – 50 AD) and Josephus (37 AD – sometime after 100 AD), still appear to support the 24-book Hebrew canon (Bruce, *Canon*, 46).
20. Barclay, *Making*, 47-48: "So long as the original apostles survived there was no need for written records of the life and words of Jesus. The apostles were the eye-witnesses who knew. They were at once the repositories and the guarantors of Christian truth. They were the living books on which Jesus had written His message." See Barclay, *Making*, 43-59 on the delay in writing, the end of the oral tradition, and the need for written literature.
21. Quoted by Eusebius, *The Ecclesiastical History* 3.39, cited by Bruce, *New Testament Documents*, 29; Gamble, *Canon*, 26-27.
22. See Birger Gerhardsson, *Memory and Manuscript: Oral Tradition and Written Transmission in Rabbinic Judaism and Early Christianity* (Grand Rapids: Eerdmans, 1998); cf. Barclay, *Making*, 56.
23. Some believe there was an original collection of the sayings of Jesus, perhaps written in Aramaic, Jesus' spoken language. Scholars sometimes refer to such a document as "Q" (German *Quelle*) as a possible source of our Gospels written in Greek. See, e.g., Barclay, *Making*, 73; Bruce, *New Testament Documents*, 37-39: a fragment of Papias reads: "Matthew, compiled the Logia in the 'Hebrew' speech, and every one translated them as best he could."
24. Barclay, *Making*, 66.
25. Lightfoot, *How*, 21.
26. Aland and Aland, *Text*, 49; Barclay, *Making*, 65.
27. Bruce, *New Testament Documents*, 25, with n. 1; Ewert, *Introduction*, 119; Gamble, *Canon*, 43; Barclay, *Making*, 65.
28. Barclay, *Making*, 65.
29. Marcion was branded a heretic and excommunicated in the second century by the church at Rome. His collection or "canon" of scripture only contained ten of Paul's letters (which appear to have been edited) and an edited Gospel of Luke; he rejected the whole Hebrew Bible and the rest of the New Testament books. Many believe that the church began formulating a concrete list of New Testament books as a necessary

response to Marcion. Barclay (*Making*, 83-84) suggests that the canon was closed, at least in principle, as a response to the spiritual/prophetic claims of Montanus (between AD 156 and 172), who at one point said, "I am the Father and the Son and the Paraclete." On the potential influence of Marcionism and other theological controversies on the formation of the canon, see, e.g., Gamble, *Canon*, 59-67.

30. Bruce, *New Testament Documents*, 25; cf. also Dungan, *Constantine's Bible*, 43-44; Barclay, *Making*, 80 regarding Marcion's collection. Sheler (*Is the Bible True?*, 19) says, "It is known from second-century sources that Paul's letters were being copied and widely circulated among the churches of Asia Minor by no later than the early decades of the second century, along with what were described as 'memoirs' of the apostles, which later would become known as the 'gospels.'" Aland and Aland, *Text*, 49: "Unlike the Gospels, the letters of Paul were apparently preserved from the first as a collection. At first there were small collections in individual churches; these grew by a process of exchange until finally about the mid-second century the Pastoral letters were added and the collection of the fourteen Pauline letters was considered complete."
31. Barclay, *Making*, 74; Ewert, *Introduction*, 121.
32. Bruce, *New Testament Documents*, 23; cf. Barclay, *Making*, 74.
33. Barclay, *Making*, 74.
34. Lightfoot, *How*, 83-84; Gamble, *Canon*, 28-29; Barclay, *Making*, 75: "Justin Martyr (A.D. 110-165) quotes copiously, although not accurately, but practically never from anything other than our Gospels."
35. Bruce, *New Testament Documents*, 23-24; Gamble, *Canon*, 30-31.
36. Barclay, *Making*, 75-76. Gamble (*Canon*, 31-32) contends that the defensive nature of Irenaeus's remarks implies that the idea must have been somewhat of an innovation. Others don't take it that way (see, e.g., Barclay, *Making the Bible*, 75-76). Irenaeus's statement shows, at the very least, that there was enough precedent for him to make and believe (as evident by its force) the argument for a fourfold Gospel. Ewert, *Introduction*, 127: "Clement of Alexandria (died 215) knew many gospels, but he gave the highest place to our four canonical Gospels." Like Irenaeus, Jerome later used the four corners and rings of the Ark of the Covenant as a symbol of the four Gospels (Barclay, *Making*, 76).
37. Barclay, *Making*, 75-76: ". . . midway through the second century our four Gospels held a place of undoubted and unquestioned authority within the Church."

38. Aland and Aland, *Text*, 50: "Acts, however, was probably at first associated with the Gospels (cf. p^{46}, and also Codex Bezae Cantabrigiensis)."
39. Bruce, *New Testament Documents*, 24-25. Acts appears to have been separated from Luke to form "The Gospel" collection (see Bruce, *New Testament Documents*, 24).
40. Lightfoot, *How*, 84.
41. Besides that of "the heretic" Marcion (AD 140) who intentionally excluded all books with significant Jewish influence (Bruce, *New Testament Documents*, 22).
42. It "curiously" adds the Wisdom of Solomon after the two Epistles of John (Bruce, *New Testament Documents*, 22, with n. 2) and includes the Apocalypse of Peter, which it describes as "apocryphal," with a note that some refuse to have it read in church (Bruce, *New Testament Documents*, 22-23, with n. 1); see also *Gamble*, Canon, 32-33.
43. Keating, "Criteria," 7, citing Hans von Campenhausen, *The Formation of the Christian Bible* (trans. J. A. Baker; Philadelphia: Fortress, 1977) 271, 275-76; Ewert, *Introduction*, 126: "Generally speaking, then, twenty-two books of the NT were accepted in the Western church by A.D. 200."
44. Metzger, *Canon*, 75; Barclay, *Making*, 84: "So, then, by the end of the second century the Church had reached a position in which the Canon of the New Testament was well on the way to being defined, and in which in principle it was agreed that the production of sacred Scripture had come to an end." Barclay (*Making*, 86) offers this summary:

    "So, then, by A.D. 300 it is quite certain that the New Testament contained the following indisputable books—the four Gospels, Acts, fourteen letters of Paul including Hebrews, 1 Peter, 1 John, and the Revelation with just a tinge of doubt. Still on the fringe of the New Testament were James, 2 Peter, 2 and 3 John, Jude, although Jude was included as early as the Muratorian Canon. We must be quite clear about these books against which there was a question mark. Their usefulness for life and doctrine is not in question; they were freely used and freely quoted; there is no question of their rejection. Eusebius supplies a list of books which were definitely rejected—the Shepherd of Hermas, the Apocalypse of Peter, the Letter of Barnabas, the so-called Teaching of the Apostles. Although

Eusebius and Origen list these books as disputed, they never suggest discarding them."
45. Gamble, *Canon*, 50; Barclay, *Making*, 85.
46. Origin includes the Epistle of Barnabas, the Shepherd of Hermas, the *Didache*, and the "Gospel according to the Hebrews" among the questioned works (Bruce, *New Testament Documents*, 25).
47. On Eusebius and his categories, see Dungan, *Constantine's Bible*, esp. 54-93; Barclay, *Making*, 85-86.
48. Gamble, *Canon*, 53.
49. Sheler, *Is the Bible True?*, 20.
50. Gamble, *Canon*, 54-55; Barclay, *Making*, 43.
51. And possibly the Council of Rome in AD 382 (our reference to the Council of Rome is secondary). The Council of Laodicea in 363-64 AD appears to have approved a collection of 26 New Testament books (omitting Revelation), though the actual list of books may have been added later. What was approved at the Council of Carthage in 419 AD concerning the New Testament canon was accepted by the Council of Nicea II (AD 797) and later by the Council of Trent (1545-63). These councils approved what is considered the modern Roman Catholic canon, including the apocrypha. Other denominational councils followed suit in articulating their official canons.
52. Bruce, *New Testament Documents*, 27; Gamble, *Canon*, 55-56; Dungan, *Constantine's Bible*, 134. The Council of Laodicea (363 AD) forbade the reading of non-canonical books, as if which ones would have been known (Ewert, *Introduction*, 129). A list that may have been added later includes 26 of our current New Testament books, omitting Revelation; the Old Testament included the 22 books of the Hebrew Bible plus Baruch and the Letter of Jeremiah.
53. Bruce, *Canon*, 215.
54. Sheler, *Is the Bible True?*, 20: "Apostolic connection, conformity to the 'rule of faith,' and acceptance and usage in the churches had been the keys. Conciliar action and papal decree had only ratified what had already become apparent"; Gamble, *Canon*, 56.
55. Lightfoot, *How*, 84-85. Similarly, F. F. Bruce (*New Testament Documents*, 27) offers this observation:

> "One thing must be emphatically stated. The New Testament books did not become authoritative for the Church because they were formally included in a canonical list; on the

contrary, the Church included them in her canon because she already regarded them as divinely inspired, recognizing their innate worth and generally apostolic authority, direct or indirect."

56. For discussions, see Lightfoot, *How*, 88-95; Ewert, *Introduction*, 73-83. A good, recent overview of the Old Testament Apocrypha can be found in Evans, *Ancient Texts*, 9-25; a classic study is Nickelsburg's, *Jewish Literature between the Bible and the Mishnah*.
57. See Lightfoot, *How*, 91-95 for a good presentation of why these books are rejected.
58. Ewert's (*Introduction*, 74) succinct phrase.
59. The Greek Orthodox Church includes 3 and 4 Maccabees, 1 Esdras, Odes (which includes the Prayer of Manasses), and Psalm 151.
60. Cf. Lightfoot, *How*, 93.
61. Ewert, *Introduction*, 77.
62. Martin Luther included apocryphal books in an appendix that he called the "Apocrypha" in his German translation, but he also moved Hebrews, James, Jude, and Revelation to the end, seeing them as less than canonical. Similarly, the apocrypha was originally included in the King James Version. When used by Catholics, "deuterocanonical" does not mean *less* canonical; only that they became canonical at a secondary, that is, later time.
63. There were other ancient texts, often written in the name of some well-respected leader of the Jewish people like Moses or Enoch; these books are referred to as the Pseudepigrapha, which means "pseudo-" or "false-writings." A good overview can be found in Evans, *Ancient Texts*, 26-75; the classic collection is *The Old Testament Pseudepigrapha*, edited by James H. Charlesworth.
64. For an overview of these, see Evans, *Ancient Texts*, 256-67. The classic collection of these works is *New Testament Apocrypha*, edited by Wilhelm Schneemelcher. These works are sometimes also called "pseude-pigrapha," as in this citation from Cyril of Jerusalem (writing in 347 or 348 AD): "The four Gospels alone belong to the New Testament; the rest are pseudepigrapha (that is, written under assumed names and falsely attributed to great apostolic figures) and harmful" (*Catecheses* 4.36; cited in Barclay, *Making*, 74).

Chapter 1

65. An exception is the Ethiopian Orthodox Church, which recognizes as canonical the Shepherd of Hermas, 1 Clement, Acts of Paul, and several other Old Testament books.
66. In addition to the books specifically on the topic of the canon listed at the end of this chapter, helpful overviews can be found in Bruce, "The Canon of the New Testament," in *New Testament Documents*, 21-28; Lightfoot, "The Canon of the Scriptures," in *How*, 81-87; Ewert, *Introduction*, 123-34; Sheler, "Canon and Content: The Bible as Sacred Scripture," in *Is the Bible True*, 15-21.
67. Sheler, *Is the Bible True?*, 15. On the historical use and meaning of the word "canon," see Dungan, *Constantine's Bible*, 26-29.
68. Bruce, *New Testament Documents*, 21.
69. The following is taken from Bruce, *New Testament Documents*, 18-19; cf. Aland and Aland, *Text*, 48-49.
70. Gamble (*Canon*, 67) says that the church "engaged in a reflective evaluation of its literary and theological heritage." Dungan (*Constantine's Bible*, 69, 78-79) makes these comments: "Keep in mind that Eusebius and his predecessors sifted through more than 100 writings that had been cited or used as supposed apostolic writings, by some person or group, during the previous 250 years . . ."; "The fundamental purpose of the entire orthodox Scripture selection process was to identify, with all the certainty their methods would permit, exactly those writings bequeathed to posterity by Jesus' apostles."
71. On the "criteria of canonicity," see Gamble, *Canon*, 67-72; Dungan, *Constantine's Bible*, 61-93; McDonald, *Canon*, 401-21.
72. Barclay (*Making*, 64-65) outlines the stages of how a book became canonical:
    > "It has to be written; it has to be widely read; it has to be accepted as useful for life and for doctrine; it has to make its way into the public worship of the Church; it has to win acceptance not simply locally but throughout the whole Church; and finally it has to be officially approved by the voice and decision of the Church."
73. See Barclay, *Making*, 60-61 for emphasis on the role of a book in public worship as the first step toward canonicity.
74. Irenaeus, *Against the Heresies* 3.1.1; Eusebius, *The Ecclesiastical History* 3.39.15.

75. Irenaeus, *Against the Heresies* 3.3.3 (cited in Dungan, *Constantine's Bible*, 45, with n. 34); see also Eusebius, *The Ecclesiastical History* 3.3.3 (cited in Duncan, *Constantine's Bible*, 61) and cf. Dungan, *Constantine's Bible*, 45-49, 54-93.
76. A succinct summary of this idea is presented by Corey Keating, "The Criteria Used for Developing the New Testament Canon in the First Four Centuries of the Christian Church" (Fuller Theological Seminary Paper, 2000) 1-15, published online at http://www.coreykeating.com/SeminaryPapers/SeminaryPapers.html.
77. Cf., e.g., Dungan, *Constantine's Bible*, 83: "For Eusebius, it meant this: Was the writing in question actively used by the orthodox Catholic bishops in all of the main apostolic succession churches in public worship and as a source for theology and church government, from earliest times down to Eusebius' own day?"
78. McDonald (*Canon*, 405-21) identifies and discusses these criteria: Apostolicity, Orthodoxy, Antiquity, Use, Adaptability, and Inspiration as a corollary rather than a criterion of canonicity.
79. Barclay, *Making*, 78.
80. Many other fragments from as early as the fifth century AD have also been discovered (Ewert, *Introduction*, 92).
81. Ewert, *Introduction*, 91; Lightfoot, *How*, 69-70, 75.
82. Because of the care used in copying the manuscripts, Jewish scribes did not think older manuscripts any better than newer ones. Once they became worn, were copied and no longer needed, they were deposited in synagogue storage rooms and later reverently buried with elaborate ceremony (Ewert, *Introduction*, 85-86).
83. Though most of the texts found at Qumran are very fragmentary, there is a full copy of the book of Isaiah called the Great Isaiah Scroll.
84. Lightfoot, *How*, 76-79. The discoveries also revealed multiple lines of textual tradition, however (see Ewert, *Introduction*, 94).
85. Ewert, *Introduction*, 95.
86. There are many sources that could be consulted and studied on the integrity and reliability of the text of the New Testament. A nice introduction to textual criticism as it applies to the New Testament can be found in Lightfoot, *How*, 27-80. The classic, scholarly studies of textual criticism are Metzger, *The Text of the New Testament,* and Aland and Aland, *The Text of the New Testament.* See Elliott, "Text of the New Testament," 227-53 for a recent overview; also Bruce, *New Testament*

Documents; Sheler, *Is the Bible True?*; and Childers and Parker, *Transmission and Reception* for overviews and discussions of several related topics.

87. On the threefold witness (manuscripts, ancient translations, and early church leaders/writers) to the text of the New Testament, see Metzger, *Text*, 36-92; Aland and Aland, *Text*, 72-217; Ewert, *Introduction*, 135-46, 163-82.

88. For example, Daniel Wallace recently made reference to an upcoming publication by E. J. Brill (in 2013) about new manuscript discoveries, including a first-century fragment from the Gospel of Mark (see, e.g., "Discovery of the Earliest New Testament Manuscript?!?!," *Earliest Christianity: Perspectives on the development of Early Christianity* [Feb.6, 2012]: http://earliestchristianity.wordpress.com/2012/02/06/discovery-of-the-earliest-new-testament-manuscript). If the first-century date is verified by scholars, this would be a remarkable discovery that will challenge some views of the chronology/dating of New Testament books.

    Carsten Peter Thiede (based on initial work of Jose O'Callaghan) has issued a stream of publications asserting that some of the small papyrus fragments from Cave 7 of Qumran are actually pieces of New Testament documents; in particular Mark 6:52-53, pushing the date back to around 50 AD, which would make these the oldest surviving pieces of the New Testament. He makes a similar claim regarding the need to redate the Magdalen Fragment (of Matthew) to as early as 60 AD. Most current scholars have not been persuaded by Thiede's arguments. For a sampling of his work, see Carsten Peter Thiede, *The Earliest Gospel Manuscript?: The Qumran Papyrus 7Q5 and Its Significance for New Testament Studies* (Exeter [Devon, England]: Paternoster Press, 1992); *Rekindling the Word: In Search of Gospel Truth.* (Valley Forge, PA: Trinity, 1995); Carsten Peter Thiede and Matthew d'Ancona, *Eyewitness to Jesus: Amazing New Manuscript Evidence about the Origins of the Gospels* (New York: Doubleday, 1996).

89. Metzger, *Text*, 38-39; Aland and Aland, *Text*, 84-87; Bruce, *New Testament Documents*, 17-18.

90. Metzger, *Text*, 37-38; Aland and Aland, *Text*, 87.

91. Metzger, *Text*, 39-40 ("Herbert Hunger, the director of the papyrological collections in the National Library of Vienna, dates p^{66} earlier, in the middle if not even in the first half of the second century . . ." [40, n. 1]); Aland and Aland, *Text*, 87.

92. Metzger, *Text*, 41.

93. Metzger, *Text*, 42-48; Aland and Aland, *Text*, 106-8.
94. For this type of information, see Bruce, *New Testament Documents*, 16-17; Ewert, *Introduction*, 139.
95. Bruce, *New Testament Documents*, 15-17.
96. Metzger, *Text*, 86; cf. Bruce, *New Testament Documents*, 18-19.
97. On ancient versions of the Old Testament, such as The Samaritan Pentateuch, the Aramaic Targums, and the Septuagint, see Evans, *Ancient Texts*, 155-66; Ewert, *Introduction*, 99-111. For discussions of ancient versions of the New Testament, see Metzger, *Text*, 67-86; Aland and Aland, *Text*, 181-217; Ewert, *Introduction*, 163-82.
98. Metzger, *Text*, 67; Aland and Aland, *Text*, 181: "The early versions... start from about A.D. 180."
99. For a summary of the journey of the Latin Bible to England, including before and after Jerome, see Daniell, *The Bible in English*, 23-27.
100. Metzger, *Text*, 75-76.
101. Aland and Aland, *Text*, 187-88, 196; Dungan, *Constantine's Bible*, 127; Daniell, *The Bible in English*, 26; see Daniell, *The Bible in English*, 25-26 for a brief summary of Jerome and his importance for the English Bible.
102. Bruce, *Canon*, 225; for a summary of the thousand year reign of the Vulgate, see Rawlings, *Trial by Fire*, 27-31.
103. Ewert, *Introduction*, 179.
104. Ewert, *Introduction*, 178; cf. Rawlings (*Trial by Fire*, 30):
    "In its long history it has exerted an incalculable influence not only on the piety but the languages, literature and art of Western Europe. It inspired Dante, Leonardo da Vinci, Raphael, Michelangelo, and the sculptors of Chartres. When printing was invented, the first book to come from the press of Johannes Gutenberg of Mainz, Germany, in 1454/1455 was Jerome's Latin Vulgate."
105. Ewert, *Introduction*, 179; Rummel, "Renaissance Humanists," 289-90.
106. Metzger, *Text*, 76.
107. Daniell, *The Bible in English*, 9 (see quote in n. 108 below). See Moynahan (*God's Bestseller*, xviii-xix) for a brief overview of the journey (of Bible translations) from Jerome to Wycliffe, including reference to the pre-Wycliffe English versions.
108. As Daniell (*The Bible in English*, 9) expresses it:

> "The necessary next stage, the translation from the originals into the many spoken languages of the known world, was blocked by the increasing power of the Bishop of Rome. He claimed supreme authority over the whole Church as pope (an authority always denied by the Orthodox churches to the East), and decreed that the Bible could exist only in the assembly of Latin translations made by Jerome about 400.... The Old and New Testaments did not just take second place to the pope's authority: as far as the ordinary faithful man and woman were concerned, they largely disappeared."

109. Though commenting specifically on the influence of imperial politics on the church, Dungan's (*Constantine's Bible*, 125) line captures some of the same sentiment: "Were not their voices [Jesus, Paul, Jeremiah, etc.] snuffed out, encased in heavy leather bindings of the lavishly illustrated codexes, lying on cold stone altars in giant stone buildings?"

110. Cf. Daniell's (*The Bible in English*, 7-9) discussion of "The Bible and the People."

111. Ewert, *Introduction*, 129: "It should be said straight off that no council ever made a book of the NT canonical. They simply affirmed those books that the church through long usage had found to speak with the voice of the living God." Speaking of the Old Testament, Barclay (*Making*, 40) says,

> "The books of the Old Testament took their place as sacred Scripture, not because of the *fiat* or decision of any council or committee of the Church, but because history and experience had manifestly and effectively demonstrated them to be the word of God. These were the books in which men had met God in the times which tried men's souls, and in which they had discovered the strength and the comfort of the Almighty. When any council gave any decision in regard to any book or books of the Old Testament, it was simply repeating and affirming that which experience had already proved. Such councils did not make these books into sacred Scripture and into the word of God; they simply recorded the fact that men had already mightily found them so."

112. Barclay, *Making*, 93-94.

Chapter 2

The Bible Set Free

The importance of the Bible in the culture of the world should not need to be spelled out. The Jewish and Christian Scriptures, flowing together as they do, have for two thousand years flooded into all levels of Western living, a permeation greater even than the classical inheritance from Greece and Rome. The Bible has been high, often supreme, in its influence. . . . if by some hideous accident at the divine computer keyboard the "delete" key were pressed for the Bible, much of the content of Western culture would disappear and it would shrivel like a deflating balloon.[1]

Not only has the Bible been fundamental in the making of Western culture as a whole, but it's important to us personally as families and individuals.

How many Bibles do you have at your house? If you're like me, you have several, maybe a bunch. And how much did they cost? Some are pretty expensive, others cost next to nothing, and some are free, received as gifts or awards or passed down in families. We don't think much of it, but it's really a priceless treasure to be able to sit down any time we want, open the Book, and see what God says. Isn't that incredible? It's an indescribable privilege and blessing. But how did it happen? How did we get from the ancient copies of the Bible in Greek and then in Latin, with only a select few having access to the words of scripture, to the place where we can all have our own personal copies to read and use any time, any way we want? And what does such freedom mean?

Chapter 2

A Dream Come True

> For in every small point of the sacred page, so many meanings fly on the wings of virtue, such stores of wealth are accumulated, that only he can fully exhaust them whom God has inspired. Shall not therefore the Word given to the unlearned be as *pearls before swine*, when we know them to be fitted neither to receive it, nor to give out what they have received? Away with this idea, and let it be rooted out. *The ointment ran down from the head, even to the skirts of his clothing*: waters flow from the spring, not from the mud of public ways.[2]

So said Walter Map, an Englishman, who saw some of the earliest Waldensian translations of the Bible. These translations were the result of the influence of Peter Waldo (1140–1218), a rich man from Lyons in east-central France, who paid a priest named Bernardu Ydros to translate portions of the Bible. (Waldo later gave away his wealth out of commitment to Christ.) The impact started a movement in southern France, Italy, and Spain that came to be known as the Waldensians (or Waldenses). Similar to the followers of John Wycliffe ("Lollards": more on this shortly), these common folks traveled the countryside—delivering their ideas of strict adherence to the gospel in villages, open places, houses, and churches of their day—armed with the words of scripture (the basis of their movement and their message) that they had memorized from portions of the Bible translated into their own languages. Having attended the Third Lateran Council in 1179, Map pronounced his view on the futility and danger of putting scripture into the hands of the common people.[3]

As the movement spread, official opposition grew in proportion. In July 1199, Pope Innocent III returned a letter from the archbishop of Metz (in northeast France) who requested authorization for the repressive measures he was about to take. While complimenting the desire of anyone to understand and live by the holy scriptures, Innocent III went on to say,

> The secret mysteries of the faith ought not therefore to be explained to all men in all places, since they cannot be everywhere understood by all men but only to those who can conceive them with a faithful mind, for what says the apostle to simple people? *Even as babes in Christ I have fed you with milk and not with meat.* For such is the depth of divine scripture, that not only the simple and illiterate, but even the prudent and learned, are not fully sufficient to try to understand it. *For many seek and fail in their search*, whence it was of old rightly written in the divine law, that *the beast which touched the mount should be stoned* lest, apparently, any simple and unlearned person should presume to attain to the sublimity of holy scripture. *Seek not out the things that are above thee.*[4]

What if you were told that? Let's put it another way: can everyday folks read and understand the Bible for themselves? In the days when the Bible was first becoming available for everyone to read, many didn't think so. But not everyone.

> I vehemently dissent from those who would not have private persons read the Holy Scriptures, nor have them translated into the vulgar tongues. I would wish that all women—girls even—would read the Gospels and the letters of Paul. I wish that they were translated into all languages of all people. To make them understood is surely the first step. . . . I long that the husbandman should sing portions of them to himself as he follows the plough, that the weaver should hum them to the tune of his shuttle, that the traveller should beguile with their stories the tedium of his journey.[5]

These are the words of Erasmus of Rotterdam (1466-1536), a sixteenth century Christian humanist, from the Preface (*Paraclesis*—meaning exhortation) to the first printed edition of the Greek New Testament, published in 1516. Because of his work in translating and publishing the Bible in its original languages, Erasmus was accused of

Chapter 2

having laid the egg that Martin Luther hatched,[6] believing everyone should have access to the Bible in his or her own, everyday language.[7]

More than a century before Erasmus, John Wycliffe (1324-84) championed a similar view, affirming the authority of scripture over that of the church and its traditions.[8] Credited with making the first English translation—and often now referred to as the "'morning star' of the Reformation"[9]—with a team of followers called Lollards (pejoratively, at first), Wycliffe circulated hand-written copies of scripture in English throughout the countryside of England.[10] In direct confrontation with the church of his day, Wycliffe affirmed the Bible as the only true religious authority and asserted the right of every person to examine the Bible for himself or herself, believing that true understanding comes from those who approach it with humility and love, "for Christ did not write his laws on tables, or on skins of animals, but in the hearts of men."[11]

William Tyndale (1494-1536) believed whole-heartedly in making the Bible available to the common people. Exasperated at Tyndale's ideas served up over dinner, a "learned" religious leader said that we would be better off without God's laws than the Pope's. Reacting with fiery passion and emerging determination (which he would live out the rest of his life), Tyndale responded: "If God spares my life [he had to run for his life from the authorities on numerous occasions], before many years pass I will make it possible for a boy behind the plow to know more Scripture than you do."[12]

Bibles don't cost much these days—unless you get the really nice, leather-bound, thumb-indexed, personalized . . . version. And many of us have those because our Bibles are important to us, as they have been in Western civilization from the beginning. In the United States, you can get "give-away" copies of the Bible for next to nothing, however, and they are freely available.

I received a catalog in the mail this week from CBD (Christian Book Distributors), a popular, Christian book distributor. The choices of Bibles, as well as books about the Bible, are staggering. (Bear with me as I give you a longer description than is probably necessary.) There were 13 pages of English versions of the Bible. I started to count the actual number of different versions, but gave up, the number was so high and the print so small. Page 1 featured the NLT Study Bible, ESV Study Bible, NIV Study Bible, Ryrie NASB Study Bible, NASB Hebrew-Greek Key Word Study Bible, NKJV Chronological Study Bible, and the NIV Adventure Bible, among others. Some come in the standard-size edition, others in the new personal-size, in hardcover, soft leather-look, green, indexed, soft leather-red, soft leather, black, burgundy, genuine leather, etc.—with an assortment of styles and options. Page 2 has the *NLT Slimline Reference Bible, Graduate Edition*, with special features like the words of Christ in red. The *HCSB Graduate's Bible* is available, as is the *TNIV College Devotional Bible*. There's the *NLT New Believer's Bible*, the *NASB New Inductive Study Bible*, the *NIV Archaeological Study Bible*, the *NIV Quest Study Bible, The Word: The Bible from 26 Translations* . . . ("Etcetera, etcetera, etcetera," as the King of Siam in *The King and I* would say).

And there are many, many more: all sorts of types, styles, special features, and accessories. (Perhaps it would be better just to have you do an internet search on "English versions of the Bible"; you'll see what I'm talking about.) I think my favorite title in this catalog was the *NKJV New Spirit-Filled Life Bible for Women* (I wonder what a Bible that wasn't "Spirit-Filled" would be like. Maybe that's the . . . *for Men* version). There was also the *NKJV Personal-Size Giant-Print Reference Bible* (and I wondered how "Giant-Print" and "Personal-Size" go together).

The list of Bible translations and options is seemingly endless. Not only is there a plethora of printed Bibles for reading, there are also numerous types of audio and electronic Bibles—for spuds and pods and pads and phones . . . The whole catalog contained 64 pages of every kind of Bible resource imaginable. In addition to translations of the Bible itself, there're books about the history, content, and impact of the Bible. Commentaries in single volumes and massive sets. Books on outreach and discipleship, personal and spiritual growth, prayer, favorite authors from favorite churches, on women and by women, devotionals, inspirational reading, autobiographies and biographies . . . (believe it or not, I cut out 4 lines) . . . systematic theology, reference tools, software, Christian music . . . And the list goes on and on.

A book by Beth Moore called *Praying God's Word* caught my eye because it reminded me of Erasmus. Erasmus looked forward to the day people could use the very words of scripture to sing and pray. I wonder what he would think of Stormie Omartian's *The NIV Power of a Praying Woman Bible*, designed to help women seek the Father in his word. Though this catalog didn't advertise a lot of music—the distributor produces another one for that—contemporary Christian music has a host of songs (many that we use in our assemblies) that contain the words of scripture in the lyrics. Erasmus envisioned followers of Christ relieving the weariness of their journeys—and he was speaking literally—by reciting or singing the words of scripture (Sandi Patty has a CD called *Songs for the Journey*. And, of course, Christians have been doing this long before Sandy Patty).

If you're interested in studying the Bible in the original languages, the catalog has Greek and Hebrew tools galore. One Bible software package boasted of having 160 Bible translations and reference works; another, of 112 Bible translations in 32 languages! The choices of Bibles and Bible tools is no less than astonishing. They even had a copy (a facsimile) of the 1560 edition of *The Geneva Bible*—the Bible used by Shakespeare and brought to the U.S. by the Puritans and Pilgrims (just think, it was read on the decks of the *Mayflower!*).[13] It influenced the translation of the King James Version more than any other source and—get this—retained 90% of William Tyndale's original English translation![14]

The accessibility of the Bible in English and many other languages is wide and getting wider all the time. In fact, the choices can be rather confusing and almost overwhelming. (Years ago, our local newspaper ran a story called "Which Word?" with the caption: "Bibles today come in a confusing variety of translations and reader-oriented formats.")[15] There's no doubt that the dreams of the Reformers—Protestant and Catholic alike—for the Bible to be available to everyone in the everyday language of the people (and I'm talking now about English in particular) so that we can have free access to the words of God in scripture have come true—beyond their wildest imaginations. At last count, at least portions of the Bible have been translated into more than 2,400 languages.[16] In his history of the English Bible published in 2003, David Daniell says that since Tyndale's first printed Bibles, 350 new translations of the entire Bible have been translated from the original Hebrew and Greek and published in English, along with thousands of translations of the New Testament alone.[17]

For centuries now, "the folks" have indeed sung the words of scripture as we plowed the fields (as Erasmus envisioned) or programmed computers (to make an historical jump). Believers often worship God with the very words of the Bible, listening and singing as we ride on our bikes, drive in our cars, or soar through the air, plugging the words of scripture into our ears via electronic gadgets and apps of various sorts (the number of which will only increase as time goes on and technology advances). To put it briefly, *for most of us, the Bible is freely available.* We can own personal copies and read them whenever we like. What a tremendous gift and blessing! It *is* a dream come true, an unspeakable gift! (I wonder—to pause for a second—if such a gift carries a reciprocal responsibility.) It's such a blessing and has been accomplished so wonderfully that *we can hardly imagine it otherwise.* Like a Gideon Bible in the dusty drawer of a hotel or small, green New Testaments handed out to passersby on the corner of a busy intersection, the Bible is so commonplace today that we don't think of its presence or readability as a gift or an issue—in fact, we don't think of it. It's just there. But believe me, *it was otherwise;* there was a time not so long ago when it wasn't here, and I'd like for you to think about that for a little while. *Free access to the words of scripture now taken for granted was expensive—very expensive.* Many of us have little idea how much it cost.[18]

Chapter 2

How Much for My Own Personal Version?

The idea that the Bible should be available to everyone, to read in his or her own "vernacular" (the everyday language of the people) was a fundamental premise of the Protestant Reformation.[19] It started with some key individuals and swept through the fields of change that ripened across Europe during the age of Renaissance and Reform (roughly 1300-1600).[20] Traceable in part to the general rediscovery of language and learning toward the end of the Middle Ages, interest in the Bible grew most particularly out of the efforts of the people to free themselves from the oppressive control of the church and politics of that time. For nearly a thousand years, the Bible was only available in Latin, and only for a few (the scholar and the cleric); and not just in Latin, but one particular version of the Bible called the Latin Vulgate, that over time had become so inaccurate and corrupt[21] as to be used as part of the strong arm of the church to dominate and control the people. As Daniell and Rawlings put it, ". . . both Old and New Testaments were locked away from the people, the Bible considered too sacred to be touched by any but the most learned." "It was a text suited only for priests, dusty, locked up in Latin, safely beyond the reach of the average Englishman."[22] When outspoken leaders began to envision and produce new translations of the Bible—in order to breathe spiritually, so to speak—the church responded with almost inconceivable, vicious and violent opposition.

"Our Father who art in heaven, hallowed be thy name . . ." What if you'd never heard those words? Or what if you would be arrested or even killed for saying them out loud in English? Hard to imagine, isn't it? But it was once that way. Let me highlight a few extraordinary people and events.

Pope Martin V was so infuriated by the teachings and influence of John Wycliffe that in 1428 he had Wycliffe's bones dug up, burned, crushed, and scattered in the river, 44 years after his death.[23] What was his crime? In addition to his outspoken ideas, Wycliffe and his followers ("Lollards") had spread written manuscripts of English translations (from Latin) in the late 1300s. These manuscripts circulated illegally for almost 150 years before the first printed English

Bible appeared. In order to deal with these "Bible-men," in 1401 (at the urging of Thomas Arundell, the Archbishop of Canterbury) Parliament passed a law called *De Haeretico Comburendo* ("On the Burning of Heretics") that made heresy punishable by burning at the stake. This is why it was such a big deal for those who wanted to make the Bible available to the common people through these "heretical" translations. In 1408 Arundell created the *Constitutions of Oxford* (to deal with these translations), which said,

> It is a dangerous thing, as witnesseth blessed St. Jerome to translate the text of the Holy Scripture out of one tongue into another, for in the translation the same sense is not always easily kept. . . . We therefore decree and ordain, that no man, hereafter, by his own authority translate any text of the Scripture into English or any other tongue, by way of a book, libel or treatise; and that no man can read any such book . . . in part or in whole.[24]

The penalty was severe: violators were

> to be accursed eating and drinking, walking and sitting, rowing and riding, laughing and weeping, in house and in field, on water and on land . . . Cursed be their head and their thoughts, their eyes and their ears, their tongues and their lips, their teeth and their throats . . .[25]

No mercy was to be shown, under any circumstances. Those who simply read the scriptures in English were to "forfeit land, cattle, life, and goods, from their heirs for ever, and so be condemned for heretics to God, enemies to the crown, and most arrant traitors to the land."[26]

When John Hus, one of Wycliffe's most influential followers, was burned at the stake in 1415, they kindled the fire with Wycliffe's hand-written English versions. Think about that for a minute. They used hand-written copies of the Bible in English, those being spread throughout England for the good and salvation of the people, to start the fire. How hot burned the resistance to a free Bible! (Places where Wycliffe's followers were to be burned came to be known as "Lollard pits."[27]) As Hus was brought from the cathedral of Constance to a stake prepared for him on the banks of the Rhine, they led him past a bonfire of his own writings that had been set ablaze in the cemetery.[28]

Another example: As a boy of 11, the dramatist John Bale watched a young man burned to death in Norwich for possessing the Lord's Prayer in English. *Foxe's Book of Martyrs* records that seven followers of Wycliffe (six men and a woman) were burned at Coventry in 1519 for teaching their children and family the Lord's Prayer and the Ten Commandments in English rather than Latin.[29]

English translations were often confiscated and burned by the hundreds. Hard to believe, isn't it? On the other hand, this wasn't the first time this sort of thing had happened in history. They've tried to burn the Bible and those who believe in it on numerous occasions. In 303 A.D., for example, the Roman emperor Diocletian tried to eradicate Christianity from the imperial capital once and for all. He ordered the burning of all the Bibles in the city, along with all the churches and homes where they were found. Christians who refused to offer sacrifices to the pagan gods were arrested and put in jail. Torture and bloodshed ensued. In December of 303, "Galerius prevailed upon Diocletian to pass a fourth edict commanding all citizens to offer sacrifice to the Emperors on pain of death. Large numbers of Christians accepted death rather than comply."[30] But the books of the Bible didn't disappear. In fact, within three years, Diocletian was gone, and the new emperor, Constantine, became a Christian and welcomed the Bible into the heart of the Roman Empire.[31]

Back to our story of the English Bible. William Tyndale was so devoted to the cause of putting the Bible into the hands of the common people that he offered to turn himself in to King Henry VIII and never write another book if the King would give his official endorsement to a vernacular Bible for the English people. Stephen Vaughn—an English merchant sent by Thomas Cromwell, the King's advisor, to find Tyndale and tell him that the King wanted him to come back to England out of hiding—told Cromwell, "I find him always singing one note."[32] To the King's offer of mercy, Tyndale repeated that refrain:

> I assure you, if it would stand with the King's most gracious pleasure to grant only a bare text of the Scripture [that is, without explanatory notes called glosses] to be put forth among his people, . . . I shall immediately make faithful promise never to write more, not abide two days in these parts after the same: but immediately to repair unto his realm, and there most humbly submit myself at the feet of his royal majesty, offering my body to suffer what pain or torture, yea, what death his grace will, so this [translation] be obtained.[33]

The King declined. In 1535, after being hunted for years, Tyndale was betrayed by a pretend friend, imprisoned for 18 months, garroted (strangled to death with a chain instead of being burned alive—out of distinction as a scholar),[34] and his body finally burned at the stake. They had already killed him, but they burned him anyway (as with Wycliffe, to rid the earth of every last molecule of a "heretic"). A horrible way to die, but for Tyndale probably not as painful as having to witness young men burned alive who were converted by reading his translation and books: his closest friend, John Frith, was arrested in London, tried by Thomas More, and burned alive July 4, 1531 at the age of 28; as was Richard Bayfield who ran the ships that took Tyndale's books to England.[35] To give one more gruesome example, John Tewkesbury, converted by reading Tyndale's *Parable of the Wicked Mammon*, was whipped in Thomas More's garden, had his forehead squeezed with small ropes till blood came out of his eyes, then sent to the Tower where he was racked until he was lame, and finally burned alive. Thomas More "rejoiced that his victim was now in hell, where Tyndale 'is like to find him when they come together.'"[36] For seeking to put the Bible into the hands of the common people, More believed they would burn in hell, and thus rejoiced to send them on their way. In 1543 Parliament passed an act to ban the use of Tyndale's New Testament and made it a crime to read it publicly to others.

Chapter 2

The bloodshed resumed under the reign of Queen "Bloody" Mary (1516-58), as hundreds were burned at the stake,[37] including John Rogers, assistant and successor to Tyndale, and Thomas Cranmer, the Archbishop of Canterbury who hired Myles Coverdale (another assistant of Tyndale) to publish the Great Bible. But—and here's the stirring part—all this could not stop the coming of the English Bible. It came. English versions were often smuggled into England in bales of cotton, sacks of flour, and bundles of flax. So hungry were the people for the scriptures that when John Colet, an Oxford professor and son of the Mayor of London, started translating and reading the Bible publicly in English, within six months 20,000 people packed Saint Paul's Cathedral in London to hear the words of God in a language they could understand, with at least that many more outside trying to get in. Just think, a sixteenth century mega-church, born of hunger—no, starvation—for the word.[38]

My purpose here is not to give you a detailed history of the English Bible,[39] but to help you see how our deep river of choices for owning and reading the Bible in English—how freely they sit around our churches, homes, and living rooms—flows from the blood and ashes of those who gave themselves for this cause. (I encourage you to do some reading on the history of the English Bible. It's well worth the time.) Most of us know very little of the horrible price paid many times over so we could have copies of the Bible today. No longer was the Bible to be reserved for the educated scholar, available only to the pious priest, chained to pulpits of cathedrals and scriptoriums of monasteries. On the contrary, Reformers dreamed of a Bible that was free and accessible to everyone. They lived for it; they died for it. They believed in it so much that, like the pages of the precious Bible manuscript Tischendorf pulled from the waste basket, many of these Christians were "committed to the flames" to make it a reality.

We should have tremendous respect and utter appreciation for the men and women who gave themselves to make the Bible available to us, because—and this is the point—it wasn't always that way. Even when the Great Bible was published in 1539, it was distributed to every church, "chained to the pulpit." There was a time

. . . not so long ago . . . when regular folks did not have access to the Bible.[40] It took great courage, great education and scholarship, great passion and devotion—to the point of real-life burning and bloodshed—to put the Bible into our hands. Calling upon Christ for such strength, while waiting in prison in Constance before his death, John Hus said this prayer:

> O most holy Christ, draw me, weak as I am, after Thyself, for if Thou doest not draw us we cannot follow Thee. Strengthen my spirit, that it may be willing. If the flesh is weak, let Thy grace precede us; come between and follow, for without Thee we cannot go for Thy sake to cruel death. Give me a fearless heart, a right faith, a firm hope, a perfect love, that for thy sake I may lay down my life with patience and joy. Amen.[41]

What they laid down, we pick up gratefully and freely to the immeasurable enrichment of our lives and the eternal salvation of our souls. What would life be like without our Bibles?

Chapter 2

Christianity's Dangerous Idea

The dreams of the Reformers for a freely available English Bible have certainly come true. Through the King James (1611) and other versions, Tyndale's English translation influenced Bible reading for several hundred years.[42] Some believe he had more to do with shaping the modern English language than anyone else, even Shakespeare: Tyndale is sometimes called the "architect of the English language."[43] As Daniell puts it, "The great change that came over England from 1526, the ability of every ordinary man, woman and child to read and hear the whole New Testament in English, accurately rendered, was Tyndale's work, and it's importance cannot be overemphasised";[44] "Tyndale's gift to the English language is unmeasurable."[45] "English-speaking Christians look back with rejoicing at the miracle of the English Bible."[46]

Now—to complete our brief historical journey—imagine Tyndale (or Wycliffe or Erasmus) walking into a Bible bookstore today for the first time. Can you see the look on his face? I suspect he would be amazed and overwhelmed. How quickly and deeply would tears of gratitude flow for having been a tool of God to bring his voice to the people?[47] And how cool it would be to look him in the eyes, shake his hand, hug his neck, and say "Thank you!" The Bible once chained to pulpits and locked behind thick walls of language and lecterns has indeed been set free, and I would like to remind us of how we got from there to here. The next time we open our Bibles and begin to read in English, perhaps we should take a moment to say a prayer of thanks to God for those who made it possible. Then, as we read, *let's be sure we don't subject ourselves to a new form of spiritual slavery!*

Like Wycliffe, Erasmus, Tyndale, and others, I believe it is a wonderful thing for the Bible to be available to us all. Who could think otherwise? No longer is the Bible controlled and suppressed by the church or other institutions, at least not physically. It may be suppressed by something else, however. You've heard of "unintended consequences"? There is an unintended—perhaps inevitable, though not necessarily unanticipated—consequence of our freedom of access to the scriptures. Less known for its visionary insightfulness than the dreams and predictions of Erasmus and Tyndale, this potential outcome was in fact one of the stated reasons behind the opposition to the efforts of the Reformers to put the Bible into the hands of the people.[48]

Obviously, the main reasons the church of the day opposed the efforts to make the Bible available were religious and political—the potential loss of control that would ensue if people could see for themselves what the Bible really said.[49] There were others, though.[50] At the time, illiteracy was high and some believed that English was too crude and unworthy of the exalted language of God's word. (Tyndale put the kibosh to that idea, and we later discovered that the Greek of the New Testament was actually the "common"—*koine* in Greek—language of the people of that day.) Some believed that translating would allow errors to creep into the text; so, it would be safer not to translate.[51] Many believed that it was simply beyond lay people to read and understand the Bible for themselves:[52] "Common people spoke the vernacular; they were expected to leave the interpretation of Scripture to their betters, and be content with what was mediated to them through the priests."[53] Lynne Long offers a nice summary of the climate and the concerns:

> "Reading" the Bible, in the sense of interpreting its meaning, was historically considered to be the province of scholars and theologians. The pre-Reformation Bible was written in Latin and Greek, and this provided a natural barrier that prevented misreading or misinterpretation, since access to Scripture was through sermons, or priests' explanations. Even when the vernacular Bible was first available in print, there genuinely remained . . . "the abiding fear of common access to the Scriptures."[54] This fear was partly due to a perceived loss of power and authority on the part of the mediators of the text, but it was also due to the idea that reading without a mediator might lead to heretical interpretation. Heresy meant damnation, and was to be avoided at all costs, including, if necessary, restricting access to the text.[55]

This concern was voiced in various ways and is the point that's important here: if the Bible were in English and each person could read it for himself or herself, then everyone would become his own interpreter. And what if they get it wrong?[56] Did you catch that? There was a fear that everyone would have his or her own interpretation and might misunderstand the Bible? They might read and miss the point? Sound familiar? *A key element of inkblotitis was anticipated by some who opposed making the Bible available to everyone.*[57] With no one in authority to guide them, "The resulting free-for-all of interpretations was bound to be an inferno of souls lost, a present hell of heretics destroying Christian heritage, and seething sedition."[58] A comment made by John Stokesley (1475–1539), Bishop of London, boldly highlights an aspect of this idea. In 1534, when Thomas Cranmer (1489–1556), Archbishop of Canterbury, spearheaded an effort to create an approved translation of the New Testament (as opposed to Tyndale's) by leading bishops of the day (a projected "Bishop's Bible"), Stokesley replied,

> I marvel what my lord of Canterbury meaneth that thus abuseth the people in giving them liberty to read the scriptures, which doth nothing else but *infect them with heresies* [my emphasis]. I have bestowed never an hour upon my portion, nor never will. . . . for I will never be guilty to bring the simple people into error.[59]

Others said similar things. In the early fifteenth century, an opponent of John Wycliffe wrote of his horror that "the Gospel that Christ gave to the doctors and clergy of the Church," Wycliffe made available to lay men and women: "And so the pearl of the Gospel is scattered abroad and trodden underfoot by swine."[60] During the early phase of the Reformation, Melchior Cano (1525-60), a Spanish Dominican writer, vigorously disputed the idea that ordinary people could read and understand the Bible for themselves. Roberto Bellarmine (1542-1621) argued that the Bible is difficult to interpret, "a fact that Protestantism tried to conceal by following a herd instinct and pretending that this amounted to divine guidance."[61] In 1553 Cardinal Reginald Pole (1500-58) ". . . abhorred religious argument and the spirit of self-sufficiency which he believed indiscriminate Bible-reading by lay people was likely to encourage."[62] Johannes Eck (1486-1543), a German theologian and defender of Catholicism during the Reformation, had similarly accused the leaders of the Protestant Reformation of claiming the controlling influence of the Holy Spirit to justify their diverse and even contradictory interpretations of scripture.[63] Rule IV of the preface to the Roman Index of 1564 sums up the viewpoint, declaring, "If Bibles in vernacular languages are permitted to all without discrimination there will result, due to human imprudence, more damage than profit."[64]

In his recent history of the Protestant Reformation called *Christianity's Dangerous Idea*, Alister McGrath develops the view that free access to the Bible, based on the idea that all Christians have the right to read and interpret the Bible for themselves, lies at the heart of the Protestant revolution.[65] The idea was "dangerous," McGrath argues, because it was uncontrollable:

> The dangerous new idea, firmly embodied at the heart of the Protestant revolution, was that all Christians have the right to interpret the Bible for themselves. However, it ultimately proved uncontrollable, spawning developments that few at the time could have envisaged or predicted.[66]

Even among the leaders, Bible interpretation (the issue of authority) became "the Achilles' heel of the Reformation."[67]

Have you ever thought about the countless number of different churches and denominations in the world today? Compare that to the relatively few types of churches before the Bible was freely available.[68] Of course, the more readers you have, the more interpretations you will have. That's why the problem is a modern one to some extent (coming after and via the printing press). Ever since the Bible became a personal tool in the hands of all the people, freely available in our churches and our homes, there has also developed a naturally concurrent, rising flood of individualism and subjectivism in (the results of) our Bible reading. We might even call it "personalism": my own Bible. McGrath makes the same point, suggesting that the "outbreak of the Peasants' War in 1525 brought home to Luther that this new approach was dangerous and ultimately uncontrollable. If every individual was able to interpret the Bible as he pleased, the outcome would only be anarchy and radical religious individualism."[69] Witness radically different expressions of Christian spiritualism, theological systems or schools of thought in academic settings; different types of churches on opposing street corners; each person having his or her own individual interpretation or opinion on controversial teachings of scripture; a sort of popular mishmash of Christian doctrine in contemporary churches; denominational boundaries and religious division based on what we think a certain verse means or doesn't mean.[70] Many tears and even blood has been shed over what some folks think a verse means against what someone else sees in it.

Inkblotitis springs from "Christianity's dangerous idea." Now, don't get overly alarmed. That doesn't mean it's a bad idea or that the Bible shouldn't be available to everyone. Almost all powerful things, capable of good, can also be harmful if used poorly. Are knives bad because they can cut and cause injury? What about medicine, which we depend on daily to save lives? Many die from overdoses or misuse. *Powerful things are by nature dangerous things.* For the most part, I've found this to be a basic truism of life: the more powerful something is—the greater its potential for good—the greater the potential for harm. This is the proverbial "double-edged" sword. For example, perhaps the most powerful, at times uncontrollable, experience of humankind, the ability to conceive and participate in the creating, shaping, and steering of new life, is laden with the most extreme risks—the death of one's child being the most devastating event a person/parent can endure, not to mention the dangers and heartaches of teenage rebellion. *Yet we keep on doing it.* Why? Because it has so much to offer.

Saying that putting the Bible into the hands of the common people is dangerous does not of itself mean it's bad. Eternal salvation to many, dramatic life-change, spiritual growth, service to the poor and the oppressed, deep and lasting friendship and community, inspiration and hope, comfort and encouragement in the face of devastating heartaches and struggles, freedom and life to the fullest: these are one side of the dangerous idea—the double-edged sword—of a free Bible. The other side—the dark side—comes from inkblotitis.

In conclusion, there was a side effect, an unintended consequence, to making the Bible available to everyone that Wycliffe and Hus and Erasmus and Tyndale and Luther and many others didn't anticipate[71]—a very ironic side effect that over time has come to have deeper and more spiritually profound consequences than we know or would like to admit. In some ways, we have gone from the tyranny of the *institution* to the tyranny of the *individual*—or, to put it another way, to the tyranny of the subjective or even the personal.[72] All tyranny results in captivity to the status quo and worse, and, when it comes to the way we read and use the Bible, *we've been captivated by the subjective*. The change flows with modern culture and in relation to the Bible is a result of the pervasive influence of inkblotitis. It affects us as Christian communities; it affects us as individual believers.

This new tyranny is surprisingly not altogether unlike the situation that existed in the late Middle Ages when the institution's control of the text asserted "that ordinary Christians had no need of an English Bible, as his or her faith was strengthened by biblical wall paintings or stained glass in the churches, or by biblical plays . . ." Summaries, snippets, and images from liturgies, sermons, plays and paintings were enough. "Yet such paintings or glass, of Adam and Eve, Noah's ark or the Crucifixion, could represent only the smallest fragment of the Bible."[73] How ironic that something as wonderful as free access to the Bible, made available to us at so great a cost, has in many cases become a tool for biblical illiteracy, spiritual self-protection, hateful division, and even violence, as *the tyranny of the self again reduces the Bible to summaries and snippets and images*. The "ties that bind" come not from the Bible itself, but the way we read and use it.[74]

Chapter 2: The Bible Set Free

Chapter Resources

Mozley, J. F. *William Tyndale*. London: S.P.C.K., 1937.

Bedouelle, Guy. "Biblical Interpretation in the Catholic Reformation." In *A History of Biblical Interpretation: The Medieval through the Reformation Periods*, pp. 428-49. Edited by Alan J. Hauser and Duane F. Watson. Grand Rapids: Eerdmans, 2009.

Dahmus, Joseph H. *The Prosecution of John Wyclyf*. New Haven: Yale University, 1952.

Daniell, David. *The Bible in English: Its History and Influence*. London: Yale University, 2003.

William Tyndale: A Biography. New Haven: Yale University, 1994.

Deanesly, Margaret, *The Lollard Bible and Other Medieval Biblical Versions*. Cambridge: Cambridge University, 1920; reprint ed., 1966.

"The Significance of the Lollard Bible." The Ethel M. Wood Lecture delivered before the University of London on 12 March, 1951. London: The Athlone Press, 1951: published online at http://www.medievalchurch.org.uk/pdf/lollard_deanesly.pdf and http://www.bible-researcher.com/wyclif6.html.

Dungan, David L. *Constantine's Bible: Politics and the Making of the New Testament*. Minneapolis: Fortress, 2007.

Foxe, John. *Foxe's Book of Martyrs*. Edited by W. Grinton Berry. 1563, 1570, 1576, 1583.

Gibbs, Lee W. "Biblical Interpretation in Medieval England and the English Reformation." In *A History of Biblical Interpretation: The Medieval through the Reformation Periods*, pp. 372-402. Edited by Alan J. Hauser and Duane F. Watson. Grand Rapids: Eerdmans, 2009.

Gonzalez, Justo L. *The Story of Christianity: The Early Church to the Present Day*. Peabody, MA: Prince, 2007 (originally published in 2 vols; New York: HarperCollins, 1984, 1985).

Hudsen, Anne, *The Premature Reformation: Wycliffite Texts and Lollard History*. Oxford: Clarendon, 1988.

Latourette, Kenneth Scott. *A History of Christianity*. 2 Vols. Revised ed. Peabody, MA: Prince, 1997.

Lewis, Jack P. *The English Bible/From KJV to NIV: A History and Evaluation*. Grand Rapids: Baker Book House, 1981.

Long, Lynne. "Scriptures in the Vernacular Up to 1800." In *A History of Biblical Interpretation: The Medieval through the Reformation Periods*, pp. 450-81. Edited by Alan J. Hauser and Duane F. Watson. Grand Rapids: Eerdmans, 2009.

McGrath, Alister. *Christianity's Dangerous Idea: The Protestant Revolution—A History from the Sixteenth Century to the Twenty-First*. New York: HarperCollins, 2007.

Moyhahan, Brian. *God's Bestseller: William Tyndale, Thomas More, and the Writing of the English Bible—A Story of Martyrdom and Betrayal*. New York: St. Martin's, 2002.

Muller, Richard A., and Thompson, John L., eds. *Biblical Interpretation in the Era of the Reformation: Essays Presented to David C. Steinmetz in Honor of His Sixtieth Birthday*. Grand Rapids: Eerdmans, 1996.

Murray, Stuart. "Biblical Interpretation among the Anabaptist Reformers." In *A History of Biblical Interpretation: The Medieval through the Reformation Periods*, pp. 403-27. Edited by Alan J. Hauser and Duane F. Watson. Grand Rapids: Eerdmans, 2009.

Piper, John. "Always Singing One Note—A Vernacular Bible: Why William Tyndale Lived and Died." 2006 Desiring God Conference for Pastors. © Desiring God. Website: desiringGod.org, specifically at www.desiringgod.org/resource-library/biographies/always-singing-one-notea-vernacular-bible.

Alfred. W. Pollard, ed., *Records of the English Bible: The Documents Relation to the Translation and Publication of the Bible in English, 1525-1611*. Oxford: Henry Fowde, 1911.

Rawlings, Harold. *Trial by Fire: The Struggle to Get the Bible into English*. Wellington, FL: Rawlings Foundation, 2004.

Schreiner, Susan E. "'The Spiritual Man Judges All Things': Calvin and the Exegetical Debates about Certainty in the Reformation." In *Biblical Interpretation in the Era of Reformation*, pp. 189-214. Edited by Richard A. Muller and John L. Thompson. Grand Rapids: Eerdmans, 1996.

Shelley, Bruce L. *Church History in Plain Language*. 2nd ed. Nashville: Thomas Nelson, 1995.

Tyndale, William. *The Obedience of a Christian Man*. Edited with an Introduction and Notes by David Daniell. London: Penguin Books, 2000.

Notes

1. Daniell, *The Bible in English*, 1; cf. Rawlings, *Trial by Fire*, 13-16.
2. Walter Map, *De Nugis Curialium*, M. R. James (Oxford, 1914) xxvi (cited in Deanesly, *Lollard Bible*, 26-27).
3. Deanesly, *Lollard Bible*, 18-57.
4. Cited in Deanesly, *Lollard Bible*, 30-31.
5. From the *Preface* to the first edition of the Greek New Testament, 1516. For citations and commentary on this important passage, see Daniell, *William Tyndale*, 67; *The Bible in English*, 117; Deanesly, *Lollard Bible*, 11-12, 386; Rawlings, *Trial by Fire*, 69.
6. See, e.g., Shelly, *Church History*, 313; Daniell, *William Tyndale*, 67; Rawlings, *Trial by Fire*, 70.
7. Cf. McGrath, *Christianity's Dangerous Idea*, 25; Rawlings, *Trial by Fire*, 69.
8. On the influence and impact of Wycliffe and his followers, see, e.g., Deanesly, *Lollard Bible*, esp. 225-97; Daniell, *The Bible in English*, 66-95. Daniell (p. 106) tells the story of an ordinary farmer named Murdoch

Nisbet of Hardhill in Ayrshire (southwest Scotland), who, in spite of the threat of severe punishment, kept and read a Wycliffe manuscript secretly in a vault that he dug below his farm. His painstakingly revised and edited translation of the New Testament (from Wycliffe's English version) was the earliest Bible in Scots and became the treasured inheritance of his family—now preserved in the British Library. Daniell comments, ". . . the story of Nisbet's making his New Testament is a demonstration of the passionate dedication of communities to Wycliffite Bible translations."

9. According to Daniell (*The Bible in English*, 70, with n. 13), the phrase is John Bale's in 1548 (*Illustrium maioris Britanniae scriptorum [. . .] Summarium* [Ipswich, 1548]: f. 154v). Rawlings (*Trial by Fire*, 57) interprets the epithet with a list of the major elements of the Reformation that first appeared in Wycliffe: "Before Huss, Luther, Zwingli, and Calvin, Wycliffe was 'a voice crying in the wilderness.'"

10. It's uncertain how much of the actual translating was done by Wycliffe himself or by his followers (McGrath, *Christianity's Dangerous Idea*, 214); for the idea that Wycliffe inspired others rather than translated himself, see Hudson, *The Premature Reformation*; Deanesly, *Lollard Bible*, 240, 248-49; Daniell, *The Bible in English*, 69-83 ("Whether any translating at all was done by Wyclif is not known: there is no convincing evidence. It remains unlikely."); Gibbs, "Biblical Interpretation," 381-82.

11. Shelley, *Church History*, 229; cf. Rawlings, *Trial by Fire*, 48-49. Shelley also includes the following statement by Wycliffe: "The New Testament is of full authority, and open to the understanding of simple men, as to the points that be most needful to salvation. . . . He that keepeth meekness and charity hath the true understanding and perfection of all Holy Writ." Free access to the Bible, Wycliffe affirmed, would give rise to "government of the people, by the people, and for the people." McGrath (*Christianity's Dangerous Idea*, 214) says that this was one of Wycliff's best-known slogans, "shamelessly plagiarized by Abraham Lincoln."

12. Foxe, *Book of Martyrs*, 138-39; language of the quotation from Shelley, *Church History*, 268.

13. Shelley, *Church History*, 293-94.

14. See, e.g., Lewis, *English Bible*, 22 (Dr. Lewis actually cites an estimation of 92 percent); Daniell (*The Bible in English*, 151-52; 805, n. 13), citing others, suggests that the actual amount is 83 percent.

15. Jennifer Lowe, "Which Word," *Kansas City Star* (Oct 12, 1995).
16. Modern biblical translators continue to live out the quest of the Reformers to make the Bible available to all peoples, since there are still many places and languages where the Bible needs to be taken. See the information provided by the United Bible Society (http://www.ubs-translations.org/about_us/#c165) and the Wycliff Bible Translators (http://www.wycliffe.org/About/Statistics.aspx) for summaries of the current status of Bible translation. In 1999, Wycliff Bible Translators announced Vision 2025, a project that aims to see Bible translation begun by 2025 in every remaining language community that needs it. The vision of Wycliff Bible Translators "is to see the Bible accessible to all people in the language they understand best" (http://www.wycliffe.org).
17. Daniell, *The Bible in English*, xiii. Daniell later (p. 13) makes this statement:
    > "There have never been more translations into English available than there are now. Even the list of recommended versions, from one mainstream theological position, lists fifteen published versions of the entire Bible for study, and ten of them, all significantly different, appeared after the end of the Second World War."

    On the proliferation, availability, and impact of the Bible in English, see Daniell, *The Bible in English*, 120-32; 162-63: "In Britain in the eighteenth and nineteenth centuries, the records show over twelve hundred different Bible editions, largely of the KJV. It ceases to be possible to calculate numbers printed, now running into millions"; see also his chronological list of English Bibles from around 650 AD through 1997 (pp. 843-51); cf. Rawlings, *Trial by Fire*, 13-16.
18. See Rawlings, *Trial by Fire*, for a readable summary of "The Struggle to Get the Bible into English."
19. See Daniell, *The Bible in English*, xix-xx. McGrath (*Christianity's Dangerous Idea*, 2; see also, e.g., 2-5, 17-36, 199-241) argues throughout his history of the Protestant Reformation that this is the fundamental (and "dangerous") idea that distinguishes Protestantism: "The dangerous new idea, firmly embodied at the heart of the Protestant revolution, was that all Christians have the right to interpret the Bible for themselves."
    > "The idea that lay at the heart of the sixteenth-century Reformation, which brought Anglicanism and the other Protestant

churches into being, was that the Bible is capable of being understood by all Christian believers—and that they all have the right to interpret it and to insist upon their perspectives being taken seriously."

20. Movement toward a vernacular Bible has an interesting and complex history; see Long, "Scriptures in the Vernacular," 450-81 for an introduction to the topic.

21. When he first read the New Testament in Greek, Thomas Linacre's reaction was telling; he wrote in his diary: "Either this [the original Greek] is not the Gospel . . . or we are not Christians" (the quotation is recited often, e.g., http://www.greatsite.com/timeline-english-bible-history). On the corruption of the Vulgate and the need to return to the Greek and Hebrew sources, see Gibbs, "Biblical Interpretation," 382; Daniell (*The Bible in English*, 12) includes a frequently recited comment by the Catholic scholar William Lindanus (born 1529), who wrote of "the errors, vices, corruptions, additions, detractions, mutations, uncertainties, obscurities, pollution, barbarisms and solecisms of the vulgar Latin translation." The errors were highlighted by the number of changes (about 400) Erasmus made to the Vulgate and his elucidations of those errors in his *Novum instrumentum* (see Daniell, *The Bible in English*, 116-17).

22. Daniell, *The Bible in English*, 9; cf. also xx; Rawlings, *Trial by Fire*, 49.

23. Actually ordered in 1415 at the Council of Constance. See the Preface ("On the Burning of Heretics," ix-xxv) to Moynahan's *God's Bestseller* for an engaging presentation of these events; also Dahmus, *John Wyclyf*, 153-54 (cited in Lewis, *English Bible*, 20); Lewis, *English Bible*, 19-20; cf. also Daniell, *The Bible in English*, 73.

24. Moynahan, *God's Bestseller*, xxii; also Pollard, *Records*, 79-81; Daniell, *The Bible in English*, xiv, 75. I owe some of the flow of my summary to Piper, "One Note."

25. Moynahan, *God's Bestseller*, xxii.

26. From the 1563 version of *Foxes Book of Martyrs*, cited in David Brown, "Foxe's Martyrs," http://logosresourcespages.org/History/foxes.htm, 9.

27. Moynahan, *God's Bestseller*, xxv: "'Lollards' towers' were prepared for the imprisonment of the Bible men, in the palaces of English bishops and in the archbishop of Cantebury's great palace at Lambeth; and 'Lollard pits' were assigned as the places where they were to be burnt."

28. Moynahan, *God's Bestseller*, xxiii-xxiv.
29. Tyndale, *Obedience*, 202, n. 8.
30. Dungan, *Constantine's Bible*, 58.
31. Sheler, *Is the Bible True?*, 10.
32. Daniell, *Tyndale*, 217.
33. Daniell, *Tyndale*, 216; cf. also *The Bible in English*, 151.
34. Daniell, *The Bible in English*, 156.
35. Piper, "One Note," 11. Moyhahan, *God's Bestseller*, 260: Thomas More wrote on December 4, 1531 that Bayfield "the monk and apostate [was] well and worthily burned in Smythfelde."
36. Moynahan, *God's Bestseller*, 261.
37. According to Daniell (*The Bible in English*, 192), John Rogers "was the first of almost three hundred martyrs under Queen Mary." The story of John Rogers is inspiring and heart-wrenching. His wife and 10 children were left in desperate need, and his urgent pleas to speak briefly with his wife before his burning were rejected (Daniell, *The Bible in English*, 192).
38. Concerning Wycliffe's handwritten copies, Moynahan (*God's Bestseller*, xix) comments, "The new English Bibles were eagerly sought after—it was said that a man would give a cartload of hay for a few sheets of St Paul..."
39. An internet search on "History of the English Bible" yields plenty of quick, introductory overviews; for overviews of the early history of the English Bible, see Lewis, *English Bible*, 9-34; McGrath, *Christianity's Dangerous Idea*, 17-36, 214-18. For more thorough studies, see Rawlings, *Trial by Fire*; Daniell, *The Bible in English*.
40. Unfortunately, it is still very much true that Christians suffer great persecutions in parts of the world today, as Paul Marshall's (with Lela Gilbert) *Their Blood Cries Out: The Worldwide Tragedy of Modern Christians Who Are Dying for Their Faith* (Dallas: Word, 1997) clearly displays.
41. Shelley, *Church History*, 232. It's reported that Hus's last words were, "In 100 years, God will raise up a man whose calls for reform cannot be suppressed." One hundred and two years later, Martin Luther nailed his famous 95 theses to the church door at Wittenburg.
42. Daniell, *The Bible in English*, 156: "Every one of the thousands of English versions round the world goes back to Tyndale's fundamental work in Worms and Antwerp. His was a dazzling achievement."

43. Cf. Daniell, *The Bible in English*, xiii-xvii on the importance of the Bible in English. Daniell (xvii) calls the King James Version of the Bible "the world's most important written text"; also Rawlings, *Trial by Fire*, 13-16.
44. Daniell, *The Bible in English*, 157; see pp. 157-59 on the importance of Tyndale's work.
45. Daniell, *The Bible in English*, 156.
46. Daniell, *The Bible in English*, 158.
47. Daniell (*The Bible in English*, 156) highlights Tyndale's uncertainty and faith, speaking of his "dazzling achievement": "Of its success he knew nothing."
48. In response to the Protestant emphasis on *sola scriptura* ("only scripture") and the right of each individual to read and interpret the Bible, the Council of Trent (1546: *De reformatione*) decreed that
    "... no one, relying on his own prudence, twist Holy Scripture in matters of faith and morals that pertain to the edifice of Christian doctrine, according to his own mind, contrary to the meaning that holy mother the Church has held and holds— since it belongs to her to judge the true meaning and interpretation of Holy Scripture—and that no one dare to interpret the Scripture in a way contrary to the unanimous consensus of the Fathers...." (cited by Bedouelle ["Biblical Interpretation," 431]).
    The Council of Trent did not, however, "pronounce on vernacular translations of the Bible" (Bedouelle, "Biblical Interpretation," 434).
49. Daniell (*The Bible in English*, 110) gives this indictment:
    "Controlled by Rome, what was orthodox Christianity in the English Church from 1409 until the 1530s was unique in Northern Europe in its narrowness and terrifying restrictions. Even in 1536, Tyndale, who broke the barriers and gave the Greek New Testament to the people in printed English, had, as well as his books, to be burned."
    "Further, again, by 1400, the Church was sanctioning beliefs and practices that were unbiblical: only trouble could follow that discovery by ordinary people" (Daniell, *The Bible in English*, 69).
50. On some of those reasons, see Daniell, *The Bible in English*, 68-69; Bedouelle, "Biblical Interpretation," 428-49, esp. 434-36; Long, "Scriptures in the Vernacular," 451, 454-55; Rawlings, *Trial by Fire*, 47-51.
51. Long ("Scriptures in the Vernacular," 454) makes this statement:

Chapter 2

> "The Lollard English Bible of the 1380s and 90s . . . set the pattern associating translation with heresy. The Lollard group was known for its use of the vernacular at a time when vernacular languages were considered inferior and unsuitable vehicles for literary and religious texts."

52. The concern goes way back: in the late tenth and early eleventh centuries, Aelfric, the foremost Anglo-Saxon scholar of his time, was reluctant to translate Genesis into (Old) English for fear that common folks might be led into immorality by "examples" found in the private lives of the Patriarchs (Daniell, *The Bible in English*, 49-50). According to Deanesly (*Lollard Bible*, 23), the first time the question of the legitimacy or legality of vernacular translations was raised was in connection with political and geographical dispute between the Eastern and Western Churches (Greek or Slavic scriptures would draw populations toward the East; Latin, towards the West). In response to a letter from Vratislaus, king of Bohemia, written in 1079, Pope Gregory VII made these comments:

> "For it is clear to those who reflect often upon it, that not without reason has it pleased Almighty God that holy scripture should be a secret in certain places, lest, if it were plainly apparent to all men, perchance it would be little esteemed and be subject to disrespect; or it might be falsely understood by those of mediocre learning, and lead to error. . . . Wherefore we forbid what you have so imprudently demanded of the authority of S. Peter, and we command you to resist this vain rashness with all your might, to the honour of Almighty God."

Citing an opponent of Wycliffe who thought that "the pearl of the gospel" should not be "scattered abroad and trodden under foot of swine" (see n. 60 below). Deanesly (*Lollard Bible*, 239-40) draws this conclusion:

> "The canon is here exactly explaining the orthodox attitude to the Bible at the time. It ought not to be accessible to lay people, but priests should explain passages from the Sunday gospels and epistles in their sermons, not translating them, but telling the story in their own words, with its moral inferences, 'the usury of their minds.'"

53. Long, "Scriptures in the Vernacular," 454-55; cf. also Daniell, *The Bible in English*, 68. Long (456) later makes this statement:

"One of the most contentious issues of the times was open access to the Scriptures as opposed to access through the mediatory priest. The strictly hierarchical nature of society of those times conflicted with the idea of equal opportunity: vernacular translation gave access to the Bible to lay people who, it was genuinely believed, had neither the capacity nor the sophistication to read the Bible. The unlearned, unwary, and unworthy reader might well misinterpret or misunderstand and be brought to heresy . . ."

54. D. S. Kastan's words (p. 57 from "'The noyse of the new Bible': Reform and Reaction," in *Henrician England in Religion and Culture in Renaissance England* [ed. C. McEachern and D. Shuger; Cambridge: Cambridge University, 1997] 46-68).

55. Long, "Scriptures in the Vernacular," 451. Daniell (*The Bible in English*, 68) points out that the church was comfortable with the sacramental value of the Latin services, concluding, "The Bible was good only when it was not understood."

56. It was taught (the doctrine is called "mediate dominion"; see, e.g., Rawlings, *Trial by Fire*, 45) that a special, divine grace is needed to understand the scriptures accurately, and that grace is reserved for the priests (cf. Daniell, *The Bible in English*, 68). Protestants would develop a similar teaching regarding the "enlightening" or "illumination" of the Holy Spirit, though such illumination is believed to be available to all Christians. See Erasmus's *Preface* for an interesting statement in this regard where he bases the work of the Holy Spirit on motive and humility (cf. "they do well who warn the common people that they should make use of the sacred volumes with religious fear, and not trust rashly to their own judgment" [*Erasmus Opera*, 1706, Leyden, v, 729; cited in Deanesly, *Lollard Bible*, 11]); cf. Wycliffe's idea that true understanding comes from those who approach the Bible with humility and love (Shelley, *Church History*, 229), as well as Tyndale's emphasis on seeking God's help "day and night instantly to open our eyes, and to make us understand and feel wherefore the scripture was given . . ." (Daniell, *The Bible in English*, 148). This is an important consideration when addressing the issue of understanding the Bible, and we'll look into it a little more in another chapter.

57. Though pointed out explicitly by opponents—as one would expect—the subjective and even destructive potential of putting the Bible into

the hands of common folks was implied and even warned against by the most ardent supporters. William Tyndale's admonitions about the use of scripture in his Prologue to Genesis is a case in point (see Chapter 4, n. 12 below; cited in Daniell, *The Bible in English*, 148).

58. Daniell, *The Bible in English*, 161.
59. Pollard, *Records,* 196-98; also cited in Daniell, *The Bible in English*, 166. Given the literature that the clergy allowed the folks to read, Tyndale countered the idea that restricting access to the Bible was motivated by concern for the readers in the Preface to *The Obedience of a Christian Man* (p. 24): "Finally that this threatening and forbidding the lay people to read the scripture is not for love of your souls (which they care for as the fox doth for the geese) is evident and clearer than the sun . . ." See pp. 15-23 for Tyndale's refutation of the contemporary arguments against a vernacular Bible.
60. Cited in Daniell, *The Bible in English*, xx, 67; Moynahan, *God's Bestseller*, xx; a fuller passage can be found in Deanesly, *Lollard Bible*, 239 (see below). The passage comes from Henry Knighton's *Chronicle* (*Knighton's Chronicle 1337-1397*, trans. G. H. Martin, Oxford: Oxford University Press, 1996). Knighton was canon at the abbey St. Mary of the Meadows, Leicester, England. Writing "of the year 1382," the text reads:

   "This master John Wycliffe translated into English, (not, alas, into the tongue of angels), the gospel which Christ gave to clerks and doctors of the Church, in order that they might sweetly minister it to laymen and weaker men, according to the message of the season and personal need, with the usury of their own minds: whence, through him it [the gospel] is become more common and open to lament, and women who are able to read, than it is wont to be even to lettered clerks of good intelligence. Thus the pearl of the gospel is scattered abroad and trodden under foot of swine, and what is wont to be the treasure both of clerks and lament is now become the jest of both. The jewel of clerks is turned into the sport of the laity, so that that has become the 'commune aeternum' of laymen, which heretofore was the heavenly talent of clerks and doctors of the Church" (Deanesly, *Lollard Bible*, 239).
61. Melchior Cano, *De locis theologicis* (Salamanca, 1563); Roberto Bellarmine, *Disputationes de controversiis Christianae fidei*, 3 vols. (1581, 1582, 1593); McGrath, *Christianity's Dangerous Idea*, 203. Cf. also Martin Bucer

as an early Protestant critic (McGrath, *Christianity's Dangerous Idea*, 208). Bellarmine's work was a three-volume synthesis of Catholic theology that functioned for years as the most complete Catholic response to Protestant issues. A contemporary response to Bellarmine was given by William Whitaker (1547-1595) in *A Disputation on Holy Scripture: Against the Papists, Especially Bellarmine and Stapleton* (trans. and ed. William Fitzgerald; Cambridge: Cambridge University, 1849). The question or "dispute" about the understandability ("perspicuity") of the Bible was a part of the broader, vigorous debate about the sufficiency of scripture (*sola scriptura*) for Christian faith and practice.

62. Eamon Duffy, *The Stripping of the Altars: Traditional Religion in England c.1400-c.1580* (New Haven, 1992) 530, cited in Daniell, *The English Bible*, xx.

63. Johannes Eck, *Enchiridion locorum communium adversus Lutherum et alios hostes ecclesiae* (1525-43), ed. P. Fraenkel, Corpus Catholicorum 34 (Münster, 1979) 81-82; *Enchiridion of Commonplaces*, trans. Ford L. Battles (Grand Rapids: Baker, 1979) 48; cited in Schreiner, "Certainty in the Reformation," 200, with n. 27; 207, with n. 49.

64. Bedouelle, "Biblical Interpretation," 435.

65. In the preface to his major work on the history of the Bible in English (*The Bible in English*, xix-xx) David Daniell presented similar ideas, but from a somewhat more positive perspective, labeling his summary of the access of common people to a vernacular Bible "A True Revolution." Daniell (*The Bible in English*, xx) says, "Access to the whole Bible in a vernacular opens up rich continents of new, and different, understanding of New Testament faith."

66. McGrath (*Christianity's Dangerous Idea*, 2) continues,
    "The great convulsions of the early sixteenth century that historians now call 'the Reformation' introduced into the history of Christianity a dangerous new idea that gave rise to an unparalleled degree of creativity and growth, on the one hand, while on the other causing new tensions and debates that, by their very nature, probably lie beyond resolution. The development of Protestantism as a major religious force in the world has been shaped decisively by the creative tensions emerging from this principle."

67. Schreiner ("Certainty in the Reformation," 207) points out that Johannes Eck detected and explicated this weakness.

68. There have always been different types of Christian groups throughout the centuries. To some extent, the same tendency to diversity and even sectarianism was evident prior to the consolidation of Christianity during the time of the Roman Emperor Constantine, as seen, e.g., in Celsus's criticism of Christianity (cf. Dungan, *Constantine's Bible*, 55-56) and illustrated by such non-orthodox groups as the Ebionites, Gnostics, Marcionites, Montanists, and others. Since common people did not have copies of biblical writings in those days, long before the inventing of the printing press, the divergent interpretations tended to come from and be associated with influential/charismatic leaders and involved not just the interpretation of the texts (though that was included) but which texts to use. Without a closed canon, texts were often "discovered" or created to support the theological views of the groups. Cf. Dungan, *Constantine's Bible*, esp. 54-55, 80 ("As time went by . . ., more and more writings allegedly by 'apostles' began to mysteriously surface . . ."), 94-125.

    On the other hand, the impact of an available Bible on the diversity of Christian groups and expressions is obvious. Deanesly (*Lollard Bible*, 2) offers the following comments:

    > "It is scarcely doubtful that the unity of Christendom was preserved till the sixteenth century only by force. Had lay people in the thirteenth century been allowed the right to read the gospels for themselves, or exposed to the temptation to do so, and had they generally been able to read, reinterpretation would inevitably have followed, and Christendom would have been divided in that century instead of the sixteenth. . . . The question of the unity of Christendom depended on the possibility of the reinterpretation of Christianity, and this depended on the accessibility of the original Christian records to the masses. It was only to these books that a sectarian teacher could appeal against the traditional teaching of the Church. . . . It is thus true to say that the history of vernacular translations, and the attitude of the Church towards them, is not a matter of merely antiquarian interest, but the central strand in the history of the unity of Christendom."

69. McGrath, *Christianity's Dangerous Idea*, 3.
70. McGrath (*Christianity's Dangerous Idea*, 219) gives this summary of the impact of different approaches to biblical interpretation:

> "It is not difficult to identify specific groups within Protestantism according to their relatively well-defined and well-defended—yet *different*—ways of interpreting the Bible. In the United States on the eve of the First World War, for example, relatively coherent and distinctive belief systems, each rigorously based on the Bible, were associated with Presbyterianism, Methodism, the Southern Baptist Convention, Episcopalianism, and Lutheranism. Reinforced by dedicated seminaries, denominational theological textbooks, and preachers, each group defended its specific reading of the Bible against the alternatives."

As McGrath points out, Pentecostalism and many other groups could now be added to the list.

This tendency toward division in Protestantism in general was prefigured to some extent within the Anabaptist wing of the Reformation, as S. Murray ("Biblical Interpretation," 418-19) observes:

> "But if each was hermeneutically autonomous and if each claimed the Spirit's anointing, who was to judge matters? Divisions—some bitter—over issues of interpretation troubled Anabaptists. The mistakes, disagreements, and poor interpretations that sometimes occurred suggest Anabaptists leaders underestimated potential problems."

71. McGrath (*Christianity's Dangerous Idea*, 3) suggests that the outbreak of the Peasants' War brought home this idea to Luther to an extent that he "tried to rein in the movement by emphasizing the importance of authorized religious leaders, such as himself, and institutions in the interpretation of the Bible." But by then, it was too late.

72. An interesting commentary on the potential of interpretive methods can be gleaned from Tyndale's criticism of contemporary Scholasticism as patently subjective and the power of theology/doctrine over interpretation (*Obedience*, 23):

> "Now whatsoever opinions every man findeth with his doctor, that is his gospel and that only is true with him and that holdeth he all his life long, and every man to maintain his doctor withal, corrupteth the scripture and fashioneth it after his own imagination as a potter doth his clay. Of what text thou provest hell, will another prove purgatory, another *limbo partum* and another shall prove of the same text that an ape hath a tail...."

Tyndale's comical point highlights that it's not so much *who* reads the Bible (in this case scholastic academicians) but *how* we read it.
73. Daniell, *The Bible in English*, xx, 107.
74. Cf. the statements by Tyndale against the scholasticism of his day (see Chapter 4, n. 12; cited in Daniell, *The Bible in English*, 148) on the effects of an overly "zoomed in" biblical focus: ". . . persecuting one another for defending of lewd imaginations and fantasies of our own invention."

Chapter 3

Why It's Hard to Understand the Bible

"Oh, earth, you're too wonderful for anyone to realize you!," Emily Gibbs exclaims in her brief return from the grave to the land of the living at the end of *Our Town*, Thornton Wilder's classic American play about the extraordinary nature of ordinary life in a small town. She then asks the telling question, "Do any human beings ever realize life while they live it—every, every minute?" As a type of omniscient narrator, the Stage Manager responds, "No—Saints and poets maybe—they do some."

We "realize" life only *some* because it's beyond us: the majestic and the troubling sides of living and dying on planet earth go beyond what we as humans are apparently able to grasp and explain, or even experience to the fullest. To the extent that life—real, hard-to-figure-out and hard-to-handle life—is sometimes difficult to understand, so the Bible is hard to understand because it reflects the complexities and ambiguities of real life, while pointing beyond the daily grind of the ordinary and the haunting confusion of the tragic to the one who sheds ultimate light on the moments and the mysteries. Truly "getting" life while we live it is difficult: our perspectives are limited and cluttered by a host of competing values and wounds, impulses and influences.

As part of its overall purpose of helping Christians and potential Christians come to believe in Jesus and enjoy the results of that faith, John's Gospel contains a striking statement of Jesus. In an immediate context of religious prejudice and criticism concerning his real purpose and as part of the developing theme of "eternal"—beyond the grave—life, even in the land of the living, Jesus says, "I have come that they may have life, and have it to the full" (John 10:10, NIV)—in other words, "that they might *realize* it." That's why

Chapter 3

the Bible is so important. It's also why the Bible is sometimes hard to understand.

Is It Hard to Understand the Bible?

Therefore, beloved, while you are waiting for these things, strive to be found by him at peace, without spot or blemish; and regard the patience of our Lord as salvation. So also our beloved brother Paul wrote to you according to the wisdom given him, speaking of this as he does in all his letters. There are some things in them hard to understand, which the ignorant and unstable twist to their own destruction, as they do the other scriptures (2 Peter 3:14-16).

Is the Bible hard to understand? The title of this chapter gives away at least part of my perspective. From the time the books of the Bible were first written and read, and especially when the Bible was put into the hands of everyday people, Bible students have wondered whether the Bible can really be understood by any and everybody. This is sometimes referred to as the "perspicuity" of scripture—a fancy word that refers to whether something is clearly expressed and therefore easily understood—and is part of the broader discussion of the sufficiency of scripture for Christians. Anyone who sits down and tries to read the Bible from cover to cover, especially if he or she is unfamiliar with the Bible, will have to admit that parts of it are not easy to understand and some parts are even baffling. In fact, if you start at the beginning with Genesis, as many people do, you may find some of the early material so foreign to American culture and modern ways of thinking that you give up, thinking the Bible is really strange or outdated.[1] (I have some interesting and provocative questions that a young friend of mine who recently set out to read the Bible for the first time asked after reading about half of Genesis. I'll share those with you in a minute.)

So, what does that mean? Does it mean that God didn't do a very good job of communicating his word to us? Does it mean that the Bible is outdated and irrelevant? Does it mean that the Bible really can't be understood by everyone and someone has to help or perhaps be the official interpreter of scripture? Does it mean that understanding the Bible sometimes takes work, even hard work? Or might it mean that the Bible—like many parts of life on this planet—is part of a complex web of reality where splendor meets slop, where passions and prejudices, choices and leadings, skills and spirit all intertwine in a highly complex, sometimes hard-to-figure-out life? . . . where beauty meets beast!? When the brilliant beauty of the only son of God became a vulnerable, sometimes soiled little boy of Mary, delivered in pain and loneliness, on a dirty stable floor surrounded by the smell and sounds of barn animals, I think we find immutable evidence that God meets us where we are. Put another way: to speak so we can listen and help us clean up our mess, God has to speak in *our* language and become part of *our* mess. There was and is no other way. This is the classic Christian teaching of the *incarnation*: God becomes human so we humans can see God. That's why the Bible is sometimes hard to understand.

Before we discuss some of the specific reasons the Bible is hard to understand, I'd like to clarify a couple of things. We can divide the process of understanding the Bible into three parts: the message, the medium or means of delivering the message (= the text), and the recipients of the message (= us). Communication can break down at each level.

Assuming for now that the content of the Bible is from God, we need to be sure we don't mistake the message for the messenger. If you asked what you need to do to be saved and someone said, "Μετανοήσατε καὶ βαπτισθήτω ἕκαστος ὑμῶν ἐπὶ τῷ ὀνόματι Ἰησοῦ Χριστοῦ εἰς ἄφεσιν τῶν ἁμαρτιῶν ὑμῶν," would you know what to do? You might if you read Greek. That's the beginning of Peter's response to the people who asked a similar question in Acts 2:37-38. Whenever we read the Bible in English, or any other language besides the original Hebrew and Greek for that matter, we're not reading the Bible as originally written. So how do we know that what we're reading is really what God meant to say in the first place? Good question. That's why we owe a huge debt of gratitude to the many individuals and organizations that have given much to preserve and translate the Bible for us. We stand on the shoulders of many gifted and hard-working believers when we read our English Bibles. And, though there are differences, you can be confident that most any of the major versions tries to be accurate in rendering the meanings of the originals.

The point is that whether something is easy or hard to understand depends a lot on the messenger, or in the case of languages, on the medium of the message. The writers of the Bible wrote in different styles, levels, and languages. Styles of communication change. Levels of reading comprehension vary. If I'm not understanding something I'm reading, it may have little to do with the content of what's being communicated and more to do with the way it's being communicated to me—the go between, the text as a messenger, in other words—and multiple things can affect it. So, when I say that some things in the Bible or some parts of the Bible are hard to understand, that doesn't necessarily mean that the content or message is hard to understand. Part of the reason some things in the Bible are hard to understand has less to do with the messages than with the means of how those messages are being delivered to us. As we often say, "It's Greek to me." Make sense? Distinguishing the message from the messenger can sometimes be helpful in pinpointing the cause of the difficulty.

Now, about the messages. Through the centuries, many Bible students have come to believe that the fundamental and essential points that God wants to communicate to us are understandable to almost anyone who can read the Bible. As in Robert Fulghum's book *All I Really Need to Know I Learned in Kindergarten*, the most profound, life-changing concepts are usually quite simple. As I get older, I'm coming to see that I'm not going to wake up one day, having learned some new secret that will solve my problems and overcome my weaknesses, no matter how many books I read. *Realizing* life is often not so much a need to *know* more—though sometimes it is—but to actually *get or do* what I already know. The being and doing is usually harder than the knowing. The most important messages about God are like that. You can be illiterate and receive just as freely the good news of Jesus Christ, be saved, and have your life changed by the power of the Holy Spirit. In fact, in the history of Christianity, many if not most, Christians couldn't read—certainly not Hebrew and

Chapter 3

Greek. A faithful messenger (a "preacher," the Bible calls him) is essential. Reading is not. The message is the important thing.

Now, having said that, I'd like to affirm, with many others, that I believe most anyone who can read the Bible can, from that reading, understand the essential messages of God's saving love for us and how we are to respond, especially if he or she has a little help.[2] Like the Reformers who dreamed of putting the Bible into the hands of the common people, I believe in the *understandability* of the scriptures. It would be intellectually dishonest, however, not to admit the points made by the Catholic counter-reformers and others—really anyone who tries to read the Bible from cover to cover—who point out the clear difficulties of understanding the Bible. A million books have been written on "How to Understand the Bible"—I'm exaggerating a little, but not much. Why? Because something—*some things*—make reading and understanding the Bible hard at times. All the different opinions as to what parts of the Bible mean, even by scholars, confirms the point. So, I'd like to list and briefly describe for you some of those things—the reasons the Bible is sometimes hard to understand. And this is important because either we can't read and understand the Bible (in which case we always need help); or the problem lies elsewhere, and perhaps there's something we can do about it. Would it be accurate to say that either we can't read and understand the Bible or we're doing something wrong?

Sometimes the content of the Bible itself is hard to understand. 2 Peter 3:15-16—quoted earlier—says that some of the things Paul writes about in his letters are "hard to understand." Mark's Gospel tells us that Jesus spoke in parables as a means of communicating to people on various levels, which is how the Parable of the Sower functions at the beginning of the teaching ministry of Jesus, giving a pictorial illustration that based on the nature of a person's heart—the seed fell on the road or path, on rocky soil, on thorny soil, and some on good soil—the mysteries of the kingdom of God were being revealed. When I say that the messages of the Bible are understandable to most people, I don't mean to imply that everything in the Bible is simple and easily understood. On the contrary, the mind of the Spirit of God goes beyond all human comprehension. So we have both: deep revelations of transcendent spiritual realities and simple, saving, life-changing truths.

For a few minutes let's focus on the hard stuff. Why is the Bible hard to understand? We'll look at six reasons. Before we begin looking into these, an admonition: please don't be discouraged by what might begin to sound like a pretty doomy-and-gloomy picture as we go. On the contrary, our purpose is to be motivated and empowered by the knowledge that we're not alone and difficulty does not mean defeat. Finally, I'd like to give you a theme word to keep in mind as we explore the difficulties (or perhaps "challenges" would be a better word): the word "distance." The concept of *distance* helps to clarify most of these reasons, though, as you'll see, it's obviously a stretch in some cases (no pun intended).

Chapter 3

Reason #1: The Scope of the Bible

I was tempted to use the word "length" instead of "scope" for the title of this segment, since, even if you're just counting pages, the Bible is a big book, and big books can be daunting. But "scope" is better. When you realize that the Bible is really a collection of books that covers the history of the world from the beginning of the universe and looks ahead to the end, you begin to see how a casual reader might get lost a time or two along the way. Add to the general time frame the fact that the books are not always in chronological order, cover different periods of history, are written by different authors to different audiences, about different topics; you begin to get a sense of the challenge involved in just picking up a Bible and starting to read. The historical and theological *distance* covered in the Bible is, therefore, one of the reasons that understanding the Bible can be difficult. From a purely historical standpoint, the Bible covers a lot of ground.

Genesis, the first book of the Bible, starts with the stories of creation and the antediluvian (= before-the-flood) fathers that go back hundreds of years before Noah's flood (2300-2500 BC). It then picks up with Abraham (about 2000 BC) and takes us through the moving of the descendants of Jacob (Israel) into Egypt. Moses, leaving Egypt (the Exodus) and receiving the Law of God, takes place more than 400 years after Abraham. That takes us to the end of the Pentateuch (the first five books) and gives us a time frame of over 2,000 years, and that's if you're taking all the dates literally. The period of the Judges then lasts more than 300 years, the Kings and Prophets another 600-700 years, with another 400 plus till we get to the time of the birth of Jesus. Now imagine picking up a Bible, flipping open to a book and starting to read. Is it any wonder that we sometimes have no good clue as to what's going on *historically* in what we're reading?

Suppose we were to start reading 2 Samuel—not that you would or should start there, but just to illustrate the point. The text says,

After the death of Saul, when David had returned from defeating the Amalekites, David remained two days in Ziklag. On the third day, a man came from Saul's camp, with his clothes torn and dirt on his head. When he came to David, he fell to the ground and did obeisance. David said to him, "Where have you come from?" He said to him, "I have escaped from the camp of Israel." David said to him, "How did things go? Tell me!" He answered, "The army fled from the battle, but also many of the army fell and died, and Saul and his son Jonathan also died." Then David asked the young man who was reporting to him, "How do you know that Saul and his son Jonathan died?" The young man reporting to him said, "I happened to be on Mount Gilboa; and there was Saul leaning on his spear, while the chariots and the horsemen drew close to him. When he looked behind him, he saw me, and called to me. I answered, 'Here sir.' And he said to me, 'Who are you?' I answered him, 'I am an Amalekite.' He said to me, 'Come, stand over me and kill me; for convulsions have seized me, and yet my life still lingers.' So I stood over him, and killed him, for I knew that he could not live after he had fallen. I took the crown that was on his head and the armlet that was on his arm, and I have brought them here to my lord" (2 Samuel 1:1-10).

Obviously, we've dropped into an engaging—sort of "in progress" report—of a battle scene. But who is David? Where in the world is Ziklag? And who are Saul and Jonathan? Why is David interested in them, and why would Saul be "leaning on his spear" and having convulsions? Wow! This is quite graphic and exciting. But where's Mt. Gilboa? Who's fighting whom, and why? What's an Amalekite? If you don't know anything about the historical context, you're pretty much lost from the get-go. Those of us familiar with biblical history take a lot of this for granted (we know something of the deep, personal reasons behind David's interest in Saul and Jonathan); my point, however, is to illustrate how much a particular scene depends on its historical context and how varied that context can be because of the historical scope of the Bible. This actually took place during the period of the United Kingdom (around 1060-920 BC) and has a lot to do with the political and relational struggles of Israel's leaders during that time, not to mention David's deep love for Jonathan and intense struggle with Saul.

Fast forward 1,000 years. We're in a small town about six miles south of Jerusalem called Bethlehem. A strange, brilliant star shines in the night sky. Why are we here? What makes this place and this night so special? How things change in a thousand years! Now suppose we're reading from Paul's first letter to the church of Christ in Corinth, almost 60 years later. Why is there a church in Corinth? What is a church, anyway? How did it get there, and why is Paul writing to them? In that letter, Paul says that he'd been told that there were quarrels and arguments among them. "What I mean is that each of you says, 'I belong to Paul,' or 'I belong to Apollos,' or 'I belong to Cephas,' or 'I belong to Christ.' Has Christ been divided? Was Paul crucified for you? Or were you baptized in the name of Paul?" (1 Corinthians 1:12-13). Who was crucified, and why? Who is Apollos or Cephas? Some Greek gods, maybe? And what were the Corinthians fighting about? Now skip forward even further to the picture of a new heaven and a new earth in the book of Revelation? What's that all about, and when is it to take place?

I suspect you get the point. The history contained in the Bible can be challenging even to experienced readers and certainly makes reading and understanding the Bible difficult at times. On the other hand, don't let that discourage you. I'm not trying to make it more difficult than it really is. The historical context of biblical books is important for understanding the books properly. Absolutely! But a general understanding of the historical timeline can go a long way toward providing a helpful framework. This is where introductory books about the Bible and summary introductions to books of the Bible are most helpful, like, for example, Gordon Fee and Douglas Stuart's guided tour, *How to Read the Bible Book by Book*.[3] On the other hand, I don't mean to imply that you have to become some kind of Bible historian to make any sense of it all. That's not the point. As we'll see later, the specifics of the historical context come mostly from reading the book itself, and had we read 1 Samuel before starting in 2 Samuel, we'd've had a much better sense of what was going on. The only point I'm trying to make here is that the historical scope of the books of the Bible, covering as much as 4,000 years, is one of the things that makes the Bible difficult at times.

Chapter 3

Reason #2: The Cultures of the Bible

A similar—but different—reason the Bible is sometimes hard to understand is the *distance* between us (our time and place) and the writing of the Bible (their times and places). Check out the following:

> Fæder ure þu þe eart on heofonum
> Si þin nama gehalgod
> to becume þin rice
> gewurþe ðin willa
> on eorðan swa swa on heofonum.
> urne gedæghwamlican hlaf syle us todæg
> and forgyf us ure gyltas
> swa swa we forgyfað urum gyltendum
> and ne gelæd þu us on costnunge
> ac alys us of yfele soþlice

Could you read it? It's an Old English version of the Lord's Prayer/Our Father, "Our Father who art in heaven . . ." That's what happened to English over a period of about a thousand years. Now, imagine 2,000 years ago when the New Testament was written in a completely different language and culture. Go back another thousand years through the Old Testament, deep into a completely different language and culture, and ask yourself how unlike modern literature might the language and customs of the Bible be. Stark differences exist even in our world today between western and eastern countries, as displayed clearly by religious and political tensions, and seen when we visit places on the other side of the globe during the Olympics or on vacation. Though modern technologies are diminishing the differences, major communication gaps still exist between contemporary peoples of the world because of cultural, religious, and political differences. Yet the Bible spanned many cultures and many centuries, a long time ago. That distance naturally creates challenges when we read the Bible today.

One of the major cultural differences comes from the languages themselves and in the way the languages are structured in a written text (both Hebrew and Greek are very different from modern English). Significant differences between a culture that existed before the invention of the printing press—an oral culture—and modern, print-based society intensifies the natural differences of syntax, style, and structure. Biblical peoples relied on oral forms of communication in almost every setting. When things were written, they were naturally written in the styles of those oral conventions and were for the most part written to be heard. Did you hear that? That's an important point.

Biblical documents were to be read to a listening audience, which means the original audiences were listeners rather than readers. Overall organizational schemes and even sentence structure tend to reflect their oral forms of expression—often more circular or concentric. Print tends toward linear thought and a lack of repetition. In English we're taught that repetition and redundancy—to repeat oneself in a short span of text or verse—is a stylistic deficiency. We are to vary the words so as not to be repetitious. (I'm obviously violating the rule!) Not so, in an ancient oral culture. You ever read something in the Bible that seemed repetitious or even sounded like something you just read a verse or two back? When that happens, you've likely reached a form of circular emphasis that grows out of their way of writing in an oral style.

Let's look at an example. Take the wording of Ephesians 3:4-9. The repetition of key words and concepts in a circular pattern around the phrase "according to the working of his power" helps to show the structure (the following is a literal translation to highlight the pattern):

Chapter 3

... you will be able **to perceive** my understanding in **the mystery** of Christ, which to other generations was not make known to men but is now revealed to his holy apostles and prophets in the Spirit

> for the **Gentiles** to be fellow heirs, members of the same body and partakers of the promise in Christ Jesus through **the gospel**
>
>> of which I became a servant according to **the gift of God's grace given** <u>to me</u>
>>
>>> according to the working of his power
>>
>> <u>to me</u> the least of all saints was **given this grace**
>
> to the **Gentiles** to preach **the gospel** of the boundless riches of Christ

and **to disclose** what is the plan of **the mystery** hidden from the ages in God who created all things

See the circular style? Where we would outline something A, B, C, D, E . . ., they might go A, B, C, D, C, B, A. Get it? The repetition is part of the outline. We don't usually write or think like that, but they did; consequently, it's a little strange to us as readers.[4] The redundancy is not just simple repetition for repetition sake, moreover, but sometimes highly artistic amplification and development of a parallel idea (this is a characteristic feature of a Hebrew poetic style called Hebrew "parallelism"). We'll talk about this more later. For now, just mark it down as one of the reasons understanding the Bible is sometimes not as straightforward as we might like. They often said things differently.

Another type of cultural difference comes from the content of the material, as biblical writers naturally wrote about issues and questions important to them that we don't understand the same or even think about. A while back, a young friend of mine enthusiastically began to read the Bible from the beginning for the first time.

(If you're in that boat and would like to read the Bible for the first time, it's probably better to start with the New Testament; then go back to the Old Testament later). It didn't take long—about half way through Genesis—before she had accumulated an insightful list of some heavy-duty questions. Here's a sampling of her questions, with only slight editing:

1. Genesis 6:4: "In those days, and even afterward, giants lived on the earth, for whenever the sons of God had intercourse with human women, they gave birth to children who became the heroes mentioned in legends of old."

   Okay . . . Now this just gets me. Who are the Giants and how come they get to be referred to as the Sons of God? I thought that was reserved for two instances #1—Jesus #2—man as a whole. Who are the heroes? Are they like Hercules? Is this a parallel to other ancient beliefs? Why does this sound like something I would read in the legends of Gilgamesh? Goliath was a Giant, right? Was he a "Son of God"?

2. Genesis 19:30-36: "Afterward Lot left Zoar because he was afraid of the people there, and he went to live in a cave in the mountains with his two daughters. One day the older daughter said to her sister, 'There isn't a man anywhere in this entire area for us to marry, and our father will soon be too old to have children. Come, let's get him drunk with wine, and then we will sleep with him. That way we will preserve our family line through our father.' So that night they got him drunk, and the older daughter went in and slept with her father. He was unaware of her lying down or getting up again. The next morning the older daughter said, 'I slept with our father last night. Let's get him drunk again, and you go sleep with him. That way our family line will be preserved.' So that night they got him drunk again, and the younger daughter went in and slept with him. As before, he was unaware of her lying down or getting up. So both of Lot's daughters became pregnant by their father."

Chapter 3

Why were Lot's Daughters not punished for getting him drunk and raping him?

3. What happened to all the fish during the flood of Noah's Ark? They are never mentioned. But it does say that EVERY living thing that was not on the boat was destroyed.

4. Genesis 9:8-16: I am not going to type this one out but basically God is admitting that he made a mistake. He is saying that he will never send a flood to destroy all living things again and gave them rainbow and all that. . . . God made a mistake?

5. Genesis 9:5-6: "And murder is forbidden. Animals that kill people must die, and any person who murders must be killed. Yes, you must execute anyone who murders another person, for to kill a person is to kill a living being made in God's image."

   Okay . . . But look at this . . . Genesis 4:15 (After God finds out that Cain killed his brother, Abel, and Cain is scared that he will be killed by anyone who finds out that he is a murderer) "The Lord replied, 'They will not kill you for I will give seven times your punishment to anyone who does.'"

   It also says later about someone who would have 7 times 77 the punishment of the one they murder (I'd have to look at the specific verse here). Can God please make up his mind?

6. Okay, I was trying to ignore that EVERYONE in the book of Genesis lives to be about 900 years old . . . but this REALLY bothered me.

   Genesis 6:3: "Then the Lord said, 'My spirit will not put up with humans for such a long time, for they are only mortal flesh. In the future they will live no more than 120 years.'"

Then AFTER that Noah lives to be 950—Shem died at age 600—Arphaxad lived 438 years—Shelah lived 433 years—Eber lived 464 years . . . and so on and so on down Noah's family tree for as far as I read.

Aren't those great questions? And real! And don't they illustrate how the content of the Bible can be foreign to us? (If you're interested, see Appendix 1 for my attempt at answering her questions.) There's more that we could talk about here, but I suspect you see clearly how the foreign languages and cultures of the Bible sometimes make it hard to understand.

Chapter 3

Reason #3: The Genres of the Bible

Thousands of years from now, excavators dig up some very old scraps of paper just outside the ancient city of Tallahassee, Florida. The artifacts were preserved in mud and concrete by an earthquake that ripped through the city in the late twenty-first century. One brief newspaper article, which appears to have been framed, reads as follows:

> **MORE GATORS TO BE HUNTED:** Applications for Florida's second alligator hunt in recent decades will be taken this week and officials plan to open more areas and increase the number of gators that can be taken. Last year was the first legal hunt in 26 years, with 2,960 alligators reported caught—well under the 3,450 limit set by the . . . This year that limit will go up to 3,900—out of an estimated population of 1 million gators.

Since alligators had long become extinct and researchers were interested in the sociological and environmental factors that led to their demise, the article is of scientific, as well as historical, significance. In a previous discovery, not far from the town of Gainesville, excavators also found what appeared to be some sort of political platform or slogan on a small piece of rubbery, contact paper, referencing the now-extinct reptiles. Though some of the letters were illegible, experts were able to decipher the content. The sticker read: "I Brake for Gators." Scientists hypothesized that evolving, political tensions gave way to a generalized aversion for gators during the late twentieth and twenty-first centuries that contributed to the extinction of the species.

What if someone from another point in history or—say—another planet who had never been exposed to cartoons or comic strips were to run across a Peanuts episode, with Charlie Brown, Lucy, Linus, and the whole gang; or a Ziggy cartoon (one that always stuck in my mind was the time Ziggy looked up prayerfully into heaven from the top of a mountain and sheepishly asked, "Have you

Why It's Hard to Understand the Bible

noticed, Sir, that the meek are still getting creamed?")? What if they knew next to nothing about the culture and circumstances of our times? Would they know how to understand what they were reading? Do you think they would "get" the punch line? Another important reason the Bible can be difficult to understand is the variety and foreignness of the types of literature the Bible contains. The genres of the Bible can create interpretive challenges for us today.

"Genre" is the category, class, or type of artistic literature, composition, or communications of various sorts, distinguished by a particular style, form, or content. Some of us are more familiar with its use in cinema. Because we are at home in our own movie-watching culture, we make significant mental and emotional adjustments easily, subconsciously, when we watch the likes of an old, John Wayne western versus a modern fantasy adventure or science-fiction epic. Animations appeal to young and old; documentaries require a certain sort of sophistication or educational bent. When we throw television into the mix, the experiences grow even wider: reality shows, sit-coms, cartoons, football games, the evening news, talk shows, you name it. Within that mix, there are discernible types of programs that require various, sometimes subtle, shifts of mood and mindset to understand and enjoy the experience. We make the adjustments naturally because we know the genres. Music has various genres as well: some like country, some like ol'-fashioned rock and roll, classical, easy-listening, etc. Similarly, theatre and art have their own sets of styles and types. Genres change and evolve over time, moreover. Electronic media—internet blogs and text messages, for example—add their own types of communication experiences. We're thus exposed to new genres as culture evolves or we experience a particular form of entertainment for the first time.

The same sort of thing happens when we read as well. We know the difference between a work of fiction—a steamy romance novel, for example—and an algebra text or a book on how to read the Bible, for that matter. Imperceptibly, we know how to read a newspaper editorial versus the Sunday comics (though some might say there's little difference between the two). Imagine reading a bumper sticker (like "I brake for Gators") as if it were a political slogan. . . . or a recipe from a cookbook. Huh? A magazine article about fashion or sports is a different experience from a collection of Rudyard Kipling's poems or an Edgar Allan Poe short story. We know the difference and how to distinguish the meanings.

As part of the wide scope and foreign cultures of the Bible, and because the Bible is a collection of works, it contains several types or genres of literature with which we may or may not be familiar. Understanding the Bible thus requires the same sort of mental adjustments we make when we move in and out of the various types of literature we read today. For most of the Bible, this is relatively easy, as the types are not all that different. On the other hand, some biblical genres are unfamiliar to us—some books as a whole and sections within books (what we might call sub-genres, like parables, for example). To the extent that the genres of the Bible are different from ours, discussion of types of biblical literature could have been included previously as a subset of (reason #2) the cultures of the Bible. I'm putting it in its own section because of the emphasis some place on it and its critical importance in a few cases.

One of the best modern guides for approaching the subject of how to read the Bible effectively, with special focus on the various types of biblical literature, is Gordon Fee and Douglas Stuart's very readable *How to Read the Bible for All It's Worth*. Fee and Stuart organize the book according to type of literature in the Bible: epistles/letters, narratives (Old Testament and Acts), gospels, parables, the Law(s): covenant stipulations, prophetic literature, psalms/prayers, wisdom literature, and the book of Revelation. *How to Read the Bible for All Its Worth* has become somewhat of a standard on the fundamentals of biblical exegesis (how to interpret the Bible) for aspiring Bible students. I recommend it to you highly. It's especially helpful with this question of the basic genres of the Bible.

Considerations of genre are certainly important for understanding the Bible properly. I do not, however, think this is the best fundamental angle or starting point from which to approach the question of how we are to read the Bible. Some people make genre the number one emphasis; I think we should focus more on the literary context (to some, this might just be a way of saying the same thing). Just as we learn the most about the specific historical context of a book by reading that book—from the literary context—so we "discover" the types of biblical literature as we read the books themselves. In cases where the book is in its entirety a specific type of literature (like a letter, for example), we can, like the historical context, learn the specifics inductively as we read (unless, of course, it's so foreign that we can't make heads or tails of it). In cases where it's a smaller part of the book (like parables, or prayers, or stories of various types), then the genre functions as part of the literary context and contributes to the overall purposes and meaning of the text, like everything else. This is not to say that knowing something about the type of literature is not helpful. Just as we assume a different sort of psychological posture when we open a letter from an old friend as when we open an electric bill, or a mystery novel, familiarity with the genre certainly contributes to good reading. This is again where introductions to the books of the Bible can be quite helpful.

On the other hand, with the exception of apocalyptic literature (primarily the book of Revelation, but also some in Daniel and the Gospels), most of the literary types of the Bible are not so foreign to us that we can't make some sense of them as we read. (This is not the case with the book of Revelation, however. Ancient apocalyptic literature is so foreign to modern Americans as to require explicit training on the nature and purposes of the genre in order to understand it properly. More on this later.) Though it's often left out completely, mentioned in passing or covered only briefly in presentations about how to read the Bible, I believe learning to read each book as a literary whole—seeking to see how all the parts fit together to communicate its primary messages—to be the first task and end-goal of good Bible reading (outside of application, of course, which is the reason we read). The more we learn about the different types of biblical genre, the better we will be positioned to experience the text as it was originally intended. You can know a lot about a particular type of literature, however, and still completely miss the point of the text you are reading.

Chapter 3

Reason #4: The Content of the Bible

We talked a little about the content of the Bible from a cultural perspective, but let's look at it from another angle. What about the content from an intellectual and spiritual perspective?

I'm having a hard time figuring out how to use our keyword "distance" with this one. The distance from the surface of the water to the bottom is called "depth." One of the reasons the Bible is sometimes difficult to understand is because of the *depth* of its topics. The intellectual, emotional, and spiritual *distance* of the Bible sometimes takes mental, emotional, and spiritual muscles to scale. How was that for effort? (I just committed a logical fallacy called an equivocation, changing from a literal to a figurative meaning of the word "depth." Interestingly, an ancient Hebrew method of interpreting the Bible allowed for such mental gymnastics as a legitimate catchword-way of connecting separate passages of scripture, which is another example of an intellectual cultural difference.) How about the distance the Bible goes into important, complex topics? But it's not just the distance or depth, is it? In some cases, it's the very fact that it's willing to talk about them at all. Add to the topics themselves the point that the writers of the Bible sometimes wrote at different educational levels and styles (reading Luke or Hebrews in Greek, for example, is a different experience than reading John or Paul), that we as readers comprise different levels, and that versions of the Bible seek to communicate at different levels, and we have all the ingredients for a rainbow-like assortment of flavors of reading comprehension.

The Bible hides from no issue, flees no challenge, tip-toes around no controversy, as the writers delve into the deepest—and sometimes darkest—crevices of human existence. Stomping around in the guts and glory of real life, the Bible pictures humanity at its lowest and at its highest. This is one of the reasons people are often drawn to the Bible. It's as real as it gets.

The time when the Hivite prince Shechem fell in love with Dinah, Jacob's daughter, and raped her serves as a good example. After raping her, he wanted to marry her; so, he asked his father to get her to become his wife. As part of a treaty-like arrangement between the Israelites (Jacob and his children) and the people of the city of Shechem (the town close to which the Israelites were camping), prince Shechem's father Hamor proposed that they make a pact of friendliness between their peoples to live together in peace, do business together, and intermarry. Then Hamor offered to pay Jacob any price for his daughter Dinah to marry prince Shechem.

Check out this verse: "The sons of Jacob answered Shechem and his father Hamor deceitfully, because he had defiled their sister Dinah" (Genesis 34:13). They said—and I'm paraphrasing—"Okay, we'll do what you ask, join together our peoples, and Shechem can marry Dinah, but only on one condition. All your males have to be circumcised." Ouch! Circumcision was very important to Israelites as a seal of religious and familial identity. Seems like a strange and rather painful price, but because of Shechem's blinding passion for Dinah, they quickly agreed. The text gives the punch line:

> On the third day when they were still in pain, two of the sons of Jacob, Simeon and Levi, Dinah's brothers, took their swords and came against the city unawares, and killed all the males. They killed Hamor and his son Shechem with the sword, and took Dinah out of Shechem's house, and went away. And the other sons of Jacob came upon the slain, and plundered the city, because their sister had been defiled. They took their flocks and their herds, their donkeys, and whatever was in the city and in the field. All their wealth, all their little ones and their wives, all that was in the houses, they captured and made their prey (Genesis 34:25-29).

Though he himself had an entangled history with deception ("like father, like son"), apparently, Jacob wasn't in on the plot because he chastised his sons from fear of what the surrounding cities might think and do.

Here we see a very real, down and dirty, story of life in the pursuit of freedom, land, family, and even God. For intrigue, Hollywood couldn't conceive it better. But it's more than a story. The

Chapter 3

depth of human questions is great: international relations (the Israelites trying to find a home and live among different types of people); love versus lust; politics and power, as Shechem and his father make personal decisions that dramatically affect all their people; marriage and family; crime and punishment; love and war. What type of response does rape deserve? Did Dinah's brothers react disproportionately? Or is everything fair in love and war? What if it were your sister, or mother, or daughter? And who is to decide and carry out the sentence? And perhaps an even bigger question: why would they act this way? Listen to Dinah's brothers' answer when Jacob scolds them for their actions: "But they said, 'Should our sister be treated like a whore?'" Whew! Good question. But—in the vein of Dr. Seuss's *The Butter Battle* book—their reaction was likely to bring more "trouble," as Jacob predicts.

You see what I mean about the courage of the Bible to present issues in the context of real life? And this is a good example of how a set of verses can be difficult to understand properly if we don't read them in light of their broader, book-level context as a whole. Taken by themselves, this and other stores can be rather confusing and even alarming about the content of the Bible and the character of its "heroes" and its God, which is why some people rail against the picture of God in the Old Testament. Seen in the overall scope of Genesis, however, the story makes much more sense.

The complex outworking of deceit in the hearts and lives of humans is one of the primary themes of the book of Genesis, as the initial deception of the serpent in the Garden of Eden and the fall of humanity as a whole finds deep and dark development in the lives of people. As part of that real-life picture of human evil, the story of Dinah graphically displays a now very ugly side of something innately good: "romantic" and "brotherly" love. The bigger picture says tough questions like these are hard to answer when dysfunctional (deceived and deceiving) human character expresses itself. The Bible never hides from this dark side, and—as you know from living in the real world—it can get awfully dark. On the other hand, just when the darkness seems to have reached the point of total blackout, a seed of God's grace finds root in the soil of a soft human heart, as a man like

Abraham—responding to God's request for his son whom he loved deeply—says, in effect, "If you say so."[5]

What topics does the Bible explore? What sort of questions does it address? The biggest and the baddest (that is, the toughest). The subjects of the Bible are the very topics that philosophers and poets have struggled (and failed) to answer throughout history. How'd we get here? What's the purpose and meaning of life? How do we get out of here? Is there a God? What's he like? Why are some things so beautiful and other things so ugly? Why does it hurt so much? Why am I so lonely? Does anyone really give a rat's rear?

One of the reasons the Bible is sometimes hard to understand is because it boldly goes where everyone has gone before, tackling the toughest questions of life. It doesn't shy away from questions about the existence and nature of God; about the origin, meaning, and purposes of life; about humans—our nature and destiny; about good and evil; the problems of pain and suffering; the futility of life and our quest to fix things; sin and salvation; death and the afterlife; heaven and hell. Though the first messages of the Bible about faith in God and "realized" life are simple, sometimes even childlike, it will take you as far as you want to go. Well, almost. The Bible is never afraid to delve deeply into these difficult topics, and it does so typically in dynamic narratives of life itself. On the other hand, the Bible doesn't give us trite, simple, or even complete answers to some of the most intriguing and infuriating questions. Implications of sin, faith, and the transcendence of God are some of the reasons why, but that's not my point at the moment. For now, I'm just trying to remind you that—in spite of its captivating and gentle, nurturing tendencies—the Bible is not children's literature. Not by a long shot. In fact, the subjects of the Bible go beyond us, and sometimes, that makes it hard to understand.

Part of Paul's purpose for writing the letter of Ephesians, expressed in his prayer for the audience, was that God would give them the ability through his Spirit "to comprehend with all the saints, what is the breadth and length and height and depth, and to know the love of Christ that surpasses knowledge," so that they might be "filled with all the fullness of God" (Ephesians 3:18-19). From God

Chapter 3

to the grave, from sin to salvation in Christ, the Bible explores the real and deep issues of life; and, as Paul implies, we need divine help to get the full dimensions of "the love of Christ that surpasses knowledge."[6]

Reason #5: The Readers of the Bible

That's one side of the coin: the difficulty that comes from the scope, depth, and transcendent nature of the topics the Bible covers. One side is the *subject;* the other side is the *subjective.* Sometimes difficulties in understanding the Bible have less to do with the writers and what's written, or with how it's delivered, than with the readers. In other words, one of the reasons the Bible is hard to understand is because *we're* the ones trying to understand it. This starts with natural differences of intellect and perspective that come from our uniqueness as individuals, progresses through the subjective nature of our personal interpretations and judgments, and culminates in the blinding effects of our needs, failures, disappointments, hurts, and resulting self-absorbedness. The Bible pictures this inordinate interest or focus upon oneself as the result of sin. The *distance* between us and God produced by sin is perhaps the strongest reason the Bible is sometimes hard to understand.

The Personal:
Individuality and Traditions of Interpretation

We see things differently. As unique individuals, both biologically and environmentally, it's natural for people to have different perspectives on life and the experiences of life. No one is exactly like you. No one has been where you've been, seen what you've seen, and done what you've done. It's part of the blessing of being a unique person, made in the image of God. It's expected, therefore, that such differences would express themselves when we analyze and interpret things. We see this every day. Ask any two individuals to describe something they've both seen, experienced, or read, and the results will never be precisely the same; though we don't want to overlook the fact that more often than not the essence or core will be the same, if the persons involved are "telling the truth." When the "stories" diverge far enough, at some point, at least one account crosses

Chapter 3

over into what we consider to be "wrong" or untrue—inaccurately representing what actually happened.

Sometimes a perspective is so influenced by personal filters (hurts, needs, blind spots, etc.) that it distorts the interpretation of a given idea or event to such an extent so as to create a misinterpretation, or what we might even call an illusion. I'm sure you've experienced this or even know of times or topics that raise your subjective temperature (or blood-pressure) to the point that you begin to take things personally that weren't necessarily intended that way (if you've been married for a while, you probably get this). When my dad and his brother start talking politics, for example, get out of the way. Normally affectionate brothers almost come to blows. And there are various levels of such personal perspective; it's even measured on personality inventories as a subjective vs. objective trait. When it becomes excessive, to the point of clearly and consistently distorting reality, we think of it as a form of mental illness. You've probably known people who took things so personally that they often distorted what other people did or said (after all, "Everyone is out to get me!"). We all do it at times—maybe all the time—to some extent. We see things through our own rose- or cloud-colored glasses. This is the subjective side of human nature. It's part of our uniqueness as individuals, but there's more to it.

Before looking at another—the darker—side of individual subjectivity, another aspect of personal perspective could be considered as a separate reason the Bible is sometimes hard to understand: what we already "know." The history of understanding we as individuals have from whatever prior reading, sermons and Sunday school, or spiritual training, and the long history of Bible interpretation within Christianity in general, naturally affect what we get out of a given passage of scripture. In other words, none of us starts with a clean slate—of course. But the deeper our own sense of the meaning of a given scripture and our investment in that interpretation (its connection to key ideas of our faith), the harder it is to see or hear it any other way.

This personal history of interpretation, which is, in effect, a form of tradition, has a counterpart in Christianity in general where we have hundreds of years of interpretive tradition. The Bible has been read and reread, interpreted and reinterpreted, explained and discussed in thousands of documents and books, sermons and encyclicals, journals and magazines, Bible classes and small groups . . . for hundreds of years, to the extent that sometimes the text begins to look more like a once-natural and stately hardwood wall covered with multiple layers of contemporary paint and paper than a living, breathing document. There are so many layers of tradition on so many biblical texts that modern commentaries often amount to collections of interpretations rather than fresh interactions with the Bible. (Stripping away the paint and paper is part of what this book is all about.) Don't misunderstand—I'm glad we have a rich history of great men and women to guide us in reading our Bibles. On the other hand, layers of interpretive tradition, both corporate and personal, can come between us and a living encounter with the text and the Spirit who inspired it.

> **Warning:** The following waxes theological. Let's hope it gives enough of a shine to the finish of our discussion (get the pun?) to make it worth the effort. So don't be bashful. Put on your waders and step on in.

Chapter 3

The Personal: The Effects of Sin

Self-Injury

A fundamental teaching of the Bible is that human nature has been marred or defaced by sin. "Sin," which I like to define as *self-injury* from the "s" and "in" (or inordinate *self-interest*—take your pick), means literally to *miss a goal* or *target* and is used in the Bible as a symbol for going against what God wants us to do. Sin means to do what God says not to do, or not to do what God wants and says to do. The Bible also portrays what God wants (sometimes referred to as "the will of God") as coming from his nature as a being of ultimate love, which means that when we go against what God says, we are violating what would naturally be good for us—real love always seeks what's best for the object of its love. That's why I like to define sin as self-injury. When Adam and Eve sinned against God in the Garden of Eden as representatives of the human race, and as we each sin as individuals, we are inflicting a devastating harm upon ourselves that causes pain and trouble, for God and us. This is something we need to keep in mind as we're thinking about why the Bible is sometimes hard to understand: we've been injured, deeply wounded by sin (in fact, destroyed, but that's another topic: God told Adam and Eve, "When you eat of it, you will die.") Even if we don't know or want to admit it, as personal, mental, emotional, and spiritual beings, we are not healthy.

The biblical account of the first sin in the Garden of Eden, usually called "the Fall," profoundly depicts some of the nature of the self-injury of sin. In the original portrait of Adam and Eve as male and female, created to live together as husband and wife, the Bible paints a beautiful picture of an outward looking, non-self-conscious sort of mutual love. After describing everything he had made—the universe, the skies, the seas, the earth, the animals—as "good" and then as "very good" once humans (as male and female) were added to the mix, God said that it was "not good" for the man to be alone. That's when it describes the creation of "woman" (Eve) as coming from the man (Adam) and being presented to him as a completion or "counterpart." Adam's very excited reaction at first sight of Eve—"This is now bone of my bones and flesh of my flesh; she shall be called 'woman,' for she was taken out of man" (Genesis 2:23, NIV)—suggests the purest form of physical and emotional attraction and is presented as the basis of marriage. Not only is Adam thrilled by Eve, the Bible then says that they "were both naked, and were not ashamed" (2:25). Many commentators have pointed out the one-another, outward focus of the marriage ideal presented in the pre-sin picture of Adam and Eve.

It didn't last. Adam and Eve decided to go against God, eating the forbidden fruit. The point I want to focus on is the result of that action. When God came along in the evening or "cool" part of the day, instead of an excited, how-great-it-is-to-see-you-again welcome, Adam hides in fear and shame. A distance has been created between the man and his God. When God asks him about eating the fruit, Adam blames Eve and even God ("the woman *you* gave me . . ."). See how one's perspective changes when wounded? Adam's idyllic, self-satisfied perspective—being rather oblivious to oneself, like when you're not hurting and you're having fun—had somehow turned inward and become defensive. Guilt, fear, and blame replaced peace, freedom, and excitement. Eve follows suit and blames the serpent, who tricked or "*deceived* me," she says. This is important because, fundamentally, sin is based on and results in deception.

The punishments for their disobedience reveal the corresponding physical consequences of a now dysfunctional world, broken by violation of the first principle of life—being what we are made to be, doing what we are supposed to do (= what God says). Extreme pain, sweat, and struggle to the point of death ("for dust you are and to dust you will return" [3:19, NIV]) symbolize the difference between the way it is now (can you relate?) and the way it was in the beginning. The resulting relational tension between the man and the woman has a physical expression in that as soon as they ate the fruit, they became aware that they were naked (self-conscious) and covered themselves with fig leaves (later, God makes them clothes of animal skins).[7] A radical change had occurred: from excited and unashamed to guilty and fearful and self-conscious; and with it, a radical change in perspective. Their perspective had turned a disastrous summersault. What was at first an "how-amazing-*you* are" part of me (such that I want to be with you forever in open, unashamed love) became a self-defensive, self-protective, self-hiding, self-covering, separated-from-God-and-each-other-by-a-wall-of-guilt-and-shame self. This is the wounded self, caused by sin.

Sin is *self-injury* because it contradicts the fundamental basis of life and health. I'm reminded of Cecil B. DeMille's comment about the law of God when introducing his famous Movie, *The Ten Commandments*. Something to the effect of "You can't break the Law [of God]; you can only break yourself against the Law." That's the point. That's what we did; that's what we do. The result is a form of *self-interest* that we sometimes interpret as selfishness, expressed either as over- or under-ego, both of which spring from the same condition: distance from God, the supremely wounded self. This is why that which is personal or subjective is often more than that; it's often—if not usually—distorted, self-defensive, and self-promoting. There is a hole in my heart—the classic "God-shaped hole"—that I can't fix or even adequately medicate. This is why we act, interact, and react with the need for self-protection and promotion, as if we're looking for something we lost. Have you ever noticed how we all seem to be constantly competing for value? The teaching of the Bible is that this is the result of our separation from God and will never be completely restored until we experience his love directly in his immediate presence. The life and teachings of Jesus bring us the knowledge of that love in as personal and close a manner as possible, and that's the purpose of the community of Christ in the church, as we begin to experience the restoration of what was lost and broken.

Deceived

As we see in the initial temptation of Adam and Eve by the serpent, sin starts with a lie, with deception: God said they would die if they ate the fruit; the serpent said "No you won't; you'll become like God." Thus, Jesus says that Satan was a murderer from the beginning, calling him "a liar and the father of lies" (John 8:44). At its root, sin is a lie—a way of thinking that goes against what God thinks and says. When we ingest that way of thinking (picture Adam and Eve eating the fruit), we are believing a lie, and, by the very fact that we have put a way of thinking into our brains that is ultimately false, we have reduced our ability to think and see clearly. Does that make sense? And it affects everything else. Sort of like a computer virus, but much worse. When deception takes root in a person's heart and becomes a part of the person when believed, everything else—the whole operating system—is messed up, with two immediate results: (1) we are no longer what we were—we are much less, our selves have been injured, and we feel the effects of that loss deeply; and (2) there is an automatic distance created between us and God because we're no longer like him—we don't think as he does anymore. Our vision for truth blurs. (You can't believe a lie without that belief resulting in systemic distortion.) The more lies we believe, the more we damage our "central processing units"—to continue the computer analogy. The more we don't do what God says, the more injured we become. That's why the sinful self is a wounded self. And wounds hurt—that's why we give them so much attention. When we hurt—if it's bad enough—our whole focus shifts to that hurt for relief and healing. That's what happened to the human race and to each of us. What was originally unselfish and destined for incredible, mutual love became subconsciously obsessed with itself, because of the pain. The result is a systemic breakdown of our thinking and feeling systems. Our focus turns inward toward the hurt, and the result is a broken, self-centered creature.

    The original sin of Adam and Eve and some of the things we do may not seem like they should create all that I've described as the result of sin. It doesn't seem like it should be that big of a deal (does the punishment fit the crime sort of thing). But take away intimacy with God, and you've created the greatest wound imaginable. Pile sin upon sin, distortion upon distortion, evil upon evil, lie upon lie throughout all the generations of all of human history, and it's no wonder that God underscores his offer of forgiveness (in Isaiah) with this clarification: "For my thoughts are not your thoughts, nor are your ways my ways, says the Lord. For as the heavens are higher than the earth, so are my ways higher than your ways and my thoughts than your thoughts" (Isaiah 55:8-9). It's also no wonder that Paul describes the ultimate result of sin as a complete reversal of perspective, where people begin honestly to think that evil is good, and good, evil (Romans 1:18-32). This is also why self-denial is at the center of Jesus' teaching: Jesus calls us to pick up our crosses and follow him on the road to death. It's not a martyr complex or some sort of morbid fascination with death. It's the beyond-the-grave realization that death to self—the wounded, always-mentally-and-emotionally-looking-out-for-#1 self—is ultimately the only path to new life (pictured as resurrection in the Bible).

As we saw briefly in the story of Jacob's daughter Dinah, the book of Genesis develops this theme of deception in the unfolding of the earliest history of the human race. We see it in many of the stories as the book seeks to show how God began working his plan to save humankind (from the downward spiral of sin and its ultimate destruction) through the lives of Abraham (whom God chooses by grace) and his descendants—in spite of the propagation of sin and its effects. One of the most important messages of the book of Genesis (and the Bible as a whole) is, therefore, that we humans are deceived and we humans are deceivers. It got so bad at one point, Genesis 6:5 says, "that every inclination of the thoughts of their hearts was only evil continually." And it's not just Genesis. The Bible repeatedly affirms that all of us have sinned and suffer the consequences of sin—not only spiritually, as some might define it—but in our minds and hearts. You can't believe a lie without having that belief change you from the inside out, resulting in a systemic condition of chronic distortion.

The portrayal of the nature and meaning of sin in Genesis is the most profound and enlightening analysis of human nature I've ever heard. How often does life confirm the hurtful, defensive, self-protective, blaming nature of our actions and reactions as we try to relate to one another outside of Eden in a broken, dysfunctional world? These are the results of not doing what God says. Bottom line: we don't think and act like we were supposed to; we have become overly self-conscious, defensive, and—now get this—therefore, overly *subjective* people. *Because of sin* (evil in us), *subjectivity is not just individuality*, not just another way of looking at something; *it's much, much more.* (Perhaps, I should say, it's much *less.*) It's distortion—though subconscious and even unintentional, but distortion nonetheless—for the purpose of helping me feel better about what I've become and what I've lost.

Still Injured and Deceived

Here's the long-winded point: when we go to read the Bible, our self-centered, self-defensive, self-protective, guilty, blaming, distorted perspectives don't just go away. Even if you don't agree with everything I've said about the effects of sin, I hope you'll admit that one of, if not the most powerful, reasons the Bible is hard to understand is because of sin and its consequences upon us as readers. This is the distance of perspective between us and God that I've been talking about.

Of course, there are individual, subjective perspectives that cause us to see some things in the Bible differently. We are unique individuals, with unique ways of thinking from all that we've seen and learned. Not unrelated are the different interpretations of biblical texts that have come from years of Christian tradition and teaching (many, many sermons, books, and Bible commentaries). These make up a part of the personal perspective of those of us who have read and studied the Bible. But what I'm saying goes beyond these. I'm saying that subjectivity wears a thick pair of self-deceived and self-deceiving glasses. I'm suggesting that the subjective is, practically speaking, a relentless, usually invisible façade of a broken and wounded self. When it comes to reading the Bible, like a pacifier that doesn't provide any real nourishment, it functions to keep us content for the time being. To put it another way, individualism, the subjective, or what I'm calling personalism, does everything it can to protect us from the (what feels like) destructive truth and to blame someone else for whatever mishap we might have been involved in.

Chapter 3

Okay, now put on your protective armor against radical statements for what I'm about to say: I think the common tendency to identify our subjective thoughts, experiences, and especially deep and personal feelings with God to be one of the greatest dangers within modern Christianity. The human tendency for the personal to function as a type of distorting filter is, moreover, one of the conditions that predispose us to inkblotitis. At the very least, it gives us a posturing toward seeing things "my way." Ironically, this is the very reason we need the Bible, and don't think that it doesn't play a role in our ability to actually get God's point when we read it. This raises the important question of the role of God's grace and the Holy Spirit when it comes to understanding the Bible. We'll talk more about that later. For now, simply add *us*—with an exclamation point—to the list of why the Bible is hard to understand.

Reason #6: The Ways We Read the Bible

To show how it fits in the current discussion, I'm including the ways we read the Bible in our list of things that make understanding the Bible difficult.[8] Since this is at the heart of inkblotitis, however, we'll explore it more fully in the next chapter. There we'll look at some of the most popular ways we read and use the Bible today, and ask ourselves the question: do the ways we read the Bible help us get God's point or do they predispose us to personal and subjective interpretations that may not be what the original writers intended?

For now, let's recap. Confirming what most of us already know from experience, we've outlined some of the reasons the Bible can sometimes be hard to understand. The wide scope, foreign and divergent cultures, multiplicity of genres, complexity and depth of real-life subjects, the subjective and protective perspectives we have as readers, and how we go about reading all contribute to the challenge of hearing God when we read the Bible.

The difficulties come from the medium, the messages, and from the readers. A message might be simple, but if it comes in a form I can't read or understand, "it's Greek to me." On the other hand, sometimes I don't have the capacity to understand, either because I don't put enough into it or something else gets in the way. The subjective and, more profoundly, the self-interest of the wounded person puts up a distorting barrier (and sometimes a strong fight) between me as a reader and the purposes and content of the Bible. The content itself can at times be hard to understand. After all, it's about God . . . and about us. It's about living and dying, and the most important things. About realizing them as we live.

Add all these to the pace and stresses of our lives, and it's no wonder that for many the Bible lies forgotten, dormant, sitting on mantles or collecting dust in dresser-drawers or back shelves of a closet. But please don't be discouraged. The point is not to overwhelm you with the difficulty, but rather to alert you to some of the—may I say—deceptive reasons the enemy uses to keep us from reading and understanding the Bible. Getting God's point might not

Chapter 3

happen automatically, but let me assure you, it's well worth the effort. In fact, as Jesus reminds us ("Man shall not live by bread alone, but by every word that proceeds from the mouth of God"), it's essential to real life. And there is divine help, if you really want to hear from God. Would God go to the trouble to send Jesus so we can realize life to the full and not help us find that life when we seek it? My purpose is not to discourage you with the difficulties of Bible reading, but to encourage and release you to the marvelous adventure of rediscovering the word of God in the books of God.

Chapter 3: Why It's Hard to Understand the Bible

Chapter Resources

Daniell, David. *The Bible in English: Its History and Influence*. London: Yale University, 2003.

Fee, Gordon D., and Stuart, Douglas. *How to Read the Bible for All It's Worth*. 3rd ed. Grand Rapids: Zondervan, 2003.

How to Read the Bible Book by Book: A Guided Tour. Grand Rapids: Zondervan, 2002.

Mozley, J. F. *William Tyndale*. London: S.P.C.K., 1937.

Tyndale, William. *The Obedience of a Christian Man*. Edited with an Introduction and Notes by David Daniell. London: Penguin Books, 2000.

Notes

1. Daniell (*The Bible in English*, 5) has a nice paragraph in the Introduction to his study on the English Bible, highlighting some of the difficulties of reading through the Bible:
   ". . . . Even sympathetic readers find long stretches of Leviticus or Numbers troublingly tedious, or passages of some of the Prophets incomprehensible. Paul at his most theological is not an easy read. At the very end of the New Testament, the book of Revelation can be read merely as accounts of hallucinations, or as foretelling imminent catastrophes. Even devout Christians can sympathise with the Scottish minister who finished his reading with the words: 'If it hadna been the Lord's will, that verse had been better left out.'"
2. When the Ethiopian eunuch was reading a passage of scripture from the Old Testament book of Isaiah while riding along in his chariot, Philip asked him, "Do you understand what you are reading?" The eunuch replied, "How can I, unless someone guides me" (Acts 8:26-40).

3. Fee and Stuart's two-book collection (*How to Read the Bible for All It's Worth* and *How to Read the Bible Book by Book: A Guided Tour*) presents some of the best material on how to read the Bible.
4. Every now and then we create similar patterns, but, as one would expect, it's usually in a poetic or rhetorical context, as when President John F. Kennedy said, ". . . ask not what your country can do for you—ask what you can do for your country."
5. This story in Genesis 22 of Abraham's offering of his son Isaac is an amazing prefiguring of God's gift of his son Jesus. My summarizing expression of Abraham's obedience with the words "If you say so" points to Jesus' own words in the Garden of Gethsemane when he prayed just before his crucifixion: "Not my will, but yours be done."
6. Paul talks about this from a negative angle in his first letter to the Corinthians, where he writes about the "carnal," "fleshly," "worldly," or "unspiritual" mind. Discussing this theme in a context of arguing and division over the presence and work of God's Spirit, he makes this impactful statement:

    "We have not received the spirit of the world but the Spirit who is from God that we may understand what God has freely given us. . . . The man without the Spirit does not accept the things that come from the Spirit of God, for they are foolishness to him, and he cannot understand them, because they are spiritually discerned. . . . But we have the mind of Christ" (2:12-16, NIV).
7. The resulting relational tension between the man and the woman may also be reflected in the statement "your desire shall be for your husband, and he shall rule over you" (3:16).
8. An interesting commentary on the potential of interpretive methods can be gleaned from Tyndale's criticism of contemporary Scholasticism as patently subjective: "Of what text thou provest hell, will another prove purgatory, another *limbo partum* and another shall prove of the same text that an ape hath a tail" (Tyndale, *Obedience*, 23). Tyndale's somewhat comical point highlights that it's not so much *who* reads the Bible (in this case scholastic academicians) but *how* we read it.

Chapter 4

The Ways We Read the Bible

> In the evening I went very unwillingly to a society in Aldersgate Street, where one was reading Luther's preface to the Epistle to the Romans. About a quarter before nine, while he was describing the change which God works in the heart through faith in Christ, I felt my heart strangely warmed. I felt I did trust in Christ, Christ alone, for salvation; and an assurance was given me that He had taken away my sins, even mine, and saved me from the law of sin and death.
>
> .... I then testified openly to all there what I now first felt in my heart. But it was not long before the enemy suggested, "This cannot be faith; for where is thy joy?" Then was I taught that peace and victory over sin are essential to faith in the Captain of our salvation; but that, as to the transports of joy that usually attend the beginning of it, especially in those who have mourned deeply, God sometimes giveth, sometimes withholdeth, them according to the counsels of His own will.[1]

These are the words of John Wesley (1703-91), founder of the Methodist movement, describing the time on May 24, 1738 when he reluctantly attended a Moravian church meeting (the church from Moravia was founded by John Hus—you'll recall him as the follower of John Wycliffe who was burned at the stake for his efforts to put the Bible into the hands of the common people).

A few years before, Wesley was on a ship headed to the New World from England, having been invited to serve as a pastor to the colonists in Savannah, Georgia. The crew and passengers endured several severe storms in the course of the trans-Atlantic journey. On one occasion, a great storm broke the mast off the ship and scared the passengers to death, including Wesley, who was—ironically— the chaplain of the vessel. Panicked and fearing the worst, Wesley stumbled into a room of German Moravians (on their way to preach to American Indians) who not only were not afraid like he and the rest of the passengers, but were singing and praying calmly (reminiscent of Jesus asleep in the boat during a furious storm).[2] When the trip ended, Wesley asked the Moravian leader why he wasn't afraid; to which he replied, "Do you know Jesus Christ? . . . do you know He has saved you?" Wesley answered, "I hope He has died to save me." The pastor added, "Do you know yourself?" Wesley replied affirmatively, but said he feared "they were vain words." Throughout his life, Wesley longed for that kind of personal, reassuring faith, one that would give him joy and peace in the temptations and storms of life. On the night he attended the Moravian meeting and felt his heart *strangely warmed*, he seemed to have found what he'd been looking for—at least for the moment.

Years removed in time but not human nature, Wesley's search for and experience of heartfelt confirmation has become a standard, not just in the arena of personal faith, but in other areas of contemporary Christianity. With roots in key reformers like Luther, Zwingli, and Calvin,[3] and especially German Pietism (see below), and in spite of the essential differences between personal faith and divine truth, Wesley's warm-heart moment has become one of the most popular approaches to how we listen to God when we read the Bible.[4]

In this chapter, I'd like to consider three common ways that we read the Bible today: (1) devotional Bible reading, (2) theological or topical Bible reading, and (3) defensive or argumentative Bible reading. Before delving into these common ways of reading, however, we should first think through some fundamental questions about *why* we read the Bible and what we're looking for when we read, since *why* we read has a significant impact on *the way* we read.

What It Means To You

You're in a small group Bible study or maybe a Sunday morning Bible class. Perhaps you're using a study-guide of some sort or someone is teaching on a particular topic. Whatever the topic or the type of group, at some point the leader has everyone open his or her Bible and read a passage of scripture that relates to the subject at hand. He or she then goes around the room and asks the now world-famous question—a question I'm sure many of you have been asked and maybe asked at some point in your Bible-study history. (It's almost the opposite of The Question that serves as an antidote to inkblotitis.) The leader says, "What does this mean *to you*?," with emphasis on "to you." (The question itself is to some extent a symptom of the hidden illness of inkblotitis.) Of course, there is an appropriate divergence of potential applications of a given set of verses, dependent on one's unique circumstances in life. But isn't the question more appropriately and profoundly "What does this mean?" Or "What did it mean to the original readers in the context of this particular book?" The personal "to you" part of the question reflects the subjective influence of our culture, the small-group setting, and our methods of reading the Bible.

Growing up in church, a favorite method of Bible education in our classes was the use of study guides, written by various teachers within our denominational framework. The guides were typically about some important aspect of the Christian faith—studies on the existence of God, features of the life and ministry of Christ (like parables and miracles), faith, baptism, the role and work of the Holy Spirit, worship, Bible history, marriage, morality, money, etc. Typically, there would be a section of teaching material, often followed by a series of fill-in-the-blank or short answer questions that called for the student to look up particular verses in the Bible in order to answer the questions. Ever do that? Think about that for a minute. How much of the context do you get with that method? And how often is Bible teaching done that way? (This form of teaching assumes that the Bible is really a single book, rather than a collection of books.) A theological point is made, with a verse or series of

Chapter 4

verses used to support the point. The leader and/or study guide provides the contextual framework for how to understand the specifics of the verses—to support the point being made, of course (this is sometimes called a "proof text"—more on this later). It might be a legitimate point, or it might be an inkblot. In fact, to the extent that we don't know the bigger-picture biblical context, it *is* an inkblot, which also shows how almost any sort of religious doctrine can be "supported" by scripture.

What about sermons? What about times of worship? What about daily devotions? What about books we read? What about . . . scripture calendars? How do we read the Bible in these situations and settings? At least daily Bible reading programs tend to go through entire books of the Bible, but not always. And they usually do little to help you remember what you read last time, much less put together the picture of the book as a whole. I enjoy the scriptures that are displayed during worship videos or songs at church. They remind me of important things. But how do I interpret them? According to the background scene on the screen or the words of the song and by what I already know—or don't know?

One of the most consistent ways—in some cases the *only* way—many of us are exposed to the contents of the Bible is from someone else talking about it—through sermons. A scripture reading often precedes the sermon. But then, how is it used? I can count the number of times on one hand—maybe I'm exaggerating—that I've heard a preacher expand and contract the heartbeat of the scripture reading as part of an inspired mosaic of a single historical encounter between God and his people—that is, within the framework of its book-level structure. Doing so does not diminish its power, I assure you. In fact, it releases the breath of God. But preachers usually preach topically (or "theologically"—more on this in a few minutes); rarely deriving their message from the literary and historical context of the book. They use scriptures that connect in some way with the theme of the day as springboards to whatever topic they want to talk about. We'll call this "pre-texting." That doesn't necessarily mean they're misusing the verses or that they're not speaking to us from God, as I've said. But how do we know? In some cases they do misuse the scriptures. And what's worse, by example they teach the people in our churches, over and over and over again, how *not* to read the Bible; or, actually, how to read the Bible in a way that's eaten up with inkblotitis. All over the world, inkblotitis is modeled and spread to the feeding sheep of the church, from pulpit to pew . . . through inkblot preaching.

    I suspect you can think of other examples of how we break the Bible up into pieces and read those pieces outside of their original contexts. Just as it's the most popular book, the Bible has to be the most dissected book in history. And—let me say—that's not always bad. Sometimes, it's the only way to do it. Of course, we can't talk about the entire meaning of every book of the Bible every time we refer to any single verse. And it's certainly helpful for finding and referencing particular teachings or discussions that the Bible is divided into chapters and verses.[5] (When Jesus cried from the cross, "My God, my God, why have you forsaken me?," he couldn't quote all of Psalm 22—he could barely breathe—and since they didn't have chapters and verses then, the first line naturally referred to the whole thing.) It's not the use of a single verse or set of verses by itself that's bad. The problem is that we have broken it into pieces for so long that we have developed a culture that doesn't seem to know how to do it any other way. What's bad is that we don't know how the verses fit into their bigger picture context. In other words, we've lost the contexts. Or, to shift the perspective, we're lost in a sea of Bible inkblots, and in this sense, we—our culture—has become biblically illiterate. When we see the big picture, on the other hand, we are certainly free to use the pieces for different purposes. Inkblotitis is not defined by reading or using a small piece of scripture; inkblotitis is using a portion of scripture without the interpretive keys of its original context. Without those keys, who knows what doors we unlock and what ships we board? The purpose of this chapter is to think about how the ways we read the Bible either prevent or promote such subjective voyages.

Chapter 4

God's First Conversations

Toward the end of the day, my wife, Cheryl, who manages a title insurance office, often shares with me some things about her day at work. Cheryl leads a group of coworkers who—like most of us at times—aren't always all that enthusiastic about their jobs and need to be motivated and "steered" from time to time. On this occasion, she steered someone a little more forcefully than usual. Within minutes of returning to their respective workstations, she got a pop-up IM (instant message) on her computer—only it wasn't intended for her. It was from the lady with whom Cheryl had just spoken, intended for one of her buddies in the office, with a stream of expletive-laden complaints about Cheryl: "Who does she think she is, that [bleep], [bleep] . . ." Only, as I said, she sent it to Cheryl by accident. (Ever done anything like that?) A few minutes later, having realized her mistake, the young lady walked sheepishly into my wife's office, where the IM was still up on the screen. It was a teachable moment, to say the least, one in which Cheryl could display the grace of Christ, while receiving a little unexpected reinforcement of her managerial duties.

What if, while Cheryl was telling me this story . . ., my mind wandered? What if I were *distracted* or *captured* by something she said in the first sentence or two—though I admit that's unlikely with this story? For example, what if her description of the encounter with the young lady reminds me of a conflict I'm having with one of my coworkers? . . . which leads to another thought about the project we're working on together, which is due next week, and it doesn't look like we're going to be able to get it done on time . . . to another thought about a particular problem I was having that day that I left unresolved and creates a sense of agitation in my spirit. My mind wanders and effectively tunes out my wife to the point I miss some, or maybe a lot, of what she's telling me. Ever done that? Ever had to admit sheepishly that you missed something someone was saying? Or maybe acted like you got it anyway (wink, wink)? An idea or event someone describes triggers a whole new idea in your mind, and you end up distracted—not really listening—to what the person is saying.

The Ways We Read the Bible

The distracting thought may be extremely important or a legitimate reaction to or furtherance of the conversation, but at that moment, you have effectively lost—tuned out—the first conversation and tuned in to something else. Though usually unintentional and a little less rude, therefore, you stop listening to the person talking to you and start talking to yourself mentally. To the extent that we have to give a great big "Huh?" when someone is done telling us something or we miss important pieces of the conversation, I think we can legitimately use the word "distracted."

This is often the way we read the Bible. We tune out God. And—prone to cover our mistakes and weaknesses—we justify it; we even anoint it, so to speak, as something sacred, as though the Holy Spirit were intentionally interrupting himself and distracting us from the first conversation God was attempting to have with us. We go so far as to *look* for verbal distractions that cause certain portions of the text to "jump out at us" and let those moments become the sole or primary focus of our conversations with God, while often having little or no idea what God was trying to say in the first place. Like walking in on the middle of a conversation already taking place, a similar sort of thing happens when we read a section of verses from the middle of a Bible book. Reading the Bible this way, we never let God finish his conversation with us. We use the text to bring up thoughts or ideas and then go off on those ideas, usually never getting back around to God's original train of thought. To exaggerate, we never let God finish his sentence. And what's really sort of puzzling: we assume it's God who is leading us away from the original train of thought. Doesn't it seem a little odd that we have to apologize to our friends and acquaintances when we do this, but turn it into a "special," even "holy," thing when we do it to God? Holy distraction? "Distracted by the Spirit" . . . from the Spirit?

If my momentary line of thought that comes from something a particular verse stirs in me or even from reading a small section of scripture in isolation from the rest of its book-level context is more sacred than the intended meaning of the author, then I would argue that we don't really need the Bible. God could use any text from any book or, for that matter, any object around us to stir a thought within

Chapter 4

us (which is, in fact, a "mystical" approach to scripture; more on this later). I wonder sometimes if this way of thinking isn't a modern way of "blessing" (= justifying) our lack of ability to sit still or stay focused for very long? Have we given sanction to our short attention spans? . . . allowed our culture to dumb-down spirituality? Could it be a modern, fast-paced, distractible, super busy, short-attention-span way of pardoning a form of spiritual laziness? "Just give it to me now." "I don't really want to have to think about it or work at it." "Have it jump off the page at me." "Whisper in my ear." "Let me *feel* it. After all, isn't that how I know when God shows up?" But what if our mental leadings are a piece of our own subjective (and may I add *broken*) psychology and spirituality, speaking to us from a myriad of complex thoughts, feelings, and experiences, spiriting us off from ourselves to . . . who knows where? All right. I'll say it plainly: what if we sometimes mistakenly identify the Holy Spirit with the human spirit? Is that possible (despite the common direction of some modern, popular theology)? And let's take it a step further: is it possible that an evil spirit or *the* evil spirit uses distractions of the urgent to steer us away from devotion to the eternal?

Of course—as I've said before—God can certainly lead us when we read the Bible, however we read it. My purpose is not to say that the Holy Spirit can't speak to us in still quiet or rocking loud voices whenever and however he wants. I would never say that. And, of course, the scriptures have legitimate, living, and immediate applications to our lives. As we'll talk about more later, if we never get to the "So what?" then it really doesn't matter how we read. What I'm trying to point out, though, is—given our potential for distraction and (throw in) the difficulties with understanding the Bible that we talked about earlier—*how we read the Bible makes a big difference with what we get out of it.* Yet, in many ways, we let the "distractions," the thoughts or reactions evoked at the moment, become our primary focus, starting point, or guiding principle; or we break up the text into such small, disconnected pieces as to amount to the same thing, tuning in and out of God's conversations with us.

The Holy Spirit has clearly spoken to us in the books of the Bible. I believe this. These are God's primary—or, I'll call them

The Ways We Read the Bible

God's *first—conversations* with us. If, however, the way we read misses the heart and purposes of God's first conversations with us, then we may need to apologize and let him finish his sentence before we pursue other, second and third level interests and impulses. I'm not saying that we don't or can't have various types of conversations with God (that's the subject of another book) or that we shouldn't apply the Bible to our lives (that's vital). What I am saying is that to the extent that we don't know the primary point or points of the book we are reading and are not seeing what we're reading within that bigger picture, we have interrupted—*tuned out*, if you will—God's first conversation with us. And if I put my own, momentary, eye-catching or heart-touching interest ahead of God's revealed message, who's in the driver's seat? (See the subjective effect of inkblotitis?) "But how do you know God's not in the driver's seat of my heart?" I don't. But I do believe he "drove" the books of the Bible to speak his messages to us. So, shouldn't our strategy be to be sure we hear the primary message of the text first? Then we'll be in a good place to know that God is indeed leading when our hearts and minds engage at various levels. As when couples dance, someone leads—let God lead. In other words, let him finish what he's saying. Then, if a particular thought or subject or application carries you beyond paper and ink, by all means, enjoy the dance!

Chapter 4

Why Do We Read the Bible?

There are really only two ways to read the Bible: in context or out of context. I think that's important enough to say again: in context and out of context are the only options for how we understand verses of scripture. Of course, there are all sorts of variations and degrees of each. Should we ever read or use the Bible out of context? Probably. The answer depends on what we mean and for what we're using it. As a matter of ongoing course, we should try to *read* the Bible in context. But there are times when we *reference*, *use* or *present* passages from the Bible, which is really not the same as *reading* it. There's no way we can present the whole of biblical contexts on every occasion we might want to refer to the Bible. For that reason, it's necessary and desirable to use verses of scripture, especially those that are more self-contained or that really do summarize some vital truth of the Christian faith. If the occasion allows, however, I believe we should do what we can to contextualize the verses and help people see the bigger picture, especially when preaching or teaching in the churches. We certainly should be learning to read and interpret passages in their own contexts so that when we do extract them, we use them properly.

Inkblotitis grows from and thrives in a culture that rarely reads Bible verses in context. Using individual verses of scripture is not the problem—we have to. I'm concerned, rather, that we live in a religious climate that even in the churches sanctions, excels in, and spreads the use—and consequently the misuse—of isolated scriptures. Naked scriptures. How embarrassing! In fact, we've come to expect a form of disconnection of the text to the point of making inkblotism the norm.[6] We expect it because we've come to accept a level of biblical illiteracy that makes the idea of always hearing or presenting a verse as part of a bigger whole seem like an impossibility. It's really not. It's just different from what we're used to. We're used to inkblots (verses), and, sadly, have come to accept and even bless the effects.

Though you probably don't think about it much (most of us just read it), styles and habits of Bible reading vary widely, ranging from those who spend the bulk of their lives pouring over the texts in the original languages so they can teach or write in professional settings, to those who only occasionally blow the dust off the cover to check a family lineage or look up some mysterious verse they've been told holds the secret to humanity's future. Most of us fall somewhere between the extremes, and our methods vary as widely as our purposes.

Historically, there have been various documented, scholarly approaches, schools of thought as to how texts should be interpreted, both for the (Hebrew) Old and (Greek) New Testaments.[7] When the Bible was put into the hands of everyone, you can imagine how the potential ways of reading it exploded. I'm not talking so much about the times or instances when we read it—I've said enough about that—but more about our purposes for reading. In fact, *how* we read the Bible depends to a large extent on *why* we read the Bible, doesn't it? The way we read depends on the reason we read, to vary the words a bit. And to say it as briefly as I can: the how depends on the why. It's a question of motive, and there's more than one legitimate reason for reading the Bible. From the makeup of the human person, we might say that we read it for intellectual (brain), emotional (heart), and practical (feet and hands) purposes.

Of course, there is no perfect system for categorizing the reasons and methods of reading the Bible, since, as complex persons, we engage with our whole selves and, consequently, do more than one thing at a time. It's probably fair to say, though, that one can approach the Bible with a primarily intellectual perspective. In this sense, a person reads or studies the Bible mostly for informational, educational, or historical purposes. This is a mental emphasis. And it makes a difference whether you approach it as a believer, with a curious neutrality, or as a disbeliever or skeptic. Typically, a believer wants to learn more about God and the history of his interactions with us, with an ultimate goal of integrating that knowledge into his or her worldview and applying it to life. (This is not always the case, though; I've been in college-level Bible classes where a significant amount of regurgitation of "facts" was prerequisite to a good grade.) Our understanding of scripture thus informs our "thinking about

Chapter 4

God," which is a good, brief definition of the word "theology." We develop our theology—at least in theory—from the Bible, though in actuality it's certainly informed by a variety of other influences. A student of history might read the Bible as a source of data about ancient times, places, peoples, and events; whereas a skeptic will likely disagree with or try to disprove the accuracy of the information (which actually shows there's more than an educational motive in play).

Most people read the Bible for more than information. Most of us read it for emotional and pragmatic or ethical purposes. In many cases, the attraction comes from how we feel. We read it for encouragement when we are discouraged; for motivation when we feel the hills are too steep or the road too long; for inspiration when sources of hope have dried up or we need to be moved by the creative winds of the Spirit of God; for comfort when our hearts are broken. And the Bible speaks to these various yearnings, as it recounts the real-life stories of God and his peoples. These emotional emphases merge with the information we learn ("information" is a little trite when we're talking about such things as the character and actions of God) to equip us for living our lives in ways that honor God and bless people. This is the practical or action-oriented emphasis of Bible reading. If what we read makes no difference in who we are and what we do, then it's rather pointless (this has something to say about inkblotitis as a condition that reduces the amount of *difference* our reading makes). We thus read the Bible to know more, to feel better, and to live more focused and fulfilled lives.

That's from a positive perspective. There are more negative reasons for reading—more negative in the sense that we use the Bible for purposes other than encouragement and growth. Once we have a pretty significant world view in place, once we have a fairly well-formed theology, we often read the Bible to remind us of that set of beliefs (which is another form of encouragement) or to defend that set of beliefs, since, after all, such important things as the goals, directions, and outcomes of life and death are at stake. How often do people read the Bible—or look through the Bible—to find things to support their way of seeing things—their "faith"? Our faith is important to us. We naturally want and need to defend it.

The Ways We Read the Bible

I suspect you can see that *the way* we approach the Bible has a lot to do with *why* we are approaching it and *what* we want to get out of it. This is so important that I'd like to come back to it at the end of this chapter. Though the categories are not perfect, let's take a little time to look closer at some of the most common ways we read and use the Bible today.

Chapter 4

Devotional Bible Reading

Besides having it read to us in pieces during sermons or Bible studies, the most common method of experiencing the Bible is when we as individuals sit down to read it, sometimes daily or periodically throughout the week. As young believers or those seeking to know more about God, we typically read out of curiosity and excitement to learn what the Bible says. As older believers, we seek to know God more intimately and often read as a form of spiritual discipline. If you've been a member of a church for any length of time, I'm sure you've been encouraged to make regular, probably daily, Bible reading a part of your ongoing spiritual life and development, to be included as part of a personal devotional or "quiet" time. Christian teachers often refer to the periodic ("regular") times that Jesus withdrew to himself to pray as a lifestyle pattern that we as followers should imitate. (At such times of exhortation, they almost always forget to point out that in the book of Mark, for example, Jesus is said to have withdrawn for such private prayer only three times in his life and at very critical—big decision, life and death—moments. Not exactly the "daily" quiet-time pattern being encouraged.)

In our times of reading and study, we seek God through his written word, and I would suggest this phenomenon of *devotional Bible reading* or *personal Bible study* is the direct and natural result of the work of the Reformers who sought to make the Bible available to us all. It is in some respects the heartbeat of the spiritual life of many Christians today, and rightly so.

I use the words "personal" and "devotional" to refer to the practice of regular Bible study to highlight some of the primary characteristics of the way we read the Bible in those times. "Personal" refers to the nature of the time or experience as being mostly private, individual, and internal. When it comes to daily devotional or personal quiet-time Bible reading, it's "God and me." This personal emphasis reflects a fundamental tenet of the Reformation, carried over into America as a nation, of individual responsibility and accountability: if each of us will one day stand before God and be judged as an individual, shouldn't we each seek God in his word?

The Ways We Read the Bible

Shouldn't we have that right and responsibility? (This was in fact why John Wycliffe was so motivated to make copies of the Bible available in English to everyone in his day). As we move from a private and personal setting to the company of others (from the bedroom or the study to the living room), the personal emphasis transfers into many small group settings as the leader highlights the individual or personal side of faith in discussions of the various meanings and applications of a scripture.

Perhaps the best way to characterize the most popular form of Bible reading is with the word "devotional." "Devotional" captures two aspects. I'm using the word loosely to refer to the commitment and passion with which many people pursue God in the scriptures. As such, devotional Bible reading is sometimes seen as part of Christian spiritual discipline for drawing close to God. We typically read the Bible out of devotion—commitment to, dedication, passion and love for God. We are *devoted* to him (although, historically, a slight shift of meaning has occurred here in the way we display or act on that devotion). We want to know and serve God. We want to know how to serve God, and there is, in fact, no better way than to seek God in his revealed word. Even when some of our earliest excitement dies down—as in a relationship when infatuation gives way to deeper forms of love—we seek God in the Bible out of a committed sense of duty or discipline, which is another form of devotion. There are times when we naturally focus on and express that devotion, and thus the word "devotional" has come to refer to (usually brief) periods of time when we express our devotion through worship or other spiritual activities. (It used to refer more to the application of biblical teachings to daily living, as we'll see in a minute.)

Though not always including worship in the sense of clear expressions of adoration and love for God, the word "devotional"— like church or "worship services" in general—has come to be used for times of spiritual interest when we devote ourselves to contemplation or expressions of our faith (Bible study, meditation, prayer, worship). When applied to private settings—and really public, for that matter—"devotional" tends to emphasize the passionate or emotional side of our faith and, when combined with an emphasis on *personal* quiet time, often carries a sense of brief or momentary encounters with God. In other words, "devotional" often has an *in this moment* flavor with respect to dedication and service to God.

Pietism

Much of the way we read the Bible in our culture today—in particular devotional Bible reading—has historical roots in an influential movement within Christianity known as Pietism (or sometimes German Pietism). Pietism was a movement that grew out of the Lutheran side of the Protestant Reformation during the late seventeenth and eighteenth centuries. In contrast to forms of Christianity that emphasized the intellectual and/or ritual sides of the Christian faith—a religion of liturgy and form or "of the head"—Pietists believed that Christianity should be a personal faith based primarily on experience and emotion, deeply committed to the practical side of living out Christian values in daily life—thus, a "religion of the heart" ("and hands," we could add). The name "Pietist," at first used as a pejorative (a critical nickname), comes from emphasis on personal devotion and practical piety.

Philipp Jakob Spener (1635-1705) is sometimes called "the father of Pietism." Spener promoted the revival of the life of the church of his day through personal change of heart, emphasis on devotional and small group Bible study ("little churches within the church"), and the application of Christian principles to daily life. These pietistic emphases of Spener were taken up and disseminated to various corners of Protestantism through the likes of John Wesley, who founded the Methodist movement, and Alexander Mack, the Brethren movement.[8] In addition to small groups that emphasized personal accountability, Wesley believed that Bible study and prayer functioned as a means of God's grace to transform believers into better and better expressions of the love and grace of God. It begins—and this is important—in the inner person.

The Ways We Read the Bible

Describing the occasion when he heard a reading of the preface to Martin Luther's *Epistle to the Romans*, as you recall from the beginning of this chapter, Wesley wrote the now famous words, "I felt my heart strangely warmed." This deeply personal experience of the heart that was such a life-changing experience for Wesley—though sometimes more diffuse and less dramatic—has become commonplace in private and public life of Christians today. When we factor in the previous mystic influence (which emphasized more direct or beyond-the-senses interaction with God),[9] as well as modern "holiness" or charismatic flavorings, we can easily see how the personal, momentary, and emotional side of the Christian experience finds a strong place in modern devotional ways of reading and applying the Bible.

I would not disparage the emphasis on personal experience and responsibility for living out our Christian faith emphasized in the teachings of Pietism. This was certainly an important, historical correction to a stale, repetitious liturgy or benign confessional theology. Personal devotion and practical piety is an essential part of what it means to be Christian. My problem is how it has affected the way we read and understand the Bible. To put it another way, when it comes to the purpose and meaning of the practical expressions of our faith, personal devotion took a left-turn or—perhaps more accurately—a slow, elongated curve.

Let me explain. Instead of "piety"—practical devotion—being the desired result of our hearing and understanding God's word, doing good came to be identified with the act and moment of reading itself. Bible reading thus becomes an act of devotion. Not reading to see and understand the times and places God interacted with us in history, to hear from God in an historic sense, so that I can be energized and transformed with the same Spirit in my contemporary world; but an act of "doing what is right" in itself, since we each have our own Bibles, with an emphasis on whatever I can hear God saying to me in this moment. (Can you begin to see the influence of mysticism in this? And a movement toward Bible reading as a sort of mystical—not educational—experience or sacrament? Not because it is performed well, but simply because it is performed.) We read, God comes. Or, with a little more explanation: we read, (and regardless of how we read or what we're getting out of it) God comes (and does something to us or for us). In this way of thinking, it's almost as if the Bible has become a charm and the words of the Bible an incantation. Read the words (or perhaps rub the book—just kidding) and poof!

When God Shows Up

From the Christian Pietists, Catholic mystics,[10] Wesley, and others,[11] not only did the Reformation make the Bible available to us all in the common language of the people, but it also gave us an emphasis on heart-felt, deep devotion to God in our personal and public life; and, not ironically, this emphasis came to be applied in our use of the Bible. I have no problem with Bible reading as a Christian discipline or a personal, inspirational experience. How could I? My concern is that the Reformation and subsequent history has not taught us to keep the two separate: my personal experience of God through faith and my reading of the Bible. With all its contributions to the history of Christianity and its undeniable impact upon the world as we know it, perhaps the greatest failing of the Protestant Reformation is that it put the Bible into our one hand and a parallel personal, passionate, and practical faith in the other, but left out the boundary between the two.[12] That boundary is the work and presence of God's Holy Spirit in history and thus in the text. *The Bible is not a personal book in the same way that faith is personal. It is, on the strongest contrary, the word of God, revealing to us the objective and eternal truths of God, which always impact the here and now.* Nonetheless, "warmed hearts" have come to be a sign that God is truly present in the moment and as proof that he has in fact "showed up" in our reading and our worship.

This is a common way of putting it today. In public worship or even in private, we speak of God "showing up" when we want to emphasize something we consider to be especially filled with God's Spirit of truth and grace. Like Wesley, we gauge that moment—the measure of God's presence—chiefly by having our hearts strangely warmed or the hair stand up on the back of our necks. Yet I would ask, is God not the God of the brain as much as of the heart? Is he any less present when truth comes in more cognitive forms, as opposed to the emotional? Are facts sometimes not hard and cold? Is the scholar any less a Christian when explaining an old Greek word than a dancer enraptured within a moment of intense praise? Does the kingdom of God have less room for the physician than the poet, or the fisherman than the song-writer? Of course not! The Bible indicates that God "shows up" any time a group of people (or an individual, for that matter) seeks his presence and blessings. In one sense, he never leaves; we do. Worship doesn't create God's presence; it calls our attention to it.

On the other hand, I think I know what people mean when they talk about "God showing up," and there were indeed times in history and in the Bible when God made himself present in a more direct way (like Moses and the burning bush, to prophets like Jeremiah, and the apostles on the Day of Pentecost). These were the exceptions and not the rule, however. In either case, God's presence was not determined by the people's awareness of it or a particular style of reaction to it. Likewise, God's presence in his word or worship today is not determined by my awareness of it or—with due respect to Wesley—by my heart being "strangely warmed." It might be for me. It might be a special or even sacred moment for me personally when I become aware of it—as it was for Wesley—but that's not what defines the origin or even the outcome of the experience. *Being strangely warmed is only one legitimate reaction of a host of thoughts, feelings, and actions that an encounter with God through his word can and should have.* Of course, the truth I learn must be applied to me personally, or why learn it? And, of course, I will be more motivated when it touches me deeply. But my emotion does not equal God's presence, and I don't have a personal encounter with God just because I read from the Bible.

In the footsteps of Pietism—to get back to our main topic—devotional Bible reading tends to seek a personal, heartfelt sort of encounter that often has little or no concern for the intended meaning of the text. What would God like to say to me *now*? is the ruling question. Thus we begin to make the momentary experience the end in itself, applying the principle of personalism or sanctified subjectivity to Bible reading. That's the "left turn" I was talking about. I'm certainly in favor of an emphasis on personal responsibility and passionate devotion to God—one that results in (even daily) Bible study, prayer, and efforts to grow in the grace and knowledge of our Lord Jesus Christ. There's nothing wrong with immediate, heartfelt application of God's word to my life. This is our purpose and our passion—for each of us to hear God and be changed by him—and it's a natural extension of the effort to put the Bible into the hands of the common people.

But this really gets to the heart of the matter. If faith is personal, if someday I will stand before God as an individual—if judgment is personal—isn't reading and understanding the Bible personal? Yes, to a certain extent. We all have that great privilege and responsibility. But that's very different from saying that we all have the right to arrive at our own personal or private interpretations. See what I'm saying? The question "What does this mean to you?" is a symptom of this idea. Personal, devotional Bible study has become a means, not of hearing God's *eternal* truth that was expressed in his first conversations with his people, necessarily, but of fanning the embers of whatever personal passion burns beneath my spiritual flames, that day, that hour, that moment. Those passions might be wonderful, but do you see how using the Bible that way undercuts the foundation of our ability to see and know what God really wanted to say to us in the first place? We place the emphasis on second and third level conversations, which, as we have seen, might be distractions or—in the worst possible case—diversions of the enemy. And if a generation of believers reads the Bible that way, and another, and another, what can result, but erosion, confusion, atrophy, immaturity, and eventually even spiritual anarchy?

The Random-Point Method

Reading the Bible with a momentary focus on what God is saying to me now without knowing how a passage fits into its book-level context is really only one step removed from what might be the most obvious example of a purely subjective Bible reading—the random-point method. Have you ever opened the Bible to a random place, closed your eyes, and pointed to a random verse with the question, what would God like to say to me?

When I was in college, I had a roommate who was studying to be a preacher, totally committed to giving his life to God. David, my roommate, was a rather recent convert to Christianity, having come from a life of drugs and various unchristian behaviors. One day in our dorm room, he told me the story of "cabin fire," his pre-conversion experience with the Bible.

Not long before becoming a Christian, David was seeking God and struggling with the question of giving his life to God. On a cold, dark night, he was at a cabin alone with a hot fire burning in the fireplace. He was also high on drugs at the time. In this rather strange setting, sitting close to the fire, my roommate took his Bible and performed the random-point method of hearing from God. He opened the Bible and expectantly pointed to a specific scripture, honestly believing that whatever it said was what God wanted him to do in his decision to become a Christian. His finger landed on 1 Corinthians 13:3: "And though I bestow all my goods to feed the poor, and though I give my body to be burned . . ." That was it. At just that moment, he could hear the crackling of the logs in the fireplace and feel the heat of the fire burning hot against his skin. The drugs, his sincere search and question, the heat of the fire all merged in his thinking, as he came to the conclusion that God was asking him to give his body to be burned. *That* was what he had to do. (I don't know what happened to the first part about giving his money to the poor—I guess it's 'cause he didn't have any.) Exactly how he was to give his body to be burned, he didn't know, but that was God's word to him. He laughed about it later as he told me the story, having come to a better understanding of 1 Corinthians 13 and God's desires for his life.

I tell you that story not to criticize anyone who sincerely seeks to know God and hear his voice or has used the random-point method, or to say that God didn't use that moment to help my friend in his search. I tell you the story to highlight one of the potential extremes of personal Bible study. Like Wesley—well, maybe not quite like Wesley—my friend's heart was strangely warmed, almost literally. But what he took from that moment was not the voice of God, and this brings us to the heart of the matter.

There is a crucial moment and/or point of danger where language (what we hear and read) becomes meaning—a place where—speaking figuratively—we come into the room and open our Bibles with the goal of hearing God and welcoming his Spirit into our hearts; while at the same time, competing values and voices seek to distract us from the truth we really need to heal our souls. The enemy seeks to use our personal beliefs, emotions, biases, dysfunctions, hurts, confusions, and every form of emotional and spiritual brokenness (remember our discussion about the effects of sin) to conceal the truth from us and divert our hearts from God. And he often does it with moments of diversion and distraction. The very first thing someone has to do to hear God or Jesus or Paul, or anyone else for that matter, is to stop long enough to listen. However subtle or small the distraction may seem—rationalization of something inherently destructive but that we like to do and really don't want to give up; a quick glossing over of self-serving tendencies, lack of love and grace toward others; reinforcement of a point of doctrine that divides us from other believers—a journey of a thousand miles begins with a single step, you know.

Now—to get you to think about it for a minute—is it possible that the enemy could "warm" our hearts, if that would accomplish his deceitful and destructive goals? Or, to put it another way, why is heart-warming only a God-thing? I understand that if something reaches to the depths of our souls and moves us deeply to be better, then chances are we've struck a godly chord that comes ultimately from being children of God, made in his image. But how big of a step is it to go from "being warmed" to "feeling good," and, as Christians, we've always believed that just because something feels good ("if it feels good, do it.") doesn't make it right or good.

Here's the main point: feeling our hearts strangely warmed has become one of the primary goals/methods of participating in spiritual activities, such as reading the Bible; yet, of itself, it has no ability to guarantee or confirm the presence and voice of God in what we take away. Of course, we don't all use the random-point method on a regular basis. We do, however, often put the focus on what God is saying to me now, here in this moment, which often becomes a way of reading the Bible that strips away much of the picture God has painted to clarify the meaning of his conversations with us, to teach us what he wants us to know. Though I know this is going to sound harsh or even somewhat sacrilegious, I'll say it anyway: devotional Bible reading often focuses so much on the moment, so much on a small portion of God's conversations with us, that it's as if I interrupt God on a regular basis and continually put the focus on what I want to hear and talk about. In other words, on me. How sadly ironic that "hearing from God" can become self-talk! Even if God transcends our rudeness to work with us spiritually as we strive to know and serve him—and I strongly believe that he does—shouldn't we be still and quiet long enough to let him speak? . . . to let him finish what he was saying in the first place?

To summarize: much of our personal, devotional Bible reading today is either ritual or mystical.[13] For those of us with strong desires "to get things right" and leanings toward legalism, personal Bible study can become a ritualistic act of piety—doing what is right—and not a Spirit-filled journey into the mind and heart of God. It's my Christian duty. To that extent, Bible study is replete with the temptation to inkblotitis. For more emotional or intuitive types, the extent to which we don't see what we're reading within the bigger picture context of the book-level message God delivered to us is the extent the experience becomes mystical and inkblotitis, our normal way of reading the Bible (can we call it a chronic illness?). The more the meaning comes from our moments, based on second- or third- or even fourth-level conversations with God, the more our Bible reading becomes a tool of the subjective, the more our feelings of being strangely warmed become sessions of personal conversations—more like prayer at best and talking to ourselves at worst—than listening to God in his word. Prayer that comes from the heart is great, but when do we hear from God? Given the brokenness of our world and our souls, only the Word of God can give us the healing we seek and need. I don't know about you, but I want to hear from God.

Theological Bible Reading

Recently my family and I were traveling to Grandma and Grandpa's for Thanksgiving. Even though my youngest is a teenager now (my oldest is away at college), we still drive at night out of habit we learned when the kids were little. While driving through the night, I was listening to one of those late night radio programs where you can hear all sorts of strange viewpoints on almost any topic imaginable. This particular night the host was interviewing a man who was an expert in exo-theology (I didn't know the word either, but it has to do with "extraterrestrial"). He was of the belief that the earth had been visited many times by highly advanced civilizations of aliens. From that perspective, the gentleman interpreted everything in the Bible—every reference to God and angels, that is—as if they were references to aliens who had visited and through their advanced technology performed "miracles" on earth. It was a theology of extra-terrestrial origins of life and religion on earth. He saw everything through those thick lenses. That was his governing "topic."

While the program made for some interesting—if a bit nutty—listening, it was terribly abusive to the intended meaning of the biblical texts. For example, because the Hebrew word for God in the beginning of Genesis is plural (*elohim*; "In the beginning *Gods* created the heavens and the earth"), the guest asserted that this actually referred to a race of super-advanced alien beings, in spite of the fact that one of the main points of Judaism and the book of Genesis is the view of a singular God (monotheism), as opposed to the polytheism (belief in many gods) of the day and culture. (Nor did he attempt to explain the use of the third person singular verb with the plural subject.) The program helped to keep me awake as I drove, but it was a clear example of reading the Bible through thick, theological glasses.

Though not as obviously biased as this exo-expert, *theological* Bible reading is what we often do when we read sections of the Bible that focus on a particular topic or theme. In one sense, "theological Bible reading" could be used as a label to describe any sort of reading that doesn't hear verses in light of their book-level context. In other

Chapter 4

words, any time the context is not familiar enough to us to act as the primary scaffolding to build and shape the meaning, we fall back on what we already know/think as interpretive keys, that is, on our own theologies. So in a broad sense, "theological Bible reading" could be used as a synonym for inkblotitis. Of course, we always condition our reading and thinking on any subject by what we already know. That's why the context is essential if we ever want to be confronted with ideas that go beyond what we already think. Kind of defeats the purpose of reading, otherwise. In a more specific sense, however, I'm using "theological Bible reading" to emphasize the times when one's reading is governed by interest in a particular theme or subject (like love, for example, or heaven, hope, joy, peace, or the nature of God, etc.) or when an already preset theology clearly controls how someone interprets a given text.

We read the Bible theologically in numerous ways, often guided by something someone else has written or said. It doesn't have to be. Sometimes we use a concordance to look up all the verses in the Bible on a given subject. "Topical Bible study," it's called; or "topical preaching" for preachers and pastors. I've done this many times, and a concordance can be most helpful. On the other hand, we're often pointed to a verse of scripture or a set of verses by a book we're reading on some topic of interest. Take marriage, for instance. The author of a book on marriage may have several references to scripture and discussions of passages of scripture that he or she uses to teach and explore how to have a good marriage from a biblical viewpoint. The shelves of Christian bookstores are filled with books on tons of topics. Sometimes we read articles in magazines or on the internet about things of interest, and, of course, this is a good thing. But—knowing what you already know about inkblotitis—how often are the verses used in such books and study guides interpreted primarily by their original book-level contexts? Or how much of what the author says to us comes from the theological constructs of the writer? Or when we look up the verses ourselves, how often do we see them in light of their book-level contexts? Theological Bible reading is reading where a subject and our previous understanding of the subject controls what we get out of it.

The Ways We Read the Bible

I received an e-mail today promoting a website where you can access any chapter of the Bible with a single click. You may have seen it. Each chapter of each book has its own link. When you click the link, that chapter opens, and then you can chose from a number of different Bible versions and translations. How cool is that! At the bottom of the page, moreover, is a list of topics called "emergency phone numbers," with links to passages from the Bible on those topics; like John 14 if you are sad, Matthew 8:19-34 if you are worried, Mark 10:17-31 if investments and inflation are hogging your thoughts.[14] (I recently received a bookmark in the mail with similar lists of verses for where to look when "You're lonely," "You're afraid," "Problems seem too big for you to handle," "You don't know what to do," and "You've lost hope"—with an admonition to "Keep this bookmark in your Bible!") When we go to these texts, we read them *for* information about the topic of interest, and, I would suggest, that if a relatively small set of verses is all we read, we will interpret them mostly *by* what we already think. In this way, topical Bible study is just another form of isolating particular texts of scripture from their contexts.

The same can be said about sermons and preachers. This is the way many, if not most, sermons use the Bible. In fact, most of the sermons I've heard in the course of my life are theological discourses punctuated by verses of scripture lifted from their original contexts (or you could say, . . . theological discourses punctuated by inkblots). Whether at the beginning of the sermon as a *pre-text* or scattered throughout as *proof-texts* to back up the point the pastor is making, sermons exemplify and implicitly teach theological Bible reading. This becomes more evident as the speaker uses the verses to illuminate the topic at hand; it's quite common for us to use isolated stories from the Bible as analogies and even allegories.[15]

At a recent weekend church service, the pastor took his message from 2 Samuel 13, the fascinating, albeit realistically violent, story of Amnon and Tamar. Amnon fell in love with his beautiful half-sister Tamar, or at least had a passionate crush on her—lust would likely be a better term—so passionate that it grew out of control and ultimately destroyed him. As the story goes, Amnon was

Chapter 4

severely depressed because he couldn't do anything about the situation, marriage to a half-sister being forbidden by law. On the advice of his cousin and friend Jonadab, Amnon concocts a plan to have his way with Tamar. Pretending to be sick (the narrative already said that he was so frustrated about the situation that he had made himself sick), Amnon has his father David send Tamar to attend him and cook for him. Having sent all the servants away so that they would be alone and in spite of Tamar's rational and tender objections, Amnon rapes her. "Then Amnon hated her with intense hatred. In fact, he hated her more than he had loved her" (13:15, NIV). He then sends her away, which was to Tamar an even greater shame than what he had already done.

The story doesn't end there. Two years later, through a similar sort of scheming plan based on simmering hatred, carried out at a festive gathering of all the King's sons; just when Amnon was feeling good from the wine, Tamar's brother Absalom has Amnon killed because of what he had done to his sister. From the ashes of one uncontrolled passion to another grows a tangled web of deceit, suffering, and death.

This is indeed a fascinating story, and one that reflects intensely fundamental elements of lust, deception, and hatred. It's easy and useful to take important lessons about these sorts of things from the story. After reading a portion of the text, the pastor used the story to teach on the subject of lust in a series of messages on relationships and sexuality.

Notice what he did—and this happens over and over again. He reads or goes through the story; he/we connect to a theme or idea in the story at points we can identify with (in this case love and lust, deceit and hatred) and then interpret the story as an analogy to things we experience. Like handles on a suitcase, the topic or theme becomes our point of connection with the story, as well as other details that we relate to our own world of experiences. This is normal. No real way to avoid it. It's the way we hear, interpret, and engage with what we hear. On the other hand, do you see how the story, disconnected from the overarching context and purposes of 2 Samuel, takes on a sort of independent life of its own, an identity that the pastor and we must then interpret by some set of ideas and values other than the book of 2 Samuel? It becomes like a parable—or an inkblot, to be blunt—that we interpret through its connections to something we know and experience, to our own mental and emotional contexts. *Isolated from its original book-level context, the story becomes a mobile analogy or allegory.* A fable on wheels. The topics are the handles we use to carry it around.

So, is that wrong? Should a pastor not use such a text to highlight the obviously destructive effects of the poor choices being made? He should. But he should do more. Otherwise—to stick with our present theme—it's only second- and third-level conversations with God. The tragedies of unbridled lust (remember King David's own encounter with Bathsheba and its consequences?), the cruelties of deception, the potential of unresolved anger—these are valid and important points. But I wonder what God's bigger-picture point might be? Is it completely contained within this brief portion of 2 Samuel, or would this text and its details take on new dimensions of meaning, possibly in favor of something even more important that God wanted to say to us, if we heard it within the context of 2 Samuel as a whole (and probably 1 Samuel since these books were originally together in Hebrew).

I hate to say it, but pastors rarely teach their audiences how to hear the scriptures as part of a bigger-picture conversation that God had and would like to have with his people. As pastors and teachers use scriptures like analogies on wheels, they are—to a large extent—responsible for the proliferation of inkblotitis in the churches. On the other hand, how exciting it is when a preacher or teacher stands up before the people, having spent time coming to see the big-picture meaning and messages of a Bible book, and delivers to his audience the inspired and interconnected truths of God. Not only are the people fed, but they are given the proverbial pole as well.

We read the Bible theologically when we read and interpret texts thematically and topically to the extent that we don't see those texts in relation to their book-level contexts. This doesn't mean we always read them wrong, but it does open us up to the dangers of inkblotitis (things like missing the main point or points, reinforcing existing beliefs that may need to be challenged or even changed, creating or strengthening division between believers, etc.; we'll look at these in the next chapter).

We read the Bible theologically also when an established set of beliefs shields us from the real, soul-shaping messages of the text. Explicit efforts to build what scholars call "systematic theology" sometimes lead young theologians to partake of a similar sort of inductive Bible reading, which, as we have said, treats the Bible more like a single-authored volume than a collection of God-inspired books. In an (sometimes subconscious) effort to maintain consistency and be loyal to defined theological constructs or doctrinal systems that have developed over time (which historically have drawn lines between the churches), not infrequently, students of the Bible simply cannot or will not hear verses of scripture according to their original contexts and purposes. If they violate the consistency of one's theology, the theology almost always wins—a method of reading that frequently leads to our next major type.

Argumentative Bible Reading

When I was a teenager, several young guys from my church would go walking through the neighborhoods from time to time, seeking to "share the gospel" with any sort of interested—or not so interested—party. We weren't always as devoted to telling the good news of the life, death, and love of Jesus as we were in engaging individuals from other church backgrounds on controversial points of doctrine and teachings of the Bible, hoping to show them the "error of their ways" and open their eyes to "the truth." Like arrows in readied quivers, we were well armed with our memorized set of scriptures, strategically pulled from here, there, and yon throughout the Bible. On one particular evening—I can't remember why we stopped there or how we actually came in contact with him—but we struck up a conversation, soon to be a rather heated argument, with the pastor of the Open Door Bible Church, not far from my childhood home. It didn't take long before we were jabbing with our recited scriptures, to which, without hesitation, he counter-punched with a set of his own.[16] Of course, ours were as plain as day and should have been completely convincing to anyone with an open mind, not to mention an open door. At least that's the way it seemed from our side of the doctrinal street. After a few minutes of quasi-heated scriptural exchanges, we parted with a mutual belief that the other was simply too closed-minded to engage in real dialogue.

Whether on the street, at the mall, or in the living room, these kinds of verbal encounters rarely result in a meeting of the minds, but—as you know—they're not uncommon. Nor is it uncommon for many of us, from different denominational backgrounds, to read and study the Bible in an effort to support, prove, or learn to prove that the things we believe are vital teachings of scripture. As in my own experience, enthusiastic young followers are often encouraged to know a list of specific verses that uphold the fundamental teachings of "the faith." After all, we are told that we "should earnestly contend for the faith which was once delivered unto the saints" (Jude 3), a verse that begs to be put into its book-level context. Even if not so aggressive as to take one's list of proof texts to the streets,

Chapter 4

argumentative or *defensive* (sometimes called "polemical") Bible reading is another common way that we sometimes approach the Bible.

Because the Bible is a big book and our faith is important to us, examining and defending what we believe is a natural and even healthy aspect of being a Christian. The apostles of Jesus and Christians throughout the centuries have been called upon to defend the true content and meaning of the teachings of Jesus. Heresy comes in many forms, and the Bible is our chief weapon against it.

Having said that, think for a minute about an approach to reading the Bible that highlights—maybe literally in yellow or underlining—a few, usually short verses in order to teach specific points. If there's any truth to the things I've been saying about the importance of interpreting verses within their own contexts, then it's certainly easy to see how this same principle—or lack thereof—applies to cases where we would use small portions of texts as proof texts to teach and argue about our favorite positions. The teaching may be accurate, and it may need defending, but how do we know? Unless we understand how the verses fit into their big-picture context, we may be highlighting and memorizing the wrong verses. I would suggest that, as a habit, this practice can become a fundamental building block of the sort of near-sighted legalism that misses the kingdom-forest for the denominational trees and majors in personal, religious minors, just as Jesus accused the Pharisees (Matthew 23 and Luke 11).

As you well know, little pieces of scripture can be taken so out of context as to support almost anything. A good, but light-hearted, example is seen in the popular musical by Joseph Stein, *Fiddler on the Roof.* Throughout the story, Tevye, a Jewish milkman and father of five daughters, refers to "the good book," humorously and clumsily, to support his religious and family traditions—the primary theme—against the unsettling encroachments of modern life. "Like the good book says . . .," Tevye frequently says.

These references to scripture take an ironic twist in the middle of the story, however, when Perchik, a somewhat radical student from Kiev, whom Tevye housed in exchange for tutoring his daughters, tells the Bible story of how Jacob acquired Rachel to be his wife.

Promising Rachel's hand in marriage to Jacob after working for him for seven years, Rachel's father Laban tricks Jacob and substitutes his oldest daughter Leah. Jacob wakes up the morning after the wedding with Leah instead of Rachel. (Exactly how that could happen, even in the darkest of bed-chambers, is an unsolved mystery of the ages. Or, I've heard it said from another angle that every new husband goes to bed with Rachel but wakes up with Leah—maybe I shouldn't have repeated that one.) Jacob ends up having to work seven more years to get Rachel, the love of his life. Perchik then draws the unexpected and funny conclusion: "Never trust an employer" (which Tevye is to him). Somehow, I don't think that's the point of the biblical story, but, as Tevye continues to display, Bible and tradition often blur together in our efforts to find balance and meaning in the real-life struggles of survival and progress—"like a fiddler on a roof." Stock scriptures worn into our minds and Bibles is one of the fiddler's most familiar tunes.

Theology formed in debate is almost always skewed in one way or another. Like a pendulum swinging to the other side of an issue, it's pushed to extremes by the mere force of its antagonism, which comes from our desire to be right and safe, just as most forms of legalism start out with good intentions. Though it's not always easy to admit, we've seen this throughout Christian history. We also see it on the streets and in pulpits where different groups of Christians come to identify themselves with particular points of teaching to such an extent that we have to build churches on different sides of the street, and it comes home in the worst way when it happens within one of those churches. If you've attended church long, you may have experienced it within your own community. Few things are worse than people who claim to love God and follow Christ who have identified themselves with a particular belief duking it out with fellow-believers who hold a different view, often over things not really even in the Bible. Church splits are ugly—very ugly. All the more when we realize how important real love and the results of that love are to the message and purposes of Jesus.

The apostle John tells us at the beginning (1:12-13) and at the end (20:31) of his Gospel, and scattered throughout, that Jesus came to give life to all those who receive him through faith. He tells us plainly (20:31) that he wrote about the things Jesus did so that his audience might "come to believe that Jesus is the Messiah, the Son of God, and that through believing . . . might have life in his name" (20:31). Within this broad purpose and context, John reports that on the night Jesus was betrayed, he told his disciples to love each other, just as he had loved them. And here's the punch line: "By this everyone will know that you are my disciples, if you have love for one another" (13:34-35). A few chapters later, in his very passionate and extremely poignant prayer, Jesus makes a brief, but almost startling request, *for us*: "I ask not only on behalf of these, but also on behalf of those who will believe in me through their word, that they may all be one. As you, Father, are in me and I am in you, may they also be in us, *so that the world may believe that you have sent me*" (17:20-21; my italics).

The results of argumentative use of the Bible are more significant that we'd like to admit, especially when it helps to split and divide the community of Christ. No less than the success of Christ's mission is at stake. As we seek to know God through faith in Christ from "their word" through the writings of the Bible, turning cut-out pieces of scripture into sharp and serrated edges for the purpose of cutting between believers seems ironically and tragically opposed to the prayer of Jesus himself about how he wanted the words of his disciples to function. If the way we read and use the Bible contributes to such, all I can say is shame on us.

Why Do *You* Read the Bible?

These are certainly not the only ways we read the Bible. There are others we could describe, including more positive and effective methods (much more on this to come). Doesn't really matter, though, because in the end, every way we read the Bible contributes to one or the other result: in context or out of context. As we have seen, many of the ways we use the Bible promote out-of-context reading: basically everything that isolates verses into separate, disparate entities. In general, out-of-context reading can be thought of as impressionistic Bible reading. I described three common ways as *devotional, theological,* and *argumentative* or *defensive* Bible reading. Replete with temptations to inkblotitis, we often use these methods to turn the pages of scripture into spiritual incense, plug-and-play analogies, or stockpiled ammo.

From one perspective, there's certainly nothing wrong with reading the Bible out of *devotion* to God or in a *devotional* frame of mind. Neither is "thinking about God"—being *theological*—while reading the Bible something to be criticized. Where better to get one's theology? And who can argue against holding firm to and *defending* what you learn from the Bible? Devotional, theological, and defensive Bible readings are only a problem when we allow the processes of being devotional, theological, and defensive to overly influence what we get out of what we read (in other words, when we let the way we read—the how—work against the reason we read—the why). Everyone uses "methods" when he or she reads the Bible—you can't get around it. The question is, does the way I'm reading help me hear God? Unfortunately, with many of our common ways of using the Bible, our understanding comes from our momentary and personal impressions of what a verse means or our established patterns of belief and ideas, instead of a careful and thoughtful reading of the book as a whole.

Think of how and when we do this: brief periods of study, sermons, small groups, devotionals, articles, study guides, books, songs, calendars, cards, etc. Mainly because of time. This is natural and inevitable. Life is busy, and we operate in shorter blocks of time

Chapter 4

than it takes to "take it all in." I understand that. It would be silly to suggest that we could do otherwise. The problem is that over time, we have forgotten that we built breaks—walls of interruption—between the sections and verses of the Bible. (An aside: this is a reason I don't like the rigidity and forcefulness with which some leaders exhort their people to read the Bible every day. Daily Bible reading is a good idea, but I'd rather have someone read once a week for an hour than daily for ten minutes, if it means he or she is going to be in a better position to hear and understand the words of God. Ideally, we can do that daily. But we need to take up some fence posts and begin to reconnect the verses and the sections so that we won't miss God's bigger points.)

In conclusion, think of any way you read and hear the Bible and ask yourself, does it isolate the text and consequently make its meaning depend primarily on my or someone else's frame of reference, or does it help me see it within its book-level, big-picture focus? Am I looking at a single piece of a disconnected puzzle; or am I seeing the piece in the context of the whole (or at least coming to see it)?

As I said earlier, a lot of what we get out of the Bible comes from our purpose for reading it. How you read is directly connected to why you read, and what you get out of it is directly connected to why and how you read. Certainly, there's more than one legitimate motive for reading the Bible. Often believers turn to target passages to meet different emotional needs. The greatest comfort for those who cry can be found in God's inspirational promises and presence. The greatest encouragement comes from the consoling words of the Comforter whose purpose was to reveal the truth and meaning of God's coming near in Christ. The greatest courage and strength to those who face ferocious giants arises from the inspirational accounts of faithful followers who stood strong against insurmountable odds and overcame, sometimes at the cost of their lives. The greatest patience and endurance descends from those who endured much, much more than we. The greatest hope, from the greatest news the world has ever heard. All from the Holy Spirit of God who stands behind and in the words and teachings of the Bible. Sometimes we read to evoke and call upon these blessings, and the living words of scripture breathe life into our deepest deficiencies more than any other written source. All these motives are good and affect what we read and how we read. But, in the end, if we always read the Bible for God to be what we want and need him to be, for us, now, or to remind of something sacred, aren't we missing something? Haven't we overlooked the most important thing? At least the first thing? Who decides what I need the most? What *do* I need the most?

The purpose of Bible reading, in my opinion, should be to hear the actual word of God. Like Mary sitting at the feet of Jesus, in contrast to her sister Martha who was "distracted with all the preparations" (Luke 10:38-42), we read to draw near to him. To see him as clearly as humanly possible, so that we might know and love him. To come close. To listen. To see. To meet with God. To hear what God says. Through the Holy Spirit, to sit in his presence and hear his word, and the word of God (incarnate in Jesus Christ, *the* Word of God) is the salvation of men and women. Since I need to be saved, I need the word of God. And here's the clincher. When we are truly confronted with the Word of God, we . . . are . . . not . . . the same. Without God, we are lost, broken, fundamentally and thoroughly confused. The purpose of Bible reading is ultimately not to confirm and support and remind and reinforce, or even encourage us in what we already know and are—it might be, if any of us had arrived. But we haven't. Far from it. We read to be changed. This is one of the very first principles of being a follower of Christ, and it's absolutely critical. We read to enter God's presence, so that God's presence will enter our persons. We read not to defend ourselves, but—in a sense—to destroy ourselves, to die so that we might live to make the Father proud and to make a real, meaningful difference in the lives of the people around us. We read to find God and fulfill the dreams and realities of his kingdom. To the extent that it's not about God, we manifest and perpetuate illness.

So here's the crucial question: Why do you read the Bible? Do you really want to get God's point? Or is there some hidden, subconscious motive or veil that distorts his voice? May I be bold enough to say that if you do not really want to meet with God, whatever the outcome; if you do not really want to hear from God, whatever the message; if you do not really want to see God, whatever the sight; to know God and be changed by that experience, then you should probably stop reading? This book is not for you. On the other hand, if you read the Bible with the hope and expectation of having God grab your soul and transform you from the inside out, for today and forever, then, don't you think we should read in such a way as to hear the clearest and see the sharpest—to promote the best possible listening?

There are many times in my life when I talk way too much. How sad, how utterly sad, when I talk over the voice of God. But how life-giving when I listen quietly and deeply and purposefully enough to understand God's first conversations with his people (so that I might join them in the eternal community and purposes of God's kingdom). The truth resonates with my soul's deepest needs, and my spirit dances with the joy of a child lost in a moment of ultimate love and protection. The truth will indeed set us free.

Hmm. I wonder how that verse fits into its original context.

Chapter 4: The Ways We Read the Bible

Chapter Resources

Bedouelle, Guy. "Biblical Interpretation in the Catholic Reformation." In *A History of Biblical Interpretation: The Medieval through the Reformation Periods*, pp. 428-40. Edited by Alan J. Hauser and Duane F. Watson. Grand Rapids: Eerdmans, 2009.

Gibbs, Lee W. "Biblical Interpretation in Medieval England and the English Reformation." In *A History of Biblical Interpretation: The Medieval through the Reformation Periods*, pp. 372-402. Edited by Alan J. Hauser and Duane F. Watson. Grand Rapids: Eerdmans, 2009.

Schreiner, Susan E. "'The Spiritual Man Judges All Things': Calvin and the Exegetical Debates about Certainty in the Reformation." In *Biblical Interpretation in the Era of the Reformation*, pp. 189-214. Edited by Richard A. Muller and John L. Thompson. Grand Rapids: Eerdmans, 1996.

Thompson, Mark D. "Biblical Interpretation in the Works of Martin Luther." In *A History of Biblical Interpretation: The Medieval through the Reformation Periods*, pp. 299-318. Edited by Alan J. Hauser and Duane F. Watson. Grand Rapids: Eerdmans, 2009.

Notes

1. From The Journal of John Wesley, which can be read online at http://www.ccel.org/ccel/wesley/journal.toc.html.
2. Wesley's description is as follows:
    "In the midst of the psalm wherewith their service began, the sea broke over, split the mainsail in pieces, covered the ship, and poured in between the decks, as if the great deep had already swallowed us up. A terrible screaming began among the English. The Germans calmly sang on."
3. See, e.g., Schreiner, "Certainty in the Reformation," 189-240. Luther believed that no one
    ". . . can correctly understand God or his Word unless he has received such understanding immediately from the Holy Spirit.

Chapter 4

But no one can receive it from the Holy Spirit without experiencing, proving, and feeling it. In such experiences, the Holy Spirit instructs us as in his own school" (Luther, *Das Magnificat*, WA 7:546.24-29; LW 21:299; referenced in Schreiner, "Certainty in the Reformation," 193, with n. 8).

Or, as Luther put it on one occasion: "You must therefore completely despair of your own diligence and intelligence and rely solely on the infusion of the Spirit. Believe me, I have had experience in this matter." (WABr 1.133.31-39 = LW 48.53-54; cited in Thompson, "Biblical Interpretation," 311).

4. The method was also seen in Monasticism (the principal "tradition of biblical exegesis in the West" until the rise of Scholasticism in the twelve and thirteenth centuries) of the Middle Ages. As Gibbs ("Biblical Interpretation," 373) comments,

"In monasteries following the various rules of their respective traditions, the monks intensely pursued what was called the *lectio divina* ("divine reading") of Scripture. Here it was not so much the text itself that was considered most important as the experience of reading it and gaining personal benefit from it . . ."

5. The Bible was divided into chapters by Stephen Langton, Archbishop of Canterbury, around 1227 AD. Rabbi Isaac Nathan divided the Hebrew Old Testament into verses in 1448 AD (following full stop markings that had been passed down from antiquity). Robert Estienne, also known as Stephanus, added verses to the New Testament in 1555, essentially maintaining Nathan's verse divisions for the Old Testament (as they had become accepted by that time).

6. I believe there is a relationship between the dissecting of the Bible into isolated verses or sayings—turning prose narrative and dialogue into oracles and proverbs—and a tendency toward mysticism and even superstition or magic in some popular expressions of Christianity today.

7. The methods of interpretation of the Old Testament at the time of Jesus is a fascinating and enlightening study. We see some of those methods used by the writers of the New Testament, as they reference and interpret their scriptures (the Old Testament).

8. On the history of these ideas in relation to Bible reading (while summarizing Martin Luther's view of "Reading in the Spirit"), Thompson ("Biblical Interpretation," 312) provides a fitting summary:

> "There is very obviously here a deep resonance with the theology of humility associated with Bernard of Clairvaux . . . as well as certain elements of late medieval German mysticism. However, the roots of this conviction are deeper than that and lie in a long tradition of *lectio divina*, 'sacred reading,' which has been shown to have been joined to the academic study of Scripture by the scholars of Abbey of St. Victor in Paris . . . The study of Scripture was in fact part of one's devotion to Christ and could not be separated from the broader contours of life lived in the presence of God. The interpreter of Scripture is first and foremost a forgiven sinner standing in the presence of his Creator, Redeemer, and Judge."

9. Like that of Jakob Böhme (1575-1624), for example.
10. See Bedouelle, "Biblical Interpretation," 440-42 for a brief discussion of mystics of the Catholic Reformation. Bedouelle (440-41) points out that in the *Spiritual Exercises* of Ignatius Loyola (1491-1556), the most widely known work of the Catholic Reformation, it's not the text that's most important, but "a landscape, a biblical episode, a parable, or even a religious setting which forms the basis for silent prayer."

> "Yet . . . at the onset of the mystical experience one finds Scripture. Verses come to mystics' minds with a new, fulfilling, existential meaning, more often, in Carmelite mysticism, culminating in a theology of Christ's cross, giving them the full vision of God's design for the world and providing the true key to interpretation."

11. Even key Reformers like Luther, Zwingli, and Calvin fell back on an immediate, personal, illuminating experience of the Holy Spirit when it comes to reading and understanding the Bible (see Schreiner, "Certainty in the Reformation," 189-215; and the citations in n. 3 above).
12. I do not mean to imply that individual Reformers or translators of scripture did not understand or support this distinction. For example, William Tyndale often uses the words "understand and feel" in his descriptions of our response to scripture, and he opposed overly individualistic (at his time, scholastic) interpretations of scripture. The following comments from his Prologue to Genesis (cited in Daniell, *The Bible in English*, 148) on the use of scripture display interesting comparisons to things I say in the course of this book:

"Though a man had a precious jewel and a rich, yet if he wist not the value thereof nor wherefore it served, he were neither the better nor the richer of a straw. Even so though we read the scripture and babble of it never so much, yet if we know not the use of it, and wherefore it was given, and what is therein to be sought, it profiteth us nothing at all. It is not enough therefore to read and talk of it only, but we must also desire God day and night instantly to open our eyes, and to make us understand and feel wherefore the scripture was given, that we may apply the medicine of the scripture, every man to his own sores, unless that we intend to be idle disputers, and brawlers about vain words, ever gnawing upon the bitter bark without and never attaining unto the sweet pitch within, and persecuting one another for defending of lewd imaginations and fantasies of our own invention."

Tyndale's emphasis on understanding the content and purpose of scripture, and not fighting over personalized interpretations does nothing to contradict and, if fact, supports my point. In short, I'm suggesting that we've reached a point where we don't seek so much to *"understand* and feel" the intent of scripture—we just *"feel"* it.

13. Bedouelle ("Biblical Interpretation," 441) provides a good description of a mystical approach to scripture:

    "Thus, mystics do no propose one particular interpretation of Scripture; rather, they willingly accept the plurality and even the multiplicity of meanings. Their experience of God leads them to an intimate, personal understanding that has no real need of contact with the actual text of the Bible. Indeed, this insight into the divine mystery, springing from mystical experience, is spontaneously directed to the contents of Holy Scripture, which are rediscovered in some way."

14. http://www.jrsbible.info/bible.htm. This changed since I wrote this to http://www.jrsbible.info and apparently removed these lists; but see also http://fbcescalon.org/Encouraging_Bible_Verses/.

15. The allegorical approach to interpreting the Bible has a long history, with its heyday being from the time of Clement of Alexandria (150–211/216) and Origin (185-254) (and the Catechetical School of Alexandria) through the Late Middle Ages.

16. This, too, is part of the Reformation heritage. As Susan Schreiner ("Certainty in the Reformation," 197) puts it in her discussion of the search for authority ("certitude") in the use of the Bible in the Reformation, "All the warring parties appealed to the guidance of the Spirit in their scriptural interpretation."

Chapter 5

Diagnosis: Inkblotitis

Inkblotitis is Christianity's dangerous disease. It's a hidden illness that comes from an odd sort of biblical illiteracy. It's odd because it germinates in the soil of scripture citation and spreads on the winds of Bible verses. It comes, in other words, from an apparent proliferation of Bible content. As a believer, you'd think I'd be happy that "the words of God" are so accessible to everyone: hoisted over highways, splattered on t-shirts, quoted by politicians, framed in greeting cards, and harnessed to online signatures. Is it really fair to call it an "illness," since by definition an illness is harmful? Is inkblotitis really so dangerous as to warrant all the fuss? Or am I just making a mountain out of a molehill?

As they say, "the proof is in the pudding" or—using our medical analogy—in the test results; and a competent diagnosis can only be reached by examining the patient thoroughly. As the infection has taken hold over a long period of time, so the exam looks back into the history of the Bible and the church. Historically and personally, the symptoms manifest themselves gradually; the outcomes appear over time. In this chapter, we'll take a bird's-eye view of some of the clinical history and test results. This will put us in a good position to consider some of the primary dangers of inkblotitis.

Dangers of Inkblotitis

- a lack of certainty about Christian teachings and practices
- misinterpreting and distorting the Bible by breaking it into pieces
- missing the main point or points by focusing on smaller points (majoring in the minors)

Chapter 5

> ## Dangers of Inkblotitis
> - reinforcing existing beliefs that may need to be challenged or even changed
> - eliminating one's ability to hear God's first conversations with his people
> - interfering with the Spirit's desire to comfort, confront, and change us
> - replacing the word of God with the word of me
> - creating or strengthening conflict and division between believers

"The Head of a Fox"

The subject is given one plate after the other and asked, "What might this be?" He holds the plate in his hand and may turn it about as much as he likes. The subject is free to hold the plate near his eyes or far away as he chooses; however, it should not be viewed from a distance. The length of the extended arm is the maximum permissible distance. Care must be taken that the subject does not catch a glimpse of the plate from a distance, since this would alter the conditions of the experiment. For instance, Plate I is frequently interpreted as "the head of a fox" when seen at a distance of several meters; at a closer range this answer is almost never given. Once the subject has interpreted the plate as the head of a fox it becomes very difficult for him to see anything else when it is brought nearer.[1]

These are the directions of Hermann Rorschach (1884-1922) regarding the procedure for administering the psychological test he invented, now known as the Rorschach Inkblot Test. The participant is given a series of "plates," each containing an inkblot. Though carefully developed and tested for interpretive potential, these blots of ink have no inherent meaning as pictures or images. They are designed to evoke responses from the observer, which are then interpreted through a complex series of categories and methods. The whole point of the test is suggestive and subjective; it is designed for the viewer to project meaning.

From our perspective, it's interesting that when viewing an inkblot, Rorschach did not want the subjects "to get the big picture," so to speak. He didn't want the test-takers to see the inkblots from a distance because the image so perceived had a controlling influence over the way he or she saw everything else: the details always then go to contributing to the mental construction of that image (the first image—a sort of primacy effect). This had the effect of reducing or obscuring the details intended to be a part of the arm-length-or-less experience. The details and sub-details of the inkblot are important for a richer subjective potential, which is the purpose of the test. The whole purpose is to evoke and accentuate what is basic and true about the personality and functioning of the person, found best, coincidentally, from an arm's length or less. The person is the goal. The test depends, therefore, on an interpretive freedom that is constrained by a big-picture—from a distance—view. (In other words, *zooming out reduces the subjective potential.*)

Do you see how we have come to treat the Bible this way? We follow Rorschach's advice well. First of all, we turn history and stories and letters and poems into isolated quotes (that is, verses) and then interpret them as plates of inkblots. At that point, we have eliminated the possibility of seeing them from a distance sufficient to get the big picture and then (naturally) understand the details as a part of that (historical and literary) picture. With misappropriated faithfulness to Rorschach's instructions, then, we allow the details and sub-details of the isolated verses free reign to evoke our subjective imaginations, each in his or her own way, shaped and defined by our mental and emotional constructs, so as not to thwart or limit the potential for personal interpretations.

For Rorschach, *projection* is the goal. But not for us! For Bible readers, *reception* is the goal. Quite the opposite. Yet, as if we are all part of some big psychological experiment, time and culture have turned the Bible into a great big pile of spiritual inkblots, interpreted by the personal leanings and leadings of energized subjectives; and, as a consequence of human nature, whether from a distance or close-up, once we see something a certain way, as Rorschach noted, it's difficult to see it any other way no matter what sort of mental gymnastics we give ourselves to. Once "the head of the fox" is there (in our minds), it's hard to get rid of.

Diagnosis: Inkblotitis

Random Access Bible Reading

When the Bible was first written—ah, see how we think of it as a single book—each book or set of books (if they were intentionally connected) was written as self-contained communications of God's interactions with and words to humans. Each book stood on its own as an independent message or word of God to its original audience and, for the most part, was intended to be read to (and therefore heard by) a listening audience, probably at a single sitting. Obviously, the chapters and verses were not a part of the original works. In fact, they were added much later. The Bible was divided into chapters by Stephen Langton, Archbishop of Canterbury, around 1227 AD. Rabbi Isaac Nathan divided the Hebrew Old Testament into verses in 1448 AD, following full stop markings that had been passed down from antiquity. Robert Estienne, also known as Stephanus, added verses to the New Testament in 1551 (and essentially maintained Nathan's verse divisions for the Old Testament since they had become accepted by that time). These chapter and verse divisions now serve as mini-addresses or memory markers that allow us to find and use the words of scripture without having to know or read large sections at a time.

As a result of the chapter and verse divisions, what's happened to the way we read and use the Bible today is a little like what happened in the electronic world with the invention of RAM—Random Access Memory. Sequential Access Memory existed before RAM—and before computers—in any sort of device that saved or stored information sequentially, meaning that you have to go through what's stored in order, sequentially, to get to any piece of data that's stored or recorded. Examples are music records, cassette tapes, eight-track tapes (if you go back that far), video-tapes, and even CDs and DVDs. (And if you get right down to it, reading and writing is a method of sequential access memory, is it not? You have to read the letters and words in order to make sense of them.) Now, we've certainly come up with ways to "jump-around" and find things stored this way more quickly when we need to (like picking up the needle of a record-player and moving the arm to another spot or fast-forward-ing to a specific place on a tape or disk), but not with the same freedom and speed that RAM allows. Random access means that we use a unique address for each piece of information, which allows us to look up that item individually, randomly, and much faster—since we don't have to "read" through the preceding information. It's random because you can "read" or access any item of information in any order, and then any other item of information from anywhere else in the system with no logical association between the pieces of data.

Does any of this sound familiar? Like what we do with scripture when we pick out verses from one book of the Bible and then another and another? Because of such wonderful inventions as computers, RAM, memory devices of all sorts, the world of the internet (the YouVersion app is a great example of modern accessibility), and the decisive division of the Bible into easily (randomly) accessed and removable verses, I'm afraid the dissection of the Bible may have only just begun. The challenge of our day and future generations is not finding things quickly or breaking them apart. Our problem is putting them back together. A shattered Bible has contributed to a shattered church and reduced its ability to speak to a shattered world. Specifically, our challenge is to overcome the habits and consequences of Random Access Bible Reading (RABR).

My teenage daughter is passionately involved in a Christian theatre organization called Christian Youth Theatre. Recently, we attended a production of the musical *Godspell*, performed by CYT South (a sister branch to our CYT North). The kids are highly supportive of each other and attend various productions around the city, especially when their friends are on stage. *Godspell* (an old spelling of "gospel") is a 1970 musical by Stephen Schwartz and John-Michael Tebelak. (You may remember the song "Day by Day" from the original cast album.) The show is a series of short stories or parables from the Gospels, especially Matthew, removed from their original settings and recast in "modern" (early 1970s) settings, language, and (musical) style. Clearly reflecting the cultural movements of the day, the collection of scenes are colorful recreations of moments and teachings from the life of Jesus, strung together with little or no overall explanation of the storyline or purposes of the biblical episodes. In fact, while watching the show, I had trouble making any big-picture-sense out of the progression of scenes and was conscious of how little I would understand if I didn't already know something of the Bible stories. The scenes were colorful, artistic, edgy; but if the authors had an overall point of emphasis through the scenes they chose and the way they connected them, I missed it. (To be fair, I probably just needed to watch it a few more times and maybe do some reading about it.)

While watching the show, however, I was touched and stimulated by some of the individual stories/parables of Jesus, which might go to support the idea that they don't really need a context, that they are context-independent or -transcendent. I would say, on the other hand, that had I not already known the content of the stories, I wouldn't have understood much at all. I suspect that was true of most of the audience. In other words, we used our already existing (mental and emotional) constructs to provide a context in place of the real context (= a substitute context) to make sense of what we were seeing. This musical is, in my opinion, a great example of inkblotitis.

As we watched the show, we were surrounded by my daughter's friends who had come to support their fellow performers. When the lights came up for intermission, a 17-year-old, highly intelligent and gifted young friend, stood up in the row in front of us and, loud enough for the surrounding few rows to hear, said, "Is that not just beyond random!?" His words poignantly echoed our experience.

Although we may often hear it said that the best way to interpret scripture is to let scripture interpret itself—that is, to let one verse explain another verse—we really don't believe that you can just pull out a verse willy-nilly from the Bible and have that verse interpret or "go with" another verse. Recently, my wife and daughter went to a women's breakfast at our church. During the message part of the morning, the speaker, encouraging the audience to dedication in their walk of faith, used 2 Corinthians 10:5: "We destroy arguments and every proud obstacle raised up against the knowledge of God, and we take every thought captive to obey Christ." When introducing the verse, however, she accidentally said "*1* Corinthians 10:5." So, many

Chapter 5

in the audience turned to *First* Corinthians. Just as the speaker finished reading the verse from *Second* Corinthians—about we Christians who are working hard to "take every thought captive for Christ"—my daughter read to herself: "Nevertheless, God was not pleased with most of them, and they were struck down in the wilderness." Laughing quietly together at the image presented by the combination of these two verses, my wife and daughter humorously realized the sometimes incompatibility of randomly selected verses. But why? Why can't 1 Corinthians 10:5 be used in conjunction with 2 Corinthians 10:5—if one verse interprets another? The answer is obvious, isn't it? And very, very important.

Neutralizing RABR—Random Access Bible Reading—means returning to the nature and experience of Bible literature as originally written and intended by the authors and, for us believers, by God. Random access to pieces of the Bible is an integral part of the climate that has produced Christianity's hidden illness. Free access was a catalytic first step—the precious gift of free access to the Bible given to us by the Reformers and translators who sacrificed to make the Bible available to us all cultivated the ground and planted the seeds. Like a soaking rain on a warm spring day, random access waters the fields, metastasizing the temptation to reading/using the Bible like inkblots; thus, spreading the infection. As we'll see when we explore the treatment for healing the hidden illness of inkblotitis, the cure is no less than a serious, if not radical, call to in-context, book by book, sequential—or what I'll call "Summit Access Bible Reading"—SABR. A SABR call to unsheathe the sword of the Spirit. Unlike the sword in *The Sword in the Stone* and the legend of King Arthur, King Jesus provides his Spirit to all of us who want it enough to open our ears: "Whoever has ears, let him hear."

What Is Inkblotitis?

By now, the answer to that question is probably obvious, but—since we've coined the term and there's a lot at stake—some formal definitions are in order. We start with the inkblot and, in particular, with the psychological test developed by Rorschach in 1921.

"Inkblot"

The Rorschach Inkblot Test, which has been used and adapted through the years, is a psychological test given to individuals using a series of inkblots to evaluate the personality characteristics and emotional functioning of a patient. From a person's initial responses and subsequent examination of the inkblots, from what the person sees (the content or meaning) and the way he or she responds to and interprets the inkblots, the therapist draws conclusions about basic personality traits and emotional/psychological functioning. The inkblot is not really a picture of anything. It has no inherent meaning. It is in a true sense, relative. It's just a shape or a "blot." To say it another way, the blot of ink has no objective meaning, but evokes subjective responses in the viewer, who thus projects meaning onto the shape. The theory is that what a person sees in the shapes, how she or he gives meaning and content to the shapes, reveals things about the person. The meaning is not in the shapes, but in the person—or in the interpretation of the shapes by the person. His or her psychological world or "context," if you will, gives rise to interpretation and meaning. This is what I'm claiming we often do with the Bible as we read and use it in today's culture.

The Bible is not a single book in the way we think of books today; nor is it a reference manual filled with definitions or collections of proverbs and aphorisms. It's more like a miniature library. The Bible is a complex collection of different kinds of books, written over a long period of time by different authors, all acting under the inspiration of God. Because its contents are important to us, we have bound it into a single volume—the Bible—and divided it into chapters and verses for easy reference and memory.

To some extent, the division of the Bible into chapters and verses was the beginning of inkblotitis (though there are certainly other ways to "take a verse out of context"), leading to the sort of random access we talked about. Of course, the chapter and verse divisions have good purposes: they allow us to find things, remember things, and mark various starting and stopping points. On the other hand, the intrinsic divisions put into the text by the verses—not a part of the original writings—act like perforations that allow us to tear out pieces of the Bible any time and any way we want. Like memory locations or addresses in a computer, we can access verses of the Bible randomly and, in some cases, instantly. These pieces of the Bible (verses and sets of verses), however we produce them and for whatever purposes, are what I mean by the word "inkblot." Small, cut-out pieces of scripture, removed from their original, book-level contexts are potentially like Rorschach inkblots that we read and interpret according to our personal sets of psychological and theological constructs more than by their Spirit-inspired literary and historical contexts. (Of course, our personal "contexts" will always be involved, but removing the meaning-shaping control of the original contexts is sort of like taking the skin off of a water balloon. The contents run out all over the place.)

"itis"

The suffix "itis" is a Latin term, used in the medical field, meaning inflammation or swelling. I'm using it in several ways. Cutting out or isolating a verse or set of verses from its original context is what I mean by the term "itis." Like perforated punch-outs, verses of scripture become inkblots when we cut them out and isolate them from their book-level contexts. In other words, the verses inflame or swell into inkblots—like a thumb hit with a hammer becomes the sole focus of our attention for a few moments—when we isolate them, giving them an identity of their own. Separating the verses is really not what turns them into inkblots, though—at least not by itself. It's the loss of context and replacement of that context with our own interpretive frameworks that makes them inkblots. From another angle, then, the isolation sets us up for the swelling—the swelling of our own subjective potential for interpreting things primarily by what we already think and know. Isolated verses swell—that is, increase—subjective hearings; or, a little pithier: substitute contexts produce subjective readings. That's the "itis" part of "inkblot-itis." As the habit of reading and interpreting verses of the Bible separated from their original contexts spread throughout the church, we can think of inkblotitis as a type of disease or illness that became systemic and pervasive, affecting us as individuals and as communities of God's people.[2]

As contextless, sound-bite use or hearing of a piece of communication, the idea of inkblotitis can be applied more broadly to any form of communication, not just the Bible. At its most basic level, inkblotitis stems from the same issues that make all communication tricky and real intimacy elusive (problems that I believe come from the destructive effects of sin upon us as persons). Norbert, a friend of mine, who was one of the first previewers of this material, noticed the frequent occurrence of a type of inkblotitis in the political arena whenever a candidate mentioned a certain buzz-word or party-mantra. It was as if the people in the audience couldn't stop and think about the issue anymore, only interpret and react based on where they were politically and ethically. In other words, the subject was closed; they had arrived, implying that the thought or position is presumed understood and true, and so there's no need to think about it anymore and listen more closely. (Does this mean that we've "lost" our minds?) Though not necessarily good, this is normal and is indeed a part of every form of communication (we don't completely start over whenever we talk, for example). We sometimes hear about it in the news when sound-bites are taken "out of context," someone protests, which actually then gives them a new, prejudicial context. (Some sound-bite punctuated talk shows provide interesting parallels to Bible-verse punctuated sermons.) When a piece of communication is taken out of context and has no real context, then the word or

Chapter 5

phrase or sentence or paragraph begins to function like an inkblot, a projective canvas for the listener's own preconceived notions, and it happens everywhere and often. The *inkblot* is the contextless item or piece of communication; the *itis* is the swelling or calling-forth of our subjective ways of thinking as a context in order to interpret it.

"Inkblot-itis"

Having said that about the parts of the word "inkblotitis," let me be ridiculously redundant for a minute with some definitions of the word as a whole (I'd like to grow and shrink, and adjust the angle of the definitions as we go) in order to highlight various nuances of this phenomenon. Inkblotitis is—or is at least caused by—reading and using the Bible in disconnected pieces. A little more elaborated: inkblotitis is reading and using Bible verses outside of the meaning-shaping control of their literary and historical contexts. Inkblotitis is the loss of the book-level context. Inkblotitis is disconnected, isolated Bible reading. Inkblotitis is impressionistic Bible reading. Inkblotitis is subjective Bible reading. Inkblotitis is—and this one gets a little more sticky—personal Bible reading, in the sense that what we get out of it comes from and belongs to the moment and to me as an individual person, as we talked about last chapter. Inkblotitis is the enlargement of our subjective potentials by verse-level Bible reading—a putting on of me-colored glasses, if you will. Inkblotitis is a verse of scripture by itself. Inkblotitis is the increased potential to misread and misunderstand God's word because of the way we are reading it.

(Continuing . . .) Inkblotitis is the swelling of self-interest to the point of interfering with our ability to listen objectively or see clearly. Inkblotitis is contextless and therefore subjective reading and use of the Bible. Inkblotitis is a potentially distorted interpretation of the Bible due to our lack of knowledge of the book-level context. Inkblotitis is a form of biblical illiteracy that comes from reading the IGB (Instant Gratification Bible). Inkblotitis is the spread of subjective Bible reading throughout the church. Inkblotitis is the greatly increased risk of not understanding the Bible by reading it in isolated verses and chapters, and the proliferation of that practice throughout the church. Inkblotitis is verse-level Bible-reading. Inkblotitis is disintegration of the Bible.

Because not hearing God or misunderstanding God has immediate and eternal consequences (we look at some of these shortly), inkblotitis can be seen as a serious condition or illness that affects both the individual person at the deepest level and the church at the widest level, since, of course, the church is made up of the people. As such, inkblotitis is a weapon of the enemy—one of the most potent and yet subtlest weapons of our day—and therefore most deadly. Inkblotitis is Christianity's dangerous disease.

Look how much we do it (separate verses from their original contexts): The preacher stands up in front of the congregation and reads a passage of scripture at the start of his sermon, then uses ideas or themes from that text as the basis of his message and exhortations. Inkblotitis. You read a portion of scripture for your daily Bible reading without remembering all that much about what you read yesterday or last week, then flip over and read some verses from another book. Inkblotitis. You look up specific scriptures to answer questions in a study guide or read sets of verses on a given topic from a devotional book or Bible concordance. Inkblotitis. You do a topical study of a word or idea in the Bible by looking at all the places that word occurs. Inkblotitis. You read a book about love or sexuality or marriage or stress or anger or finances or spiritual-gifts or God's plan for your life or anything where the author quotes verses of scripture in support of the principles she or he espouses. Inkblotitis. We run across verses of scripture cited on someone's internet blog or a church website setting forth the core values of that church. Inkblotitis. You read a novel about what's to happen in the last days where the author basis his ideas on a few isolated verses of scripture. Inkblotitis. We stand in worship together, with bits and pieces of Bible verses scattered throughout the songs or splattered on the screen. Inkblotitis. We watch beautiful worship videos with brief verses of scripture to help us in our meditations. Inkblotitis. We send cards and letters with our favorite verses. Inkblotitis. We put them on shirts and billboards and refrigerators, drawing attention to some striking or attractive feature of our faith. Inkblotitis.

Help! Is everything an inkblot? And every Bible reading bad? No, of course not. Remember that "inkblotitis" does not mean we are necessarily distorting or misusing a verse of scripture. Nor does it mean that God doesn't work around and beyond our failings. (These are important points that I hope you hear clearly.) I'm not saying that every verse or short Bible reading is necessarily a bad or misreading, or that every passage of scripture has to have a lengthy context to make any sense whatsoever, or that verses of scripture can't be used as summary reminders of our faith. Inkblotitis means that we have opened ourselves to the *possibility* of not understanding or misunderstanding the Bible by replacing the original contexts with our own personal contexts by isolating the verses. If we know the context, then we have not lost it. If we don't, then, in a real sense, we're talking about a form of biblical illiteracy, even if we know a lot of verses. The tragic flaw of Bible reading today is that the "text" often says more *about* the person reading it than *to* the person reading it. Like a Rorschach inkblot, it reveals more about the person reading it than it does about God; more to reinforce who and what we already are than to bring us face to face with a holy God of love. And relying on ourselves—the depths or pits of our personal perspectives—as interpretive keys is a little like opening Pandora's box to solve our problems, don't you think? The potential is great and dangerous, to say the least.

Does It Really Make a Difference?

Is inkblotitis really all that bad? Or am I just making a mountain out of a molehill? Since the church is the people, then its illness is my illness. As I have said repeatedly, I believe almost any Bible reading is better than no Bible reading and that God works with and around our deficiencies. My purpose is not to paint a nobody-does-it-right portrait, with a sense of fatality and gloom. My goal is to inspire a renewed passion for sitting with God through his word. My intent is to suggest that spiritual and historical developments have, over time, led us to a point where random access Bible reading has become the norm, and to contend that this type of Bible reading does indeed pose a serious threat to the church and to us as individuals.

When I say that inkblotitis is Christianity's dangerous disease, two questions quickly ask to be answered: (1) Does it—reading the Bible in small pieces—really make a difference in how a passage of scripture is understood?, and (2) Does it really make a difference for us as readers? The questions are related in that the meaning of the text—if you believe the Bible to be inspired by God—is the means God uses to reveal himself to us and show us what it means to be a follower of Jesus Christ.

Throughout his ministry, Jesus struggled with getting the heart of his messages across to his disciples. Various obstacles of what they already thought and believed kept getting in the way. Thus, the Parable of the Sower stands at the beginning of Jesus' teaching as an explanation and forecast of what happens to the word of God on the ears and in the hearts of listeners. Throughout Mark's Gospel, a tacit question hangs over the story: what kind of soil are the disciples? If Jesus had trouble communicating the word of God in person because of what was going on in the heads of the hearers, do you think we will be much more inclined to hear it clearly and freely today? Or do we have similar "earplugs"? If our own personal, subjective (self-centered and self-protective) tendencies fight hard against hearing and receiving the truth in the first place, then how much more impactful is inkblotitis as a tool of these personal, subjective, and protective tendencies? Inkblotitis is like handing a sharp sword to

Chapter 5

your worst enemy in the middle of a bloody melee—without even knowing you're doing it (were it not, of course, for God's protection). That means it's doubly dangerous: sharp and invisible. Can you think of a weapon that would be any more dangerous? I believe the enemy has taken up that sword and done great harm to us as followers and potential followers of the Lord. We'll look closer at the specific wounds in a few minutes.

When you hear or read a verse or two of scripture by itself, with little or no knowledge of the book-level context, as opposed to reading it in thoughtful connection with the remainder of its setting and story, does it really make a difference in how you might understand the verses? The question can really only be answered over time. That is, you will have to see the difference (to believe it). I would say that in some cases, it will make little to no difference. Some sentences and thoughts are rather self-contained and need little context. On the other hand, the meaning of most words is consistently conditioned and nuanced by the words around them. (How much of God's word do we want to miss or waste?) The meaning of most sentences is significantly shaped and clarified by the sentences around them. And—this is the one we respect the least in our Bible reading—the meaning of most paragraphs is reciprocally influenced, shaped, and clarified by the paragraphs around them—all of them. How do we know what a word means? How do we know what a sentence means? How do we know what a paragraph means, except by the context? We'll look at this more in chapters to come, and we'll take some time to think about the difference that in-context-reading really makes through examples and by applying the principles of book-level reading to some Bible books. To some extent, the question of how much effect the context has on the meaning of a word or sentence depends on the type of context from which the word or sentence comes, which is a question of genre.

In a broad sense, inkblotitis is the reading and use of verses of scripture in any way other than they were originally intended. How they were intended depends on what kind of "book" we are reading. In other words, it depends on the genre. "Genre" is simply the type or category of writing (or communication, to put it more broadly).

Numerous types have developed and disappeared naturally over time for various communication goals. We have prose and poetry, narrative and dialogue, books and magazines, newspapers and internet bulletin boards, letters and e-mails, legal documents and contracts, movies and TV shows, commercials and advertisements . . . You get the idea.

The Bible contains an assortment of genres. Reading the Bible as it was originally intended means that if something were intended as a proverb, then we should read it as a proverb. If as a song, then . . . as a song. If a letter, then as a letter. If a narrative or story, then as a story. If history . . . If symbolic prophecy . . . This is why some how-to-read-the-Bible books start with and emphasize the concept of genre, and this is certainly valid. But to some extent, this approach is deductive and theoretical. That is, how do you as a reader know what type of literature it is unless you read it? Or—and this is the point—someone else reads it for you and tells you? They say, "This is a letter and letters are written like this . . . So, when you read, you should think like this . . . and remember you're reading a letter." Nothing wrong with that. In fact, this is where scholars and historical research greatly help us who want to read and understand the Bible. I'm going to do some of this as well. On the other hand, I think there is something more fundamental to good Bible reading, which is at the heart and focus of this book: we need to start with the text.

How do we really know a certain book was meant to be a letter or a gospel, or anything else, for that matter, until we read it? The most important step in effective Bible reading is to read the Bible itself. That seems silly to say, doesn't it? So let's expand it a bit: the most important thing in effective Bible reading is reading the Bible as it was intended. Aha! So far, so good. This leads us to the importance of genre. But forget about genre for a second, and think more broadly, more basically. Since the Bible was given to us by God in relatively short communications—in what we call "books" (remember the word *biblia*)—reading the Bible as books is really the starting point.[3] This is the most basic thesis of this book, and it's really quite simple: hearing God most clearly means hearing his word as he spoke or inspired it, and that starts by reading the Bible—not as a book (in the way we think of books) or as broken-apart verses but—*as books*. Of course, such reading includes the historical contexts of the individual books and the integration of those books into the overall framework and unfolding story of the Bible as a whole.

Reading the Bible as books (instead of a book) is the remedy for inkblotitis, and it does make a difference. The books themselves are the meaning-controlling contexts that allow us to hear the word of God—to get God's point. They are God's first conversations with his people. If we do not know and understand them as such, we have no historical grounding as believers—only momentary, personal, and subjective impressions. This is why inkblotitis is such a serious issue. It replaces divine truth—an objective word of God—with individualized, relative experiences. "To me, this means . . ."

To see the most dangerous and graphic potential of inkblotitis, all you need do is think about the impact of replacing *God* with *me*.

History of an Illness

If inkblotitis is such a serious malady in the church today, how'd we get here? And what are the symptoms and effects on the health of the church and on us as members? In a basic sense, inkblotitis is caused by anything that removes a verse of scripture from its original context. Historically, several major events and influences helped to create the climate in today's world where inkblotitis could become the norm. We'll take a broad overview to start and then come back to more of the specifics.

A dissected book got the ball rolling. The very beginning—to be a little pedantic and overly thorough—of the process that led to inkblotitis was the collecting and binding of the books of the Bible into a single book—a tremendous milestone in the history of the world. That actually took a long time as ancient writing materials gradually evolved to the point where scrolls could be bound together into "codex" or book form, and, of course, the time it took to write and collect the documents from different places. As they began to be bound together, the question of which books belong in the Bible became paramount.

Accepting history's solution to that question as providential, we observe that it was natural and only a matter of time for these sacred texts to be treated with great respect and consequently divided into subunits (chapters and verses) for better study and remembrance. Hence, the second major cause of the climate of inkblotitis was the creation of the chapters and verses that now act like perforations, allowing us to break up the Bible in all sorts of ways. I'm glad they're there, just as I'm glad God's books were gathered into a single book, but think how much more we might be inclined to read entire books of the Bible or larger portions of books without the divisions and markers. And remember, that's the way they were originally written, to be heard by an audience on a single occasion.

A free Bible was the next step. The Protestant Reformation's emphasis on individuality ("the priesthood of all believers") and the accountability of each of us before God motivated the tremendous, life-sacrificing passion of those who gave themselves to put the Bible

Chapter 5

into the hands of the common people so that all of us could have free access to the words and teachings of scripture. When that happened, in combination with the invention of the printing press, when the Bible became freely available to all of us, the opportunities for individual reading and interpreting of the Bible exploded. Inkblotitis was a fairly predictable result—as some who opposed translating the Bible into the language of the peoples forecast.[4]

Theological and cultural factors fanned the flames. Combine a free Bible with the emphasis on personal, experience-centered faith prevalent in much of the Christian world today (with underpinnings of Pietism and other historical influences, as we talked about), and the ingredients are in place, not only for the introduction of inkblotitis into the way we read the Bible, but for it to become the standard. Personal faith is an essential of modern Christianity, as it should be; push it a little too far, however, and personal interpretation is not far behind (which then becomes one's faith, and so on). In a culture where the belief that all meaning is subjective and relative, moreover, and where tolerance to the point of intolerance are increasingly (and ironically) assumed as truth, subjectivity is anointed—at least by some—as the best we can do and even as the ideal (a church to fit everyone, on every street corner). What's more, a culture of instant gratification naturally looks for the same when it reads the Bible (the IGB, as I mentioned earlier). Add to the social and intellectual climate the difficulties of reading and understanding the Bible—things like the cultural distance between us and the writings, the complex content, and wide scope of the Bible. Multiply these by the ways we read and use the Bible—chopped up and punched out for all sorts of fast-food-style ingesting (like spiritual French fries, inkblotitis fits our frantic lifestyles). Just as the division of the Bible into verses prepared the way for its use in small slices, so the division of our lives into fast-paced, out-of-breath segments encourages us to serve them up and eat on the run. Stir in the frantic pace of modern life, then, which has to be seen as a contributing factor, and, like fresh baked cookies, the smells of personal and subjective Bible reading fill the house. Or to change the metaphor: the trees hang low with an abundant crop of inkblotitis.

These are some of the historical and cultural causes of the condition. There's also an all-important spiritual dimension. Perhaps the most potent factor, responsible for Christianity's hidden and dangerous illness, is the mind-dulling, heart-scarring allurements and effects of sin upon us as readers. In a fundamental way—fundamental to our wounded selves as sinners—we really don't want to hear what God says. Somewhere deep down, as Isaiah realized in the temple when he saw the Lord high on his throne (Isaiah 6), we know the direct and clear word of God would destroy us.

Chapter 5

The Clinical Picture: Causes and Symptoms

By definition, an illness is harmful to the patient. Most of the time, illnesses are diagnosed and sometimes even named by their symptoms. If inkblotitis really exists and is dangerous to us as believers and to the church at large, how do we know? In other words, what are the symptoms that lead to the diagnosis? And what are the outcomes of the disease? Technically speaking, the causes of an illness are different from the symptoms—a symptom is an indication of a disease or malady, caused by an infecting agent or genetic abnormality. Sometimes causes, symptoms, and outcomes get a little blurred, however, and we're not trying to be overly technical from a medical point of view. (The medical imagery is just an analogy, as you know.) Within the framework of an overall clinical history, I think it will be helpful to highlight some of the causes and most obvious symptoms of inkblotitis as part of our diagnostic journey, and when we see inkblotitis as a broad condition resulting from how the church handles the Bible, the distinction between causes and symptoms begins to disappear. With that in mind, let's examine the patient.

Concerning our use of the Bible, the first and most obvious thing we notice is the constant and pervasive dismantling of scripture into individual verses or short sets of verses, or even chapters. It cannot be denied that we have broken the Bible into thousands of pieces. This separation of the Bible into short, disconnected segments is the most obvious and determinative factor: it's both a cause and a symptom of inkblotitis. Like eating cookies or French fries, of itself and in combination with other healthy habits, reading the Bible in short pieces is not bad or harmful. But because the Bible is big and often not easy to understand, and because we are prone to self-protection and -promotion, it's a small step from breaking the Bible into pieces to using it for our own, even selfish purposes.

If we're making a comprehensive list of causes and symptoms, as I said, we have to go behind the dismantling of the Bible to the collecting of the writings into a single volume and then especially the dividing of the books into chapters and verses—both of which are obviously good things. If it's fair to call inkblotitis an "illness," don't we then have to ask the question of how something so negative can come from something so positive? How can harm and evil come from progress and things we consider to be good? Like having an indispensable, powerful immune system that somehow becomes dysfunctional and begins to attack itself in auto-immune diseases, these positive historical developments provided the basis for us to begin using the Bible in small, isolated pieces. We might think of them as preconditions of the illness; and like all attacks of the enemy, like a wolf in sheep's clothing, evil wraps itself in good things. I'll have more to say about this shortly.

Looking at the patient, then, we see a shattered Bible. In the absence of other symptoms, that might not be a big deal. Problem is, we also have a shattered church. It's been this way for so long now that we often don't really even notice, but that doesn't change the fact or the detriment of it. In many corners, we've come to accept denominationalism as a sort of "best we can do" model; however, the unity of God's people is one of the most fundamental teachings and sought-after goals of the Bible. Next to issues relating to the struggles and persecution of early Christians, it's probably the most common major theme of the New Testament, which shows its importance but also that it's never been a straightforward or easy goal. So I don't want to overstate the novelty of the problem. On the other hand, there has clearly been an explosion of separation in the church since the Protestant Reformation, which—looking back—has an easy explanation in the newfound availability of the Bible and related break from the sole authority of the Roman church (canon law). The shattering of the church on an international level is mirrored locally when brothers and sisters in Christ split and splinter over interpretations of doctrine and practice, often with scorn and condemnation for those on the other side. As Alister McGrath aptly expresses in his book *Christianity's Dangerous Idea*: "The dangerous new idea, firmly embodied at the heart of the Protestant revolution, was that all Christians have the right to interpret the Bible for themselves."[5]

Chapter 5

"Psychological Suppositionitis"

Everyone has a Bible; everyone has an opinion. You can add this to our list of causes and symptoms. We live in a time that champions individual rights, in combination with the ideas that truth is relative and meaning, like beauty, is in the eye of the beholder. And it's not limited to the secular world: Christians have become known for our ability to support all sorts of different teachings from our book. We view faith, prayer, and Bible reading as deeply personal experiences. In many circles—as we discussed—we've come to identify God's presence with various forms of emotional and heartfelt responses to a song or a scripture. We tend to think: "If it moves me, it must be from God." I'm not against being moved; I'm just pointing out the overlap between a person-focused faith and the temptations to read the Bible through me-colored glasses.

Nor is inkblotitis limited to the "common" Bible readers—as if putting the Bible into everyone's hands was the real cause of the problem, a sort of intellectual inadequacy. Various types of inkblotitis manifest themselves in scholarly circles as well. The "quest for the historical Jesus" provides a good example (as you might expect in a "scholarly" presentation, the language here is somewhat lofty; so, hang in there and we'll break it down a bit afterward):

> And this is the malady to which we must here allude—let us not dignify it with the euphemism "historical imagination." The Scientific study of the life of Jesus is suffering from psychological "suppositionitis" which amounts to a sort of historical guesswork. For this reason interpretations to suit every taste proliferate. The number of arbitrary psychological interpretations at the same time form the basis for important structures of thought; and how often do people think that the task of criticism has already been discharged by playing tuneful psychological variations on a given factual theme.[6]

William Wrede made these comments in 1901 in a book called *The Messianic Secret* (*Das Messiasgeheimnis in den Evangelien* in

German). At the time, scholars were pursuing—and continue to do so—the "real," historical Jesus. The assumption is that lying behind our gospel accounts are historical occurrences that don't really match the way they are portrayed in the Gospels. All sorts of "lives of Jesus" (books about who Jesus was) were produced, supposedly uncovering the real historical Jesus behind the Christ of faith, which actually, like our Rorschachian inkblot, revealed more about the authors than about Jesus or the Bible. Wrede's powerful, somewhat humorous, phrase "psychological suppositionitis" points out the subjectivism prevalent in those "scholarly" works.

I've witnessed this often in my educational pursuits, both in the classroom and in scholarly books. When I was working on my doctorate, it was amazing to me how some of my most intelligent professors would make such biased assumptions about what they were reading as to preclude any chance of hearing the literature on its own terms. When it comes to the tendency to break up the Bible and interpret the pieces according to firmly entrenched sets of assumptions and beliefs, inkblotitis is no respecter of persons. For academics and scholars—just like for the rest of us—the gown opens in the back (exposing our uncovered derrières).

If we honestly examine the patient, I think we have to admit that individualism and a sort of out-of-control variety and subjectivity, resulting in segregation, judgment and condemnation make up a significant portion of what outsiders see when they picture the church, at least historically. When the Bible became a right of each individual—or more accurately, when the interpretation of the Bible became the right of each individual—we have to see that as a clear symptom of a developing illness (not the right, but the results). A shattered Bible, a shattered church, shattered communities, and a shattered witness all contribute to our diagnosis.

Chapter 5

How Can Something So Bad Come from Something So Good?

We could spend a lot of time on each of these points, but I suspect we've touched on them enough in the previous chapters that you know what I mean. And let me say again that the availability of the Bible is not a bad thing. It's a wonderful gift from God. Neither does the problem come from the carefulness with which we mark the Bible into chapters and verses so that we can know and cherish its contents. It's not the right or the responsibility of the individual to pursue God in scripture, to read and interpret the Bible personally, that we should brand as the culprit. It's not an emphasis on a personal, practical, and passionate faith. These are marvelous blessings. But, like it or not, *good* things can open the door to *new* things, which may not always be so good. May I offer a personal example?

I have battled a chronic illness for about 30 years now. Though I can see now that I was predisposed to it from genetic and environmental factors, I was, nonetheless, an energetic, athletic, happy and relatively healthy teenager. I went where I wanted to go, ate what I wanted to eat, and pursued my education and goals with energy and enthusiasm. All that changed between my junior and senior years in college.

While I was working as a summer youth minister in Logansport, Indiana, lying in bed one night to go to sleep, I felt an odd sort of shooting pain. Sparing you the unsavory details, I was diagnosed with an infection and put on a broad-spectrum antibiotic. The antibiotic didn't set well. In fact, it made me sick: headache, sick stomach. So the doctor took me off that antibiotic and put me on another one. It didn't work either: excruciating headache, shaking . . . I was never the same. I was then treated with a series of on-again, off-again different types of antibiotics for the next year, and the odd thing was, the problems never got any better. In fact, they got worse. The headaches and stomach aches and an odd assortment of other symptoms increased and spread. I nearly had to drop out of my senior year of college, the symptoms and side-effects of the antibiotics were so bad.

Thus began a nearly 30-year battle with a chronic health condition that's sometimes called "Environmental Illness." It's called that because a person becomes "allergic" (intolerant or sensitive, depending on your definition of "allergy") to much of his or her environment. A dysfunctional and hyper immune system creates allergies of all sorts: to outdoor allergens, indoor chemicals and scents, even normal, everyday foods. It wasn't the original infection that caused all this for me, but the antibiotics. Actually, a side-effect of the antibiotics: Candida, a naturally occurring fungus that lives as a host in most of us. Problem is that—as yeasts and molds do—it grows by cell division exponentially and can over-colonize (a condition called candidiasis), and thus begin to take over a person's gastrointestinal flora and spread systemically to other parts of the body. This is what happened to me. As it proliferates in the gastrointestinal tract and the body as a whole, Candida begins to have toxic and chronic effects, feathering its own nest (so to speak) and producing a host of potential symptoms and conditions. It can cause chronic digestive problems; food, chemical, and environmental reactions ("allergies") of all sorts (the condition is sometimes called "Multiple Chemical Sensitivity" or MCS); and, if unchecked, the breakdown of other systems, like the endocrine system, responsible for the production of hormones and metabolism. Chronic fatigue is one of the most common results of this condition, as it was for me.

At one point in my battle, I was down to being able to eat only five foods that I knew of—I was allergic to everything else—and I ate those same foods every meal, every day (until one day, a knowledgeable doctor took those away from me, explaining that I was actually allergic to them too and they were the cause of some of my exhaustion). There were days when I could barely get out of bed by 9:00 a.m. and would then have to have a nap by 3 or 4 o'clock. I never felt good, and, as you might expect—a young father, trying to write my dissertation and lead a church—I began to be physically and emotionally drained. If it were not for finding a select group of physicians who knew about this condition (I saw many doctors far and wide), I might not be here today, and I certainly wouldn't have the quality of life that I do. By God's grace and a great, up and down,

Chapter 5

and lengthy struggle, I've been able to survive and over the last few years have had some major improvements through a serious and sustained treatment of the underlying fungus. After 25 or so years, I've actually begun to be able to eat out at a few restaurants again. You would not believe how good French fries are!

I tell you that story not to talk about myself or make you feel sorry for me, but to give an illustration of how something bad, even as bad as a serious illness, can come from something good. Antibiotics have saved hundreds and thousands of lives. They are great aids to humanity. But they can have deadly side-effects. And those side-effects can have side-effects. And the side-effects can be hidden.

This is precisely why the condition of inkblotitis is so dangerous. *Satan's best work is effective because the danger is hidden*; the temptation subtly masks the distortion that perverts the truth and causes illness and death. Evil loves to sneak its poison into otherwise good things. That's what makes them attractive and tempting. You know this. The greatest cause of inkblotitis is, therefore, not having the Bible or having it divided into chapters and verses—like fruit-bearing trees in the Garden of Eden, those are wonderful blessings. The greatest cause of inkblotitis is how we read and use the Bible. This is a critical part of the diagnostic picture.

We often read and understand verses of scripture outside of their original, book-level contexts. We do this because we don't read the whole books, because we don't know the whole books, and because we don't interpret the pieces as they relate to the whole books. This is inkblotitis. If we were not broken . . . if we were not confused . . . if we got along and all thought alike . . . if the Bible were written by a single individual in a single culture that we understood and shared, who used words and ideas the same . . . if the Spirit of God had not lived in the incarnate Christ and through his messengers inspired God's first conversations with us . . . if God revealed his will to us all personally and directly, then we wouldn't need the Bible, and we wouldn't need to understand it. It is a clear symptom of inkblotitis that we study, read, hear, and understand small pieces of the books of the Bible without sufficient knowledge of their book-level contexts to keep us from misunderstanding and misapplying those texts because of our subjective tendencies, beliefs, and attitudes.

Do you know how your favorite verses fit into the context of the book they are a part of? Do you know how they function to communicate the overall and primary messages of that book? Most people do not, and to the extent that Christians can't answer this question—The Question—this is the extent to which we have clear indications of inkblotitis. It's a form of biblical illiteracy. Like shattering a stained-glass window into thousands of shards, shattered contexts of divinely canvassed pictures produce subjectively motivated, widely-divergent interpretations of biblical texts. Imagine picking up a piece of paper that's been run through a shredder and trying to read and apply it.

Isn't it interesting that multiple shatterings in the history of the Bible evoke and promote individualism, disagreement, and division among people where friendship and love are of the essence of good and the very purposes of God in the world? Shattering and disintegration feed the fires of infection and illness. This should be no surprise to us, given the history and nature of evil. And—to be blunt—no matter how many ways we deny that we have a problem or postpone going to the doctor, it doesn't change the deep and systemic spread of Christianity's dangerous disease. Doing nothing promotes and hastens the disintegration of the Bible.

Chapter 5

Wounds to the Church

Where there's smoke, there's fire, and where there's fever, there's illness. Let's focus a little more specifically on the impact of inkblotitis on the church and then on us as individuals. These impacts or "wounds" could still be thought of as symptoms or outcomes of inkblotitis because they are damaging consequences of the disease.

As we've seen, the greatest effect upon the church may be division and the resulting consequences to the community and mission of Christ. Typically, division carries with it judgment and feelings of condemnation. People no longer call each other "friend" or "brother" and no longer join together in positive efforts to change and improve our world. We could look at many cases in point throughout the history of the church and within local communities. The process usually involves fighting, name-calling, and even violence at some level—certainly not the love and saving purposes of God in the world. In strong contrast, Jesus prayed that his followers would be one—as God and Christ are one—and thus represent God to the world. The splintering of Christendom through the ages has thus polluted our witness, undermined our mission, and drained our strength in the ongoing battles with the forces of evil. If I've learned anything in the course of my time here on planet earth, it's how much intense conflict consumes positive energy and replaces it with fear, distrust, and failure. When we fight about God and his word to us, we disagree at the deepest levels; when we disagree with spirits of self-righteousness and sectarianism, we do so with the most devastating consequences.

The shattering of the church has to be one of Satan's proudest accomplishments. To the extent the way we read and understand the Bible contributes to that end is the extent to which Satan has hidden monstrous evil in subtle crevices of some of our richest blessings. Typical! There ought to be a law. . . . The beautiful faces of masked evil stalk our gross disfigurement and ultimate destruction, however, and they pay no attention to law. We underestimate them to our peril.

With the dividing of the church into all sorts of denominations and sub-groups comes the explosion of individual preferences and personality tastes within each sub-group—supported, of course, by free access to scripture. Would it be overstating the case to say that some of the divisions in the church have come primarily from personal and/or personality differences? And on what basis does each claim the right to exist and separate from others? On the Bible, of course, often read—I would say—as Rorschach instructed. Is it just a coincidence that subjective, inkblot-like Bible reading goes to support divisions based on personality differences, when personal projection is the consistent and desired goal of contextless inkblots? I used to think that Christians were basically "better" people than non-Christians. That was before I was involved in some serious conflicts within churches. The fangs come out, as we come to appreciate the saying that Christians aren't perfect, just saved. If you ever find yourself in the middle of a church split, you might begin to wonder how some of us could even be saved. And ironically, that often becomes a fundamental issue of the division ("We are and you aren't"). In the fallout of such mission-subverting and life-consuming conflicts, the wound to the church is deep and bloody.

In addition to significant events in the history of the church, I think we can also see an effect of inkblotitis in some of our non-denominational and community churches today. Historically, one of the major outcomes of making the Bible available to us all and looking to scripture as the sole authority (in Protestant circles) has been the splintering of Christendom into many, many denominations. Over time, as these groups found meaning and identity in their particular forms of Christian beliefs, many denominational groups became more sectarian in spirit, producing more and more splinter groups with strict lines of "orthodoxy," pronouncing themselves the only ones who really know "the truth" and hence who will ultimately make it through the pearly gates. Naturally, this sort of sectarian spirit could not thrive forever in a world where people hunger and thirst for the life-giving grace of God in Christ. In a sort of counter-cultural reaction, therefore, different types of "non-denominational," "community" and "mission" churches began to emerge where the emphasis is not so much on the doctrines of the faith as on the practical and experiential. You may have heard the debates in some Christian circles over "felt-needs" ministry, where some who held strong to "sound doctrine" felt that important parts of what it means to be a Christian were being sacrificed on the altars of modernity and pragmatics. To some extent, we have repeated the historical cycle in which Pietism was born as a reaction to strict lines of confessional theology and slate liturgy. In both cases, new and—I would say—impactful expressions of Christian principles emerged in efforts to revive the heart of the message and mission. But that's not our topic at the moment.

What I want you to see now is how reading the Bible in small pieces thrives in our non-denominational, mega-church settings where the audience is made up of folks who have roots in many different denominations. Boring, traditional church drove a lot of people away; exciting and practical churches have brought many back. And think about how the collection or congregation is now different. Without a hard-nosed insistence from the pulpit about necessary sets of doctrine, and where the emphasis is often at the seeking or young-believer level of faith, many of these churches are now a sort of syncretistic amalgamation of Christian ideas, sometimes with a little New Age, post-modern, eastern religions, television-talk-show and dramatic series notions thrown in. I tend to use the phrase "pop theology" as an (admittedly poor) designation of the emerging eclecticism in Christian circles and literature. Like the alarmingly mindless responses we often see in street (walking) interviews—a popular form of checking the pulse of the people on topics and issues these days—we now have a growing form of biblical illiteracy in our culture and our churches that relies on inkblotitis as its primary or only method of exposure to the Bible. Though obviously not its only cause, I believe this popular amalgam of diffuse and often superficial Christian knowledge in some of our churches today is symptomatic of the way we read and use the Bible.

There are other negative impacts upon the church at large that we could talk about, but the ones we've touched on are probably enough to underscore the severity of the problem. Inkblotitis has negatively impacted the community, the teachings, and the mission of the church. When you think about it, that's a pretty big slice of what the church is, isn't it? especially when we compare the current conditions to the Church as envisioned in scripture—the strong, healthy, united, and growing body and bride of Christ. Have you ever had to go to work or school when you were sick? Maybe with fever? Have you ever tried to participate in sports competition when you really weren't feeling all that well? You probably didn't think and do your best. The church's battle with evil, its call to contrast and change the world, its mission to take the saving and healing love of Jesus Christ to a confused and dying world is much tougher than any football game or day job. Is it any wonder that our churches sometimes seem ineffective and weak in our communities and for our purposes? The church has a fever, and the fever burns us with debilitating weakness. Because it's been with us for some time now, we could call it the chronic fatigue of the church. And I—perhaps like you—can relate to how hard it is to do good things with enthusiasm and strength when you are chronically fatigued.

Chapter 5

Wounds to the Person

What are the effects of inkblotitis on us as individuals? In other words, how do I know if I've been infected, and what harm can the illness do? Probably the easiest test is to look at when and how you read the Bible. It's a symptom of inkblotitis to be exposed to the Bible often and/or only in pieces. Of itself, that's not necessarily a problem. A verse of scripture is not a virus. So please don't think I don't like verses of scripture. Exposure to the Bible in small pieces is just the first step, and it's *only a* step if you don't hear that verse as it fits into its bigger-picture context. Bible verses were—for the most part—never meant to be isolated sayings or moral aphorisms; they exist as part of a written document that presents a detailed snapshot of some aspect(s) of the kingdom of God. Think of Bible books as beautiful landscape paintings or pictures, but with clear scenes; or now—since we've put in all the verse perforations—as puzzles. It's symptomatic of inkblotitis if when you hear or read a verse of scripture, you do not have enough knowledge of the wider picture to see that verse as it contributes to and fits in to the context of that bigger picture. One way then to know if you have symptoms of inkblotitis is to ask yourself The Question: How does this verse fit and function in its book-level context? If you have little or no idea, that's when hearing and reading the Bible in pieces is a sign of inkblotitis.

Missing God's Point

Given this definition of inkblotitis, I suspect that most all of us have it to some degree. We probably will admit that. The question then becomes *what impact or effects does it have on us spiritually*. Does it really make a difference? Does it matter? To some extent, we won't be able to answer this question until we've spent some time reading the Bible in a different way—book by book—and learning to see the pieces as part of their collected wholes. In some cases, it won't make a lot of difference in how we understand a given verse or passage of scripture. But in other cases, it will. After some time working in the

Bible this way (with a SABR: Sequential/Summit Access Bible Reading)—reading the Bible as books—I believe you'll see the difference, and you'll be in a better position to get God's point (pun intended). The sharp point of God's sword destroys evil. Since evil lives inside us—sort of like killing cancer—the word of God has a destroying effect as part of its healing power. That's why the call of Jesus is a call to a type of self-destruction—self-sacrifice, self-denial, giving up our lives, picking up our crosses . . . The sharp point of God's sword also brings healing and life in the place of disease and death. So the question becomes the benefits of having free access to the sword of the Spirit versus the consequences of trying to fight the enemy with a dull or sheaved sword.

Majoring in the Minors

Not only does reading the Bible in context make a difference in how we understand individual verses, but it makes a profound difference on what things we see as God's most important messages to us. If my Bible reading focuses only on the individual trees that make up the forest, how will I ever see the magnificence, beauty, and overall design of the forest as a whole? Pieces of bark are important, but spending my life as a tree-bark expert prevents me from seeing and doing a lot of other things, and if my goal is not only to see the forest but to know its Creator, then tunnel-vision (verse-level) Bible reading has serious consequences. I believe one of the consequences of reading the Bible in small pieces for us as communities and as individuals is the danger of reinforcing limited, myopic, sometimes even microscopic viewpoints of God and his purposes. This can result in a legalistic or Pharisaic sort of majoring in the minors, when God has bigger plans and purposes for our lives. To some of the religious leaders of his day, Jesus said, "You strain out a gnat but swallow a camel"; ". . . you have neglected the more important matters of the law" (Matthew 23). Similarly, one of the dangers of reading the Bible in pieces is the potential of such isolated verses to enable us to put our spiritual emphases in the wrong places. You've heard the old joke about putting the emPHAsis on the wrong sylLAble? What happens when we do that with God's purposes? Is the language still intelligible as God's word? Inviting us to major in the minors, inkblotitis thus opens a dangerous path to legalism and sectarianism.

The Word of Me

Another, perhaps more fundamental, effect of inkblotitis for us as individuals comes from the center of our purposes for reading the Bible. We read the Bible to encounter God, to know him and be changed by that experience, do we not? Most of us want to hear and read the Bible to seek God. This is why turning the Bible into a pile of Rorschach-like inkblots has an almost humorous—if it weren't so serious—ironic effect. Remember, the purpose of an inkblot is to evoke that which belongs to the interpreter. It's to highlight *me*. And what is our purpose for reading the Bible? It's the opposite.

Believing, as we do, that as fallen, sinful individuals we each need to be saved, we turn to the Bible to hear from God the word (that is, message) that can save us and cause us to grow as followers. That word is God's truth, spoken over and to us, for those purposes. It was made human in Jesus Christ, passed on to the apostles and early followers of Jesus through the Spirit (that is, to the church), and then to us (the church) through the scriptures. If the church and its scriptures cannot communicate God's saving word to us, then we are lost. But it can and does. And one of the very first, most fundamental things it says to us is that we cannot save ourselves. We don't know the answers to life's most basic questions. If we would know the truth and be saved, if we would have our minds renewed and hearts restored, we must look outside of ourselves for that saving word. This is one of the most basic truths that non-believers do not yet see and many in the church seem to forget or ignore. The first step of turning to God—of conversion, of salvation, of life—is admitting that I do not know the answers. I do not know how to make life work. I do not know how to overcome the confusion, remove the guilt and shame, resolve the conflict, stop the pain, and restore hope and life. In me is death. *To find life, I must look outside of myself; I must see beyond me.* This is first and ongoing for those who seek God.

A serious wounding of inkblotitis is that we don't find the self-destroying, life-returning experiences that we seek and need when we approach God in the Bible. Reading the Bible in pieces, disconnected from the knowledge of the Holy Spirit-inspired contexts, turns that which was intended to speak the word of God to us into miniature vacuums that seek—should we say "suck out"—the world and word of me. Contextless scriptures draw or "suck" their contexts from my brain, that is, from my world, thoughts, emotions, confusions, illusions, etc.; and when I start with me, all I can hope to get is me. To the extent that my world has been changed and conditioned by God's inspired word, to the extent that it connects with the Holy Spirit living in me, this is not inherently destructive. Where I am good and things are in order, reinforcing that is not harmful. (The assumption is that that part of me has already been revived and replaced with God's Spirit.) To the extent that my word and world needs changing, however . . . to the extent that I have not arrived and the scripture I'm hearing could speak to my unhealthy condition, am I not guilty of the most basic sin? Am I not putting myself in the place of God? To speak *for* God instead of hearing *from* God; reinforcement of me in the place of revelation of God: such an enormously ironic and tragic potential impels me to be amazed at how insidiously shrewd our enemy is.

Inkblotitis is dangerous if it allows us as readers and hearers to miss God's word because of what we already think we know. ("The head of the fox," as Rorschach said, is hard to get rid of.) Don't we see this effect when people on two sides of a theological issue banish each other to the otter regions of "friendship" in Christ (or hell, to be more in tune with the emotions of the fight)? Don't we see it in us as individuals when we struggle and struggle with personal issues, weaknesses and sins—sins that never seem to get any better throughout the courses of our lives? *The ultimate, destructive effect of inkblotitis, why inkblotitis is Christianity's dangerous disease, is that it functions as a hidden, even subconscious, diversionary tactic of the enemy to encourage me to listen to myself instead of hearing from God—all the while allowing me to think I am listening to God.* Maybe I am; and maybe I'm not. The difference is too important to ignore.

The Sword in a Stone

This is what I mean when I talk about spiritual narcissism. It's not a blatant or obvious thing, usually. It's hidden—at least until it's threatened or attacked—and that's why it's so dangerous. The Bible uses the image of "eyes that don't see and ears that don't hear" to portray this condition at its worst: "hard hearts" (Isaiah 6:9-10; Matthew 13:13-15; Mark 4:10-13, 8:14-21; Luke 8:9-10; John 12:36-41). These images, based in the Old Testament book of Isaiah, occur at critical points in Mark's Gospel in raising the question of what kind of soil are the disciples. Understanding the word of God communicated in parables depends on it (Mark 4:1-34). And this brings us to a very important point. Properly hearing and understanding the word of God is not a given. If it were, perhaps no one would remain confused or lost. Throughout Matthew 23, a chapter that highlights the confrontation between Jesus and the religious leaders of his day (as part of Matthew's presentation of Jesus as the Messiah, the ultimate fulfillment and culmination of the Old Testament/the Law of Moses), Jesus refers to the religious leaders as "hypocrites," "blind guides," and "blind fools": ". . . For you cross sea and land to make a single convert, and you make the new convert twice as much a child of hell as yourselves" (Matthew 23:15). How do those who sit in the seats of religious and spiritual leadership become "blind guides"? How can such guides and those they instruct become children of hell? Scary, isn't it?

The blindness comes from the heart, but scripture can be used to protect it or even feed it, instead of healing it. When Jesus was tempted in the desert, he used quotations of scripture to counter the allurements of Satan (actually, he used an understanding and embracing of their meaning—not a mere recitation of words—and the verses point back to the basics of what it meant for God's people to be sons and daughters of God). Just as the apostle Paul pictures the word of God as "the sword of the Spirit" (Ephesians 6:17) in a fully-armored and embattled spiritual soldier, so Jesus properly understood and used scripture in his conflict with evil. But—and here's the scary part—so did Satan, use scripture, that is. "For it is written . . .," Satan said, in presenting one of the temptations, also quoting verses of scripture, which suggests, that pieces of the Bible can certainly be misunderstood and misused for destructive purposes. Perhaps you've heard the expression, "the devil quotes scripture."

As part of a strong exhortation to patience and tenacity in the faith, 2 Peter 3:14-18 includes some troubling thoughts in its concluding, powerful exhortation:

> Therefore, beloved, while you are waiting for these things, strive to be found by him at peace, without spot or blemish; and regard the patience of our Lord as salvation. So also our beloved brother Paul wrote to you according to the wisdom given to him, speaking of this in all his letters. There are some things in them hard to understand, which the ignorant and unstable twist to their own destruction, as they do the other scriptures. You therefore, beloved, since you are forewarned, beware that you are not carried away with the error of the lawless and lose your own stability. But grow in the grace and knowledge of our Lord and Savior Jesus Christ. To him be the glory both now and to the day of eternity. Amen.

Twisting scripture to one's own destruction is not a new idea. And do you suppose these folks did it intentionally or even consciously?

Properly understood and applied, scripture is the sword of the Spirit because it is the word of God—what God says. When it is misunderstood or improperly applied, it ceases to be the word of God and can actually become a tool—a sword—of Satan. The Bible and pieces of the Bible can thus become a weapon—a weapon of spiritual warfare used for all sorts of destructive purposes. Scripture is indeed a weapon, either way you look at it—a double-sided, laser-sharp sword, as Hebrews graphically portrays the significance of what God has spoken to us (long ago and in these days by his Son):

Chapter 5

"Indeed, the word of God is living and active, sharper than any two-edged sword, piercing until it divides soul from spirit, joints from marrow; it is able to judge the thoughts and intentions of the heart" (4:12-13). We've seen how an inkblot Bible sometimes functions as a destructive weapon in the church; our focus now is on how this is also true in our personal, spiritual development.

If inkblots are the only way we get the Bible, then they have the potential to take away the word of God, which is the sword of the Spirit. In the specific examples of Jesus' temptations, he used the word of God to defeat Satan in each instance. Without the word, we are left defenseless against the illusions and lies of the enemy. Can you see why the allurements of the flesh and the constant bombardment of our culture with all sorts of distortions about where and how to find life are so compelling? Hearing and knowing the Bible only in pieces creates a form of biblical illiteracy that threatens to remove the word of God from the land, and, more to the point, from our hearts and minds (even if they are easier to remember because they are short). The very personal, bloody battles with evil in which we must all engage become more and more dangerous to us in the absence of the word of God. To use a very inadequate, trivial illustration, it's worse than trying to fight Darth Vader without the Force. The sword of Satan is too dark and too powerful for us to stand against without the sword of the Spirit. One result of inkblotitis for us as individuals, then, is a new sort of biblical illiteracy that—if I may be crude for the point of emphasis—castrates us in our personal battles with evil and sin. It's as if our sword is sheaved or, even worse, stuck deep in the heart of a very personal stone.

Spiritual Narcissism

Ironically and tragically the Bible can function as a weapon of the enemy in a much more subtle, yet equally dangerous way. This brings us back to the concept of spiritual narcissism. Inkblotitis can be a subtle and sanitized form of narcissism. Spiritual blindness or hard-heartedness is, in essence, a sort of inability to get any better, at least by itself. This was the problem with some of the Pharisees and can be for any leader who leads his or her people based on misunderstanding and misuse of the Bible that flows from some deeply hidden, ulterior motives—love of power, popularity and prestige, ego, money, family, etc. But—and this is the frightening part—as we see in Mark's story of the disciples, as we see all over the Bible, and as we see all around us, it's not limited to religious leaders. Leaders bear the greatest responsibility when it comes to how we handle the Bible because they are responsible for those who listen to them and imitate them. But what about us as individuals? What about you? What about me? Most all of us have free access to the Bible, and we will all ultimately stand before God as individuals. So, in a real sense, we can't pass the buck.

And—back to the frightening part—we can see the spiritual swelling that leads to blindness and hard-heartedness duplicated in small, subtle ways whenever our previously formed opinions prevent us from hearing and understanding the word of God given to us in scripture. This is the toxic danger of inkblotitis. It allows the words of scripture to function like inkblots that evoke and reinforce what one already thinks and believes—because that's the nature of an inkblot. Remember its purpose—to illuminate and uphold me. Like small, hand-held mirrors, disconnected, contextless verses of the Bible can thus—when I understand them based on my own subjective, self-protective personal context—become, not the word of God to change, heal, and protect me, but the tool of evil to quietly and subtly seduce me to be me—to see what I see, to think what I think, to be what I am. Or . . . more passively, to *let* me be me. "After all, I'm not so bad. I'm not sure I need to change all that much, anyway. Maybe you do." The more I look, the more I tend to like what I see. And like Narcissus, who fell in love with his own reflection, the sword of the Spirit melts away in the fires of deeply wounded self-love (which is actually more vacancy and need than love). After all, who really wants to change or be changed? Who wants to be destroyed? Is that really the only way to life? Like the ring in *The Lord of the Rings*, the self-projecting echo clouds everything else and holds us captivated. Again, how satanically ironic that the freedom of the

Bible has led to new forms of spiritual tyranny and enslavement! The tyranny of the individual (a new form of traditionalism), or better perhaps, the tyranny of the self—which equals the most basic sin—is the ultimate potential of inkblotitis.

Full-blown inkblotitis is like the hard soil in the Parable of the Sower. (Younger versions facilitate rocky or thorny soil.) It's a point where all we can see or want to see comes sneakily from inside us, such that nothing really new can penetrate and take root. We become the final authority. "I" become the final authority—and I have my scriptures to prove it. How tragic to attempt to look into the face of God and see only my own reflection.

Conclusion

Diagnosis

When we examine the patient carefully, I believe there is sufficient evidence for a clear diagnosis. It starts with Jesus as the incarnate Word of God, the new humanity, then with the Church as the continuation of God's presence in the world and its mission of reflecting and extending the saving love of God in Christ. The Spirit that was in Christ was given to the Church. The same Spirit inspired the apostles and early followers of Jesus to produce written accounts of God's actions/desires targeted to various situations and needs in the early church. So revered were these books that they were collected, preserved, copied by hand, and translated into many languages (we esteem our oldest copies as invaluable treasures). Over time, the church collected the books believed to be inspired by God into a single book called the Bible. Just as the books of the Old/First Testament were for the Jews, the books of the Second/New Testament, in combination with the First, became the sacred, guiding book of Christianity.

The removal of the writings from their original historical contexts, culminating in the collecting of the books into a single book, could be seen as the very first step toward our present condition; though, of course, this was necessary if we—the church as a whole—were to have copies of them. *When the books became a book*—though very natural and, I believe, providential—we have the first, small step toward a climate that could lead to inkblotitis. When the books became a book, landscape-changing seeds were planted—seeds that carry the potential for new life and have brought salvation to many, but also that contain a hook which the evil one baits with a subtle but deadly temptation: to use pieces of scripture for unintended purposes.

So valuable are the contents of our book that we organized and carefully divided them into chapters and verses—a wonderful help, but a second step toward illness. Just as having copies of the Holy Spirit-inspired books is not a bad thing—how could it be?—

Chapter 5

neither are the chapters and verses. Like shaking hands with a congenial and well-intentioned but coughing friend, however, they are a means to exposure. *When the books were divided*, the isolation of verses became easy.

For most of the church's history, the Bible had been accessible only to the "professionals," and, though there were problems and serious abuses, the results of Bible reading were controlled by those who had access and the institutions for which they worked. Such control obviously resulted in the potential for Christians to be misled in mass, if the teacher had not done his own homework, or worse, intentionally distorted the message. (I referred to this earlier as the tyranny of the institution.) The people had no real recourse. This changed dramatically when the Bible was made available to everyone through the sacrificial work of reformers and translators, and, of course, through the invention of the printing press. *When the books became available*, we all became interpreters. Step one: collected books. Step two: divided books. Step three: published and freely accessible book.

Along with free access to the scriptures came the idea that everyone has the right and responsibility to read and interpret the Bible for oneself—one of the driving forces of the Protestant Reformation. Combine this with the emphases in modern culture that everything is relative and all meaning is subjective, and—more importantly—with the very personal, experiential, emotional, and even mystical thrusts of Pietism and other influences within Christianity today, and I think we can add to our unfolding journey ideas that promote free and personal interpretations of scripture. Step four: individual, personalized interpretations. Everyone has an opinion, or in the "immortal" words of small group leaders: "What does this mean to you?"

Given these prerequisites, is it any wonder that we've witnessed the shattering of the Bible? And, thus, we have to add the many ways that we've come to read and use the Bible in pieces, far removed from their original book-level contexts as one of the primary expressions of what came to be the rapidly advancing condition

Diagnosis: Inkblotitis

of inkblotitis. Step five: shattered contexts, or, as we've been calling it: Random Access Bible Reading—the disintegration of the Bible.

Finally, to put it all together briefly: *when the books became verses, we thereby redefined the Bible.* And now, for us as sufferers of inkblotitis, replacing the books of God with verses from the Bible, in effect, changes the word of God. I do not know anything more dangerous than that.

Let's also summarize some of the effects. Is it just a coincidence that when the Bible was given to all of us, with the conditions described above, that we've also witnessed the shattering of the church (of course, on the human side)? That's not to say that the religious freedoms and access to the Bible we share are not welcomed blessings. It's merely to point out the effect of a dissected, personalized Bible. It's also not to say that inkblotitis is the sole cause of division in the church. It's simply—in the spirit of examining the patient—observing the likely relationship between the two. New forms of eclectic amalgams of popular Christian theology are also forming in some of our largest and, in some cases, most effective churches (practically and socially). A general lack of Bible knowledge as a corollary to reading the Bible in pieces now threatens to accelerate the disintegration of the Bible that inkblotitis represents. And the loss of that knowledge is the weakening not only of the church, but of the Christian, as we stand to lose our greatest offensive weapon in our personal battles with evil. From our deepest wounds, then, Satan uses isolated portions of scripture to draw us into a subtle, self-protective and self-promoting defensiveness that sees in scripture a reflection of what we already are instead of the soul-changing image of the Creator.

There are other symptoms and effects of reading the Bible in disconnected pieces. But I think we've seen enough to come to a conclusion. It's the reason I'm writing this book. It's a serious condition. When we put the x-ray in front of the light, the picture is frightening.

A divided and dysfunctional church. Splintered local communities over, or supported by, interpretations of scripture. Distracted purposes: focus on lesser, sometimes group-identifying, features of the Christian faith. A weakened witness and model to the world. Lives that don't change. A freely available Bible: "Bibles, Bibles everywhere . . ." The shattering of the Bible into thousands of disconnected pieces: ". . . Nor any drop to drink." Reading the Bible in ways that highlight momentary experiences and personal impressions. A culture that promotes subjectivity and instant gratification. A religious climate that accentuates the personal, emotional, and even mystical as the most "spiritual." Pastors and teachers that rely on and constantly model inkblot use of the Bible. A form of biblical illiteracy that prevents us from seeing verses as part of their book-level wholes. The Bible as inkblots.

Diagnosis: . . . Inkblotitis—a serious and hidden condition of the church.

Prognosis

So what can we do? Anything? What is the prognosis?

Because of the depth and width of the infection in our culture and our habits, the prognosis could be bleak, but that's not the kind of God we know and serve. Without treatment, the condition of inkblotitis will continue to be debilitating, at best, for the church and for each of us personally, and the only cure is the resurrecting and healing power of the Holy Spirit. But, as in all things relating to human freedom and divine grace, God, amazingly and lovingly, invites and expects us to participate in the process. We participate by receiving the word of God revealed to us through scripture—simple as that. If inkblotitis is caused by the way we read and respond to the life-giving word of God spoken to us in scripture, then the treatment can only be a change in the way we read the Bible. Change—a change of heart—is always the first step in coming to God; not change that instantly enables us to do all the right things and be all that we're supposed to be instantly, but simply a change of mind that affects how we respond to God. *Responding to God starts with listening to him.* The change we need, then, is a change of heart that chooses to listen again, a sort of cleaning out of the ears, by deciding not to interrupt

God as he speaks to us or cut up his messages into disconnected sound-bites that may no longer carry the soul-shaking, sin-confronting, path-blazing, life-enriching power they once did. Because we live our lives under constant time-constraints, stresses, and pressures and are such creatures of habit, the treatment must be serious to be effective. For the church, the treatment for inkblotitis is no less than *a revolution in Bible reading.*

Finally, I believe that inkblotitis has produced a condition of biblical illiteracy in our world; or perhaps, more accurately, inkblotitis *is* biblical illiteracy. The antidote to inkblotitis, then, is a call to biblical literacy. As such, it's a new way to read the Bible. But it's really not. It's really a call to get as close to the experience and power of God's first conversations with us that we possibly can—and that's not new. But it is so distant and uncommon as to be new to many. Our treatment then is a journey back to the moments God first spoke to us. Isn't that exciting? Like going on a treasure hunt, and the treasure is greater than any ever discovered: the presence and power of new life. Think of being a fly on the wall when God showed up. But no, it's much more. Because the words are written for us too, we get to participate in that moment. And that's the secret. Not *my* moment—here, now—disconnected from that moment. But *God's* moment in history that—through the abiding work of the Holy Spirit—*becomes* my moment. The word of God to me is the same as it was to them. The impact may be different and personalized, but the soul of the message is the same. If your quest is the face of God and the impact that will have on you, then my challenge to you is to be drawn to him by the power of his word revealed to us in the Bible.

So—to take us back where we started the chapter—what is inkblotitis? Craftier than any fox, Satan uses every form of deceit and trickery to destroy us—the subtler, the better: "The head of the fox" shows up where we least expect it. Can you believe we often find it in the Bible? And once there, it's hard to get rid of.

Chapter 5: Diagnosis: Inkblotitis

Chapter Resources

Arthur, Kay. *How to Study Your Bible: The Lasting Rewards of the Inductive Method.* Eugene, OR: Harvest House, 1994.

Discover the Bible for Yourself. Eugene, OR: Harvest House, 2000.

Lord Teach Me to Study the Bible in 28 Days. Eugene, OR: Harvest House, 2006.

Daniell, David. *The Bible in English: Its History and Influence.* London: Yale University, 2003.

Fee, Gordon D., and Stuart, Douglas. *How to Read the Bible for All It's Worth.* 3rd ed. Grand Rapids: Zondervan, 2003.

How to Read the Bible Book by Book: A Guided Tour. Grand Rapids: Zondervan, 2002.

Murray, Stuart. "Biblical Interpretation among the Anabaptist Reformers." In *A History of Biblical Interpretation: The Medieval through the Reformation Periods*, pp. 403-427. Edited by Alan J. Hauser and Duane F. Watson. Grand Rapids: Eerdmans, 2009.

Rorschach, Hermann. *Psychodiagnostics—A Diagnostic Text Based on Perception.* 3rd edition. Translated by Paul Lemkau and Bernard Kronenberg. New York: Grune & Stratton, 1942.

Wrede, William. *The Messianic Secret.* Translated by. J. C. G. Grieg. Cambridge: James Clarke & Co., 1971; German edition: *Das Messiasgeheimnis in den Evangelien: Zugleich ein Beitrag zum Verständnis des Markusevangeliums*, Göttingen: Vandenhoeck & Ruprecht, 1901.

Notes

1. Rorschach, *Psychodiagnostics*, 16.
2. In his discussion of "Biblical Interpretation among the Anabaptist Reformers" (409), Stuart Murray offers this brief critique of Reformation era interpretation: ". . . if Reformers interpreted Scripture in accordance with preconceived *doctrinal* convictions, Anabaptists interpreted Scripture in accordance with preconceived convictions of *their own*." The difference has to do with who was reading/interpreting the Bible and why, but the subjective potential is obvious and is illustrated by both leaders and lay readers alike.
3. This is why the work of Gordon Fee and Douglas Stuart (*How to Read the Bible for All It's Worth* and *How to Read the Bible Book by Book: A Guided Tour*), and Kay Arthur's (see chapter sources for some examples of her work) inductive, book by book emphases are so important.
4. In his history of the English Bible, Daniell (*The Bible in English*, 127-128) provides a nice summary of what he describes as seven concerns of the Reformers, working in various countries, with the new-found authority of scripture (implied in Luther's *Sola Scriptura*): (1) confirmation of the canon, (2) establishment of the text, (3) inspiration of the Bible, (4) questions of exegesis, (5) translation of the Bible into vernacular languages, (6) circulation of well-printed Bibles, and (7) circulation of aids to Bible study. These emphases have continued in the translation, distribution, and use of the Bible, giving another angle on "the history" that brought us to the present condition of Bible reading in the church. In other words, when this was accomplished—when the Bible was freely available to the people, along with an ever-growing mountain of Bible study tools—what then?
5. McGrath, *Christianity's Dangerous Idea*, 2.
6. Wrede, *The Messianic Secret*, 6.

Chapter 6

Classic Inkblots

While doing a little after-Christmas shopping this year, I ran across a Hallmark gift book called *100 Favorite Bible Verses*. It was really quite nice—leather bound (well, at least imitation leather)—and the verses were indeed some of the most touching and powerful verses of scripture. I was tempted to buy it—not for reading and understanding the verses, but for being reminded of their encouraging power and meaning, and, of course, as great examples of inkblotitis.

Like pieces of a taken-apart puzzle, a verse or small set of verses is the normal and even the only way some are exposed to the content of the Bible. Preachers fragment the Bible and teach us how to do it by the way they deliver sermons. In fact—and please don't throw the book at me for saying this—preachers are to a large extent the primary carrier or infecting agent of inkblotitis in the churches. From one stage and pulpit to another, from Sunday to Sunday, pastors and teachers do what I call inkblot preaching/teaching. Contrarily, I believe an important responsibility of teachers in the church is to help the people under their care hear and know how to hear the voice of God most clearly. We should, therefore, model and teach effective Bible reading. And—in hopes of turning this into something positive—preachers and teachers will be a major part of the treatment program for Christianity's dangerous disease; if, indeed, we recognize and are willing to treat the condition.

In the long history of reading and interpreting the Bible and as a part of inkblot preaching, some verses of scripture have been taken out of their original, book-level contexts and highlighted so often as to become well-known, even among folks who don't read or know much about the Bible. Whether quoted in a speech, mailed in a greeting-card, or held up on a sign behind the goal posts at a football game, these are some of the most frequently dislodged scriptures.

Chapter 6

Almost any verse of scripture can be turned into an inkblot. The best way to see how this happens and the real difference it can make in how we understand a verse or set of verses is to read and study a Bible book in its entirety. With that big-picture framework, it's then relatively easy to see how a verse fits and functions—and thus speaks—in its book-level context. We'll take some extended time to examine some verses in context in our "how to" chapters at the end of the second half of our study. To give you a foretaste of this and an idea of the real significance inkblotitis can make in the way we read scripture, and as a sort of introduction to a better way of reading the Bible, I'd like to explore briefly a few common Bible-verse inkblots (or "verse-blots"). We could choose many examples, and we certainly can't look at all "100 Favorite Bible Verses"; but the following rank as some of the Bible's classic inkblots.

Preview

- No eye has seen, no ear has heard . . . (1 Corinthians 2:9)
- Love is patient; love is kind. . . . (1 Corinthians 13:4-7)
- Ask and I'll give the nations to you . . . (from Psalm 2:7-8)
- I know the plans I have for you . . . (Jeremiah 29:11)
- . . . far more than all we can ask or imagine . . . (Ephesians 3:14-21)
- For everything there is a season . . . (Ecclesiastes 3:1-8)
- Others
    - I can do all things through Christ . . . (Philippians 4:8)
    - . . . all things work together for good . . . (Romans 8:28)
    - This is the day that the Lord has made . . . (Psalm 118:24)
    - Parables of Jesus (most of them)
    - For God so loved the world . . . (John 3:16)

1 Corinthians 2:9
"Eye hath not seen, nor ear heard . . ."

But as it is written,
 "Eye hath not seen,
 nor ear heard,
 neither have entered into the heart of man,
  the things which God hath prepared
  for them that love him" (KJV).

I have a bookmark with these words printed on it: "No eye has seen, nor ear heard, nor the heart of man conceived, what God has prepared for those who love Him" (1 Corinthians 2:9). While driving home from work one afternoon, I heard a popular radio talk show host make some comments about this passage. I forget the exact context of his discussion, but the point he was making had to do with how wonderful heaven was going to be, of how much we had to look forward to, that we could live our lives with anticipation of what was to come. He used 1 Corinthians 2:9 to make his point: "Eye hath not seen . . ." I certainly agreed with his point, but not so much with the way he made it. The book of Revelation would be a great place to go to find this idea, or even later in 1 Corinthians, where in chapter 15 Paul talks about what's going to happen to our mortal bodies. But 1 Corinthians 2:9-10 actually has a different focus.

First of all, the words here are a citation, most likely from the Old Testament book of Isaiah. In a passage expressing great desire that the Lord God would come down and display his awesome presence once again, Isaiah references great times in the past when God descended upon the mountain and the mountain quaked at his presence. God himself had been with his people; he protected and led Israel. "From ages past no one has heard, no ear has perceived, no eye has seen any God besides you, who works for those who wait for him" (Isaiah 64:4). Isaiah laments the loss of the holy presence of God from among the people because of their sin and longs for his return and salvation. God's judgment is coming, but with the promise

Chapter 6

that he will bring back a remnant of his people to find his grace and presence once again. "For I am about to create new heavens and a new earth; the former things shall not be remembered or come to mind. But be glad and rejoice forever in what I am creating . . ." (Isaiah 65:17-18). Whatever Paul means in 1 Corinthians reminds him of this context and these promises.

The context in 1 Corinthians provides a framework that shapes the meaning of this potential inkblot. The immediate context presents the idea that the message of the cross is foolishness to those outside of God, but the wisdom and power of God to those being saved. This wisdom of God is baffling and indiscernible by humans on their own. It's not mighty and compelling to those outside of God who think they're important and smart: "For since, in the wisdom of God, the world did not know God through wisdom, God decided, through the foolishness of our proclamation, to save those who believe" (1:21). Ironically (to us), God chose small, "foolish," and weak things to accomplish his powerful work of true wisdom and salvation. The makeup of the Corinthian church illustrates this—not many wise by human standards, powerful, or of royal or noble birth were called—as does Paul himself. When he came to them as a missionary, he didn't speak with eloquent or sophisticated words, but simply presented to them the message of "Jesus Christ, and him crucified" (2:2). "My speech and proclamation were not with plausible words of wisdom, but with a demonstration of the Spirit and of power, so that your faith might rest not on human wisdom but on the power of God" (2:5).

The message of God is, however, wisdom and power that goes beyond human reasoning. Those who have come to know God in Christ, those who have God's Spirit—the "mature" (2:6)—possess a new sort of deeper and true wisdom from God. Now, position 1 Corinthians 2:9 in this flow of thought:

> But we speak God's wisdom, secret and hidden, which God decreed before the ages for our glory. None of the rulers of this age understood this; for if they had, they would not have crucified the Lord of glory. But, as it is written, "What no eye

has seen, nor ear heard, nor the human heart conceived, what God has prepared for those who love him"—these things God has revealed to us through the Spirit; for the Spirit searches everything, even the depths of God. . . . (2:7-10).

Our passage, then, has to do with the amazing depth of wisdom and power available to us through the Spirit of God in Christ. It's not directly or primarily—if at all—talking about heaven (though I suppose you could say heaven is included). Paul possesses that Spirit and is able, therefore, to help the Corinthians understand the amazing blessings they have in Christ: "Now we have received not the spirit of the world, but the Spirit that is from God, so that we may understand the gifts bestowed on us by God." This moves us back into the broader, book-level context (zooming out) where Paul seeks to help the Corinthian church deal with issues of conflict and division over the prevalence and use of spiritual gifts. The gifts and revelation of God's Spirit remind Paul of the promises from Isaiah, as the church experiences the return of God's presence, the new creation, and the giving of the Holy Spirit in a very special way. The Corinthian Christians aren't dealing with it very well at the moment, but there is hope for a brighter future because these things are God's things, prepared for those who "love" him (2:9), and—as we learn in chapter 13—"love is patient; love is kind. . . ."

We certainly look forward to the ultimate completion of the things no eye has seen or ear heard that God has prepared for those who love him at the end of our journey, but the point of 1 Corinthians 2:9 has more to do with the incredible gifts of God's presence among his people now—things that human wisdom could never conceive, create, or experience. Isn't it interesting how taking this verse out of its immediate and book-level contexts has the potential to turn this passage about the power of God available to us now on its head—into a forecast of the future? Inkblots are like that. I want the future, but I also want to experience fully what God has for his people in the church. One of those things is love; thus we turn to "the love chapter."

Chapter 6

1 Corinthians 13:4-7
"Love is patient; love is kind...."

A frequently quoted piece of scripture that's probably used in more weddings than any other comes from the same letter: 1 Corinthians 13:4-7:

> Love is patient, love is kind. It does not envy, it does not boast, it is not proud. It does not dishonor others, it is not self-seeking, it is not easily angered, it keeps no record of wrongs. Love does not delight in evil but rejoices with the truth. It always protects, always trusts, always hopes, always perseveres. Love never fails (NIV).

As a depiction or definition of love, these poetic and powerful words of the apostle Paul have been expounded in many sermons, pledged at many weddings, posted on many refrigerators, printed or stitched in frames and displayed on many walls. They are a transcendent expression of the nature of true love, providing a marvelous standard to which we can all aspire.

Because this passage gives such a beautiful description of the universal concept of love, these verses can have a positive impact in almost any set of circumstances where someone desires to know and act in love. In other words, they fit almost anywhere. As I've said, some verses and sets of verses from the Bible stand on their own and reveal truths of God as independent units. Anyone who acts with patience, kindness, contentment, humility, etc., acts like God, and God is love.

On the other hand, are there other ways that love could be described and defined? Are there other traits that might be emphasized? Why these particular characteristics? They're certainly not the only traits of real love. What about "love sacrifices" or "seeks and pursues the object of its affection"? Of course, there are other possibilities, and these questions are really another way of asking The Question. If we answer The Question—what role do these verses play in the primary message(s) of the book?—I suspect we will have answered these questions as well.

1 Corinthians 13:4-7 provides a good example of our need to learn to zoom in and out as we read the Bible (as when working with online maps). One click out gives us the rest of chapter 13. Verses 1-3 contrasts several abilities—special spiritual abilities—with love. Speaking in (Spirit-gifted) human and angelic languages, envisioning great mysteries and all knowledge, moving mountains by faith, giving all one's money for the poor or even one's life to the flames of martyrdom—you can do any or all of these kinds of lofty spiritual acts, Paul says, but if you don't have love, they are nothing. To be valid, Spirit-gifted actions must flow from a spring of love; otherwise, they're not really what they appear to be.

From this chapter-level view, the tension between acting with and without love gives us a hint as to what was needed in the Corinthian community. Verses 8-13 (immediately following our text) continue to highlight the spiritual activities of the Corinthian Christians. Things like prophecies, speaking in tongues, and special gifts of knowledge are limited and temporary. But love is not. Coming to know this is the difference between a child and an adult. When we grow up, Paul says, we put away childish or immature things. Faith, hope, and love stay and grow with us. "And the greatest of these is love" (13:13). Zooming out just one level, then, to the immediate context of 1 Corinthians 1:1-13 gives us a small picture of a problem that needs "love is patient, love is kind . . ." applied, and it has to do with how the Corinthian Christians understand and use their spiritual gifts.

If we click out another level, we see that this chapter—the love chapter—is surrounded or sandwiched by a discussion of the meaning, purpose, and proper use of spiritual gifts, and their place in the community or "body" of Christ. Chapter 12 starts with an important thematic statement (a "disclosure" form in ancient Greek letters; we'll explore some of these "special paragraph markers" in the second half of our study): "Now concerning spiritual gifts, brothers and sisters, I do not want you to be uninformed" (12:1). Paul goes on to talk about the different kinds of spiritual gifts and how they should all be used in serving the body of Christ. Like the different parts of our human bodies, so all the people and parts and roles of a church are important for a strong and healthy church. Even the apparently least important ones—those not so prone to flashiness or attention and prominence, like speaking in tongues, prophesying, and doing miracles—are of great value in the community of Christ. In chapter 14, Paul exhorts them to "follow the way of love," as they seek and use spiritual gifts, which he then elucidates by laying down some "loving" principles of honoring the body, the church, and using spiritual gifts to its health and benefit. Chapters 12 and 14 thus surround the chapter on love and clearly imply that the Corinthians need a little—maybe a lot—of love in the way they understand the meaning and function of spiritual gifts.

If we zoom out a few more levels to the context of the book as a whole, it's not hard to see that the Corinthian church is struggling with some serious issues of conflict and division, with fighting and immorality, pride and immaturity; and the conflict centers on their understanding and use of spiritual gifts. For example, in the introduction to the letter—the Thanksgiving (1:4-9)—Paul highlights the foundational theme of spiritual gifts, reminding them of how richly they've been so blessed: " . . . for in every way you have been enriched in him, in speech and knowledge of every kind . . . so that you are not lacking in any spiritual gift . . ." He then immediately (which is somewhat unusual in Paul's letters) hits them with the first major request or petition of the letter: "Now I appeal to you, brothers and sisters, by the name of our Lord Jesus Christ, that all of you be in agreement and that there be no divisions among you, but that you be united in the same mind and the same purpose. . . ." (1:10). The rest of the letter goes to support this purpose, seeking to help them accomplish this task.

Without taking the time for a thorough study of 1 Corinthians, I suspect you can see how the chapter on love fits within this broader theme and purpose. The Corinthians are struggling. There's jealousy, quarrels, lawsuits, immorality. They are a deeply hurting and divided community. By the inspiration of God, Paul writes to them to help them "grow up" in Christ. He tells them that when they act like this, they are acting like the rest of the world—not like followers of Christ. They're acting like "babies"—not like adults, not like mature Christians. At the heart of their divisions lurks the idea that some people—some Christians—are better and more important than others, evidenced by the "spectacular" gifts of God's Spirit, creating a spiritual pecking order, so to speak. Have you ever been in the middle of serious conflict? Hurt by someone who thinks and acts like he or she is better than you because he or she has something you don't, or can do something you can't? Ever wish you had what someone else has?

This is a small window into the context within which 1 Corinthians 13:4-7 speaks. Certainly, these verses teach us things about what it means to love in a way that could be applied in almost any circumstance. But have you ever thought about the power of behaving as 1 Corinthians 13:4-7 instructs in the middle of stressful conflict and fighting? It's reminiscent of Jesus' directive to "Love your enemies . . ." (Matthew 5:44). Now imagine the appropriateness of the aspects of love that Paul emphasizes: "Love is patient . . ." That help in conflict? What about kindness? When the air in the room is thick with a tension of a loud and cutting argument, how powerful is a conscious choice of being kind—instead of hateful? Envying, boasting, and pride—see how these were at work in the community at Corinth and how they are the opposite of genuine love and humility?

Continuing along this line, how appropriate are the following words: "Love . . . . does not dishonor others [some Corinthians wouldn't wait for and eat with some others], it's not self-seeking, it's not easily angered, it keeps no record of wrongs. Love does not delight in evil but rejoices with the truth. It always protects, always trusts, always hopes, always perseveres"? See the point and the compelling logic? Remember, Paul said at the beginning of the chapter that no matter what sort of wonderful or grandiose spiritual act one performs, if it's not based on love, it's meaningless. But if it's based on love—and don't miss this—it will behave as verses 4-7 say. They're claiming to be spiritual giants, but acting like spiritual midgets. In the presence of such behavior, genuine love is absent. In the face of real love, on the other hand, such conflict cannot continue, division will die, and they will become "united in the same mind and the same purpose." This is Paul's goal, that they might put away "childish ways," and come to understand and use the power of God's Holy Spirit in the way of love. This is the context and purpose of his description of love.

You can apply 1 Corinthians 13:4-7 almost anywhere. It's an appropriate and high standard for any marriage or relationship. But—and here's the real question—are we willing to take it into our conflicts and fights, and come out the other side "with the same mind and the same purpose" (which actually implies something profound about genuine spirituality; see the next paragraph)? The challenge is even greater than we thought, isn't it? 1 Corinthians 13:4-7 was part of the solution to problems of conflict, hurt, and division in the Corinthian church. It will serve us well in similar situations.

But let's take it even a step further. 1 Corinthians 13:4-7 gives us powerful tools for dealing with conflict, but it also says something profound about the nature of Christianity. How important is the idea of real love when it comes to how we grade our "religious" activities? What is true spirituality? The point here is similar to one of Jesus' major points in the Sermon on the Mount. Spiritual activity that is like God and pleases God comes from a heart of love (which looks and acts like 1 Corinthians 13:4-7), not from doing religious looking things (which often carry self-serving motives), no matter how spectacular or even attributable to gifts of the Holy Spirit. If we miss that point from 1 Corinthians, we may not be nearly as motivated to learn to act with real love, no matter how many times we define it by 1 Corinthians 13:4-7. Like force fields from the dark side, Bible inkblots frequently keep us from getting to the heart of the matter.

Psalm 2:8
"Ask . . . and I will give you the nations . . ."

You said, "Ask and I'll give the nations to you."
O Lord, that's the cry of my heart.
Distant shores and the islands will see your light, as it rises on us.

Some will recognize these as words from a popular Christian song from Hillsong United (written by Reuben Morgan) called "You Said."[1] It's a catchy song, recounting and exclaiming some promises of God—"You said . . ."—that appear to be taken from various Bible verses. It follows the lyrical pattern of expressing something that God has said as a promise, with the phrase "You said" (unfortunately, the song comes with little punctuation on the CD cover, except for ellipses):

You said ask and you will receive . . . whatever you need . . .
You said pray and I'll hear from heaven . . . and I'll heal your land . . .
You said your glory will fill the earth . . . like water the seas . . .
You said lift up your eyes . . . the harvest is here . . . the kingdom is near . . .
You said . . . ask and I'll give the nations to you . . .
   O Lord that's the cry of my heart . . .
   Distant shores and the islands . . . will see your light, as it rises on us.

O Lord I ask for the nations . . . (4 times)

If you've ever sung the song with a group of excited Christians, you don't need me to tell you that it's artistic and powerful; it's performed and experienced as such frequently by Christians everywhere. I have so experienced it, in particular in settings where the theme is about missions or evangelism—our great commission responsibility of taking the gospel to the world—which seems fitting, given the structure and build of the song: the end repeats the refrain "Oh Lord, I ask for the nations." The music and the moment evoke powerful feelings of renewal, purpose, and motivation. Be assured, I'm not here to criticize those moments or the use of a song with scriptures to help create them.

The song does, however, aptly illustrate several of the things we've talked about regarding the use of randomly selected, isolated scriptures. It illustrates further the common tendency for us to treat the Bible this way in our music. I'm not intending to place a heavy burden on Christian songwriters here—that they, too, must be "Bible scholars" before they can be inspired to write and lead us in worship. I'm just using this particular song as one of many examples of what's common, even normal in our use of scripture. Songs should remind us of things we believe that are important to us—no problem with that. Singing and worshipping is a different experience than reading the Bible—got you. The problem comes, however, when we don't know the contexts of the verses used in the songs (and that applies to writers and singers). When that happens, the context of the song and the experience becomes the primary lens through which we view these scriptures, and the gist of the song provides, or at least influences, our understanding of that piece of scripture (see if you are familiar with the book-level contexts of the verses cited below).

This song appears to be based on several verses from the Bible (I say "appears" because I have no firsthand knowledge of the writer's intentions, but am commenting as a general hearer/user of the song). The first "You said" ("Ask and you will receive, whatever you need") could come from several texts, most likely Luke 11:9-12 and/or Matthew 7:7-11,[2] and reflects promises from Jesus about hearing us when we pray ("Ask, and it will be given you . . ."). Continuing that theme, the second "You said" ("Pray and I'll hear from heaven, and I'll heal your land") appears to be taken from 2 Chronicles 7:14: ". . . if my people who are called by my name humble themselves, pray, seek my face, and turn from their wicked ways, then I will hear from heaven, and will forgive their sin and heal their land. . . ." The excerpt in the song is really ". . . pray . . ., and . . . I'll hear from heaven . . . and heal their land." There's quite a bit in those dots, not to mention what the immediate and book-level contexts of 2 Chronicles indicate about this promise. Perhaps the third "You said" ("Your glory will fill the earth like water the seas") comes from Habakkuk 2:14 (note the reference to "the nations" in 2:13): "But the earth will be filled with the knowledge and the glory of the Lord, as the waters cover the sea." When? Why? What is Habakkuk talking about? The next ("You said lift up your eyes . . . the harvest is here . . . the kingdom is near . . .") sounds like Jesus talking to his disciples after his conversation with the woman at the well in John: "But I tell you, look around you, and see how the fields are ripe for harvesting" (John 4:35); or of the sending out of the seventy on one of the first missionary endeavors (Luke 10:1-12; also Mark 6:6-13; Matthew 10:5-15). That "the kingdom is near" could come from numerous places (like Luke 10:9, 11; Matthew 10:7), as Jesus proclaimed, "The time is fulfilled, and the kingdom of God has come near; repent, and believe in the good news" (Mark 1:14).

We could talk about how the song uses each of these Bible verses in relation to its original context, but I'd like to focus on the next "You Said"—the one that becomes dominant by position and repetition in the song.

> You said . . . ask and I'll give the nations to you . . .
> O Lord that's the cry of my heart . . .
> Distant shores and the islands . . . will see your light, as it rises on us.

This is the cry of my heart, the song says, several times, and then actually makes the request, several times, at the end: "Oh Lord I ask for the nations." It's no wonder this song has become popular and has a dynamic impact on those singing it. We do indeed want to be faithful to our charge to take the gospel to all the world, and we pray that God will stand behind us and bless those efforts.

This last "You said" comes from Psalm 2:8: "Ask of me, and I will make the nations your heritage, and the ends of the earth your possession." The New King James Version renders it in lyric format:

Chapter 6

> Ask of Me, and I will give You
> The nations for Your inheritance,
> And the ends of the earth for Your possession.

The book of Psalms is unique among books of the Bible library in that it's one of the few made up of a collection of shorter, independent pieces; in this case, "psalms"—songs and prayers—written mostly by King David (with some others like Solomon, Asaph, Ethan, Heman, and the sons of Korah). They reflect much of the history of ancient Israel in poetic form and have been used in Jewish and Christian worship through the ages. Reading the whole psalm quickly reveals the disparity between the use of Psalm 2:8 as a motivation to missions and its book-, in this case, song-level meaning. Perhaps the best way to show this is simply to repeat the psalm in full, with our excerpt highlighted. Here's the NIV rendering:

> Why do the nations conspire and the peoples plot in vain?
> The kings of the earth take their stand and the rulers gather
>   together against the Lord and against his Anointed One.
> "Let us break their chains," they say, "and throw off their fetters."
> The One enthroned in heaven laughs; the Lord scoffs at them.
> Then he rebukes them in his anger and terrifies them in his
>   wrath, saying,
> "I have installed my King on Zion my holy hill."
> I will proclaim the decree of the Lord:
> He said to me,
>   "You are my Son; today I have become your Father.
>   **Ask of me, and I will make the nations your inheritance**,
>   the ends of the earth your possession.
>   You will rule them with an iron scepter; you will dash them to
>   pieces like pottery."
> Therefore, you kings, be wise; be warned, you rulers of the earth.
> Serve the Lord with fear and rejoice with trembling.
> Kiss the Son, lest he be angry and you be destroyed in your way,
>   for his wrath can flare up in a moment.
> Blessed are all who take refuge in him.

I sincerely question the effectiveness of breaking the nations "with a rod of iron" (NRSV) and dashing them to pieces like pottery as an effective evangelistic strategy. It certainly doesn't seem to fit the mood and purpose of the song "You Said."

Psalm 2 is obviously a song celebrating God's powerful adoption and endorsement of Israel's king—likely David—as his royal, anointed son. It encouraged him with the promise that he need not fear the nations, even when they conspire against him, for God stands behind him. You don't have to have a Bible degree to see this—just read it. In fact, the Lord promises the king ("You said") that he will give him the nations as an inheritance to rule and/or break as he sees fit. The promise functions, then, as an encouraging endorsement and a warning to the other nations and their kings to be mindful of the way they respond to the Lord and his anointed leader.

In a very broad sense, we can see the potential relevance of the psalm for Christian missions in that God has promised to stand with and behind his people, especially if we bear in mind that Psalm 2 has often been interpreted by Jewish rabbis and Christians alike as a "messianic" psalm, which means that it's seen as a prefigure and prediction of the coming Messiah. New Testament writers thus applied the verse to Jesus (Hebrews 1:5; Mark 1:11; Matthew 3:17; Luke 3:22). So—to be gracious to our use of the verse in "You Said"—I suppose we could reason that since Christ is the ultimate, anointed son of God—the Messiah—and, his inheritance is/will be the nations (as Ephesians speaks of the nations/Gentiles becoming joint-heirs in Christ [2:11-18]), then we look outward with great commission love and purpose. No longer do we seek to break the nations in conflict and war, but, by the grace of God in Christ, we seek to bring them into the light and love of Christ. And by such reasoning, we could "baptize" the psalm, so to speak.

I get this, I guess. But my question is do we really want to go to such lengths to justify our use of the verse? Or is it apparent that when we use it this way, we've really made an inkblot out of it by divorcing it from its original context and giving it a new one—"You Said." I don't have a problem using pieces of scripture to remind us of our faith, as I've said, but the problem here involves those of us who don't know the original context and place our song-derived interpretation of these encapsulated "promises" onto the mouth of God. Does that make sense? I'm not trying to be harsh. I just want to respect God's word to us. If your only interpretation of Psalm 2:8 comes from the mood and meaning of "You Said," then the verse has clearly become an inkblot, whose meaning is shaped in this case by the song and the experience as we sing it.

God has made many wonderful promises to us. He certainly will be with us, aid and strengthen us, especially as we go forth with the good news of the gospel—as Jesus promised just before he left and charged us with that task. He said,

> All authority in heaven and on earth has been given to me. Therefore go and make disciples of all nations, baptizing them in the name of the Father and of the Son and of the Holy Spirit, and teaching them to obey everything I have commanded you. And surely I am with you always, to the very end of the age (Matthew 28:18-20).

Ephesians 3:14-21
"... far more than we can ask or imagine..."

One of the most beautiful—and therefore refrigerator-posted—prayers of the Bible is Ephesians 3:14-21. It's an extraordinary prayer of Paul, with magnificent themes and desires for God to bless us. As a way of emphasizing God's ability to answer the prayer and bless us in ways we don't even know, it concludes by describing God as one "who by the power at work within us is able to accomplish abundantly far more that all we can ask or imagine" (3:20). How incredible and exciting! We get to pray to a God who can answer our prayers and bless us in ways we can't even imagine. It's no wonder we like this prayer and highlight it as a classic text of scripture.

The requests of the prayer are equally poetic and far-reaching. It starts with an endearing image of Paul bowing his knees before a loving heavenly Father, followed by the prayer itself:

> For this reason I bow my knees before the Father, from whom every family in heaven and on earth takes its name. I pray that, according to the riches of his glory, he may grant that you may be strengthened in your inner being with power through his Spirit, and that Christ may dwell in your hearts through faith, as you are being rooted and grounded in love. I pray that you may have the power to comprehend, with all the saints, what is the breadth and length and height and depth, and to know the love of Christ that surpasses knowledge, so that you may be filled with all the fullness of God.
>
> Now to him who by the power at work within us is able to accomplish abundantly far more than all we can ask or imagine, to him be glory in the church and in Christ Jesus to all generations, forever and ever. Amen (Ephesians 3:14-21).

Who wouldn't want the things Paul has so beautifully articulated in this prayer for the ages? ... to be strengthened in the inner person with power through God's Spirit, for Christ to dwell in our hearts through faith, to be rooted and grounded in love, to have the

Chapter 6

power to comprehend the breadth and length and height and depth . . . of the love of Christ, to be filled with the fullness of God? But here's the question: What does that mean? What do these requests mean? With each request, in unison we say "Yes!", "Amen!", and then—if we stop to think about it—wonder exactly what it was we just prayed for. What's it mean to be strengthened with power in the inner person? I think I know—maybe. How will I know? What will I feel? How do I know Christ is dwelling in my heart through faith? I believe he is and does. Do I need to ask for it? Can anyone comprehend with all Christians the full dimensions . . . of what? Can we know the love of Christ that goes beyond knowledge? If it's beyond knowledge, how can I know it? And what's it mean to be filled with the fullness of God? What is this power that's at work in us, through which God can do much more than we can ask or imagine? I can ask and imagine a lot. So does this mean I should be getting more than I ask for?

Given our tendencies to fill in the blanks with what we already think and feel, can you see how this prayer quickly becomes a great big, multi-dimensional inkblot? The only way to answer the questions without relying on our own subjective tendencies (and distortions) is to let God answer them by reading the book of Ephesians as a whole (Rule #1: see chapter 9 of Book 2) and hearing the prayer as it fits within that context (Rule #2).

"It's all good": one could argue that these are all good things that all Christians desire as part of our faith and position in Christ. So there's no real harm in isolating this prayer. To a certain extent, I agree. But remember this principle: there's nothing wrong with using excerpts of scripture to remind us and encourage us in our faith; unless—and this is the basic "unless" of this book—unless, we don't know much of anything of what the verses are about in their original book-level contexts. That's when these—or any other set of verses— become blank canvases, pregnant with the seeds of our own notions and theologies; or just lame, in a sense, lacking real power to speak to us with the word of God that changes and transforms us. Thus, we risk losing God's inspired messages.

One reason this prayer seems such an appropriate passage to be isolated from the text and used as a broad-based, Christian prayer is because the language is sweepingly broad and poetic. There are several reasons for that. Admittedly, the subjects are encompassing and potentially abstract, but that doesn't mean they don't relate to what's going on in the context of the book and the historical setting into which these words were injected. The position in the letter strongly influences the style and content, moreover. The prayer passage comes between the two major halves of the letter and forms a bridge or transition from the "thinking" to the "living" side of the context. As a transition, the prayer has a clear literary function to sum up and reinforce the first half of the letter. As a conclusion to the first half—the "theological" side—consistent with what was taught in schools of rhetoric at the time and with common sense, the writer uses conclusions to amplify in powerful, emotive and flowery language the points he wants to drive home to the audience. (We look more into these sorts of literary techniques in the second half of this study.) The language and style of a good conclusion is, therefore, by nature somewhat broad and generic, as it summarizes (captures in brief) the main points of the text. Paul often uses prayers for this purpose (can you think of a better way?). What's by nature somewhat broad and encompassing, however, is not separate from the purpose and meaning of the text. (It just makes us think it is if we don't read the whole thing.) On the contrary, it draws from and seeks to bring home the key points.

Many of the words and ideas of Ephesians 3:14-21 are important subjects throughout the book of Ephesians. We'll look more in the second half of our study at the process of tracing out and connecting key ideas in a Bible book, but briefly, let's think about a couple of these, starting with the concept of power. This prayer is packed with images of power—that's part of the reason we like it. The power starts and ends with God, and is, apparently, available to us. The Father to whom Paul prays is the father of all families in heaven and earth; from him, they get their name (3:14). The prayer ends with the image of God as able to do far more than we can ask or imagine, and that power is "at work within us" (3:20). Paul prays that the recipients may be strengthened in their "inner being with power through his Spirit." He prays, not that they might just comprehend what he wants them to understand, but that they might "have *the power* to comprehend." From reading the prayer alone, it's obvious, then, that God is powerful and that power is available to the Christians for whom the prayer was prayed—and, by implication, to us as well.

If we look through the first half of the letter, we see that power is a key theme, with several important developments. For example, at the end of the Thanksgiving section—the section in Paul's letters that functions as an introduction (more on this in Book 2)—power is outlined as one of the things Paul wants his readers to come to understand. If fact, he outlines three major topics (I call these the triadic themes of Ephesians). In Ephesians 1:15-23, Paul prays that God might give them a spirit of wisdom and revelation, that their eyes might be opened, so that they might come to understand some things. He lists three:

- the hope of his calling
- the riches of his glorious inheritance among the saints
- the surpassing greatness of his power for us who believe.

Paul's letter to the Ephesians is about the hope of God's **calling**, the riches of his **inheritance**, and his surpassing **power** for those who believe. He immediately expands the theme of power (and all three themes in general) with the following:

> . . . according to the working of his great power. God put this power to work in Christ when he raised him from the dead and seated him at his right hand in the heavenly places, far above all rule and authority and power and dominion, and above every name that is named, not only in this age but also in the age to come. And he has put all things under his feet and has made him the head over all things for the church, which is his body, the fullness of him who fills all in all (1: 19-23).

The power and the fullness that Paul talks about is in Christ and was exemplified when God raised him from the dead and seated him at his right hand, where he now reigns as head over all things for the church, which is his body. In other words, the unbelievable power of God that brought Jesus back from the dead now resides in and through Jesus as Lord of all things in behalf of the church. That's the power Paul wants the readers of the letter to know about, and it's that same power that he prays about at the end of chapter 3.

To see more of how that power is at work in Christ, one need only read the rest of the letter. We won't take the time to do that now, but . . . a couple of observations. You're probably familiar with the armor of God scene at the end of the letter (6:10-17)—the scene where the Christian soldier is admonished to put on all the pieces of God's armor for standing strong against the schemes of the devil and the forces of darkness (we could, in fact, have included this as a classic inkblot!). "For our struggle is not against enemies of blood and flesh," Paul says, "but against the rulers, against the authorities, against the cosmic powers of this present darkness, against the spiritual forces of evil in the heavenly places" (6:12). See why we might need an extra dose of God's power to stand? And *each piece of armor summarizes key ideas from the letter* about how that power of God is available to us—the belt of truth, breastplate of righteousness, shoes of peace, shield of faith, helmet of salvation, and the sword of the Spirit. As the prayer of Ephesians 3:14-21 concludes the first half of the letter, so this fully decked-out soldier of God concludes the book as a whole.

So we see major references to God's power at work in them at the beginning (1:19-23), middle (3:14-21), and ending (6:10-17) of the letter. Chapter 3:1-13 provides a concrete example of how that power available in Christ, in the church, is available to the readers to help them overcome a potential struggle with discouragement—by way of application and analogy to Paul. After describing God's hidden plan for the ages, that it was made know to Paul, how he participates in that plan by being God's ambassador to the Gentiles so that they too could be fellow heirs and members of the body of Christ, that he was given this special grace and privilege, that he serves Christ this way, and that now—even though he was writing this letter to them from prison (he was "the prisoner of Christ Jesus for the Gentiles" [3:1])—it was all *according to the working of God's power* (3:7). God had not lost control, even though some things may not have made much sense and looked bleak. The recipients' leader, their spiritual father in some respects, was incarcerated for the very reason they loved him, for bringing them the good news of Christ. Many potentially negative, life-altering emotions and responses were possible. But Paul uses this very situation to uphold his belief that God was in control and the power that was released when God raised Jesus from the dead—at work in us who believe (1:19)—was still at work in his life and circumstances. So he concludes: "I pray therefore that you may not lose heart over my sufferings for you; they are your glory." Not losing heart when things look bad—this is one of the ways Ephesians clarifies and applies the theme of God's power. What had happened to Paul was by a gift of God's grace "according to the working of his power."

The idea of comprehending (with all the saints/Christians) the encompassing dimensions (breadth, length, height, depth) of God's plan and of the love of Christ is another prominent theme in the prayer of Ephesians 3:14-21. This key theme is also clearly introduced in the Thanksgiving (1:15-21). Paul prays that God would give them a spirit of wisdom so that they could understand these very important realities about Christ and the church: (1) the hope of his calling, (2) the glorious riches of his inheritance among the saints, and (3) the surpassing greatness of his power upon us who believe. Just as the theme of power resonates through the pages of the letter and is applied specifically in chapter 3, so Paul discusses the first two themes in chapter 2. We won't take the time to work through these now, but read Ephesians 2:1-10 with the question in mind: what does Paul mean by "the hope of his calling"; and, 2:1-11 with what does he mean by "the glorious riches of his inheritance among the saints." I believe you will begin to see more of what these ideas are about in the context of Ephesians. When Paul prays that they would come to understand "with all the saints what is the breadth and length and height and depth . . . of the love of Christ," you will be in much better position to be one of those saints. As non-Jews, the readers of the letter used to be outside of "every spiritual blessing" of God (see 1:3-14), but now through God's grace in Christ (2:5: "by grace you have been saved"), they too share fully in all the hope and all the riches and all the power.

The book of Ephesians has much to say to us about the church; about being joint-heirs in Christ; about living up to our united, one body, calling; and much, much more—more than we can go into now. The point here is to encourage you to fill in the meaning of the amazing prayer of Ephesians 3:14-21 with the Spirit-inspired ideas of Ephesians, so that it won't just be a plaque on the wall or a very elaborate inkblot.

Chapter 6

Jeremiah 29:11
"I know the plans I have for you...."

"Several key religious leaders are saying it. There is a movement of God afoot, and it's exciting because it means we will be rescued soon. We have cried out to God, and he has heard us. *It won't be long now.* These men—these prophets of God—confirm that God has a plan for us. If we'll just hold on for a little while longer, we'll see his hand. So we're holding on and looking expectantly to that future with a great hope."

What is God's plan for your life? Next to John 3:16, Jeremiah 29:11 may be the most often quoted Bible verse. I often hear it quoted from the NIV: "'For I know the plans I have for you,' declares the Lord, 'plans to prosper you and not to harm you, plans to give you hope and a future.'" Anyone who knows something of the Bible knows that this is indeed the way the Lord feels about us. He loves us and wants our good. He goes to the utmost lengths to save us and heal us and strengthen us (Luke 15; Romans 5:8; Romans 8:39). There are many scriptures in the Bible that express God's undying, extreme love and care for us. Jesus said that the very hairs of our heads are numbered (Matthew 10:30; Luke 12:7). That God has plans to give us hope and a future is not surprising or in doubt.

I think it's the "plans" part that makes these verses so appealing, especially in light of a heart-felt desire to be significant and the fear that our lives may not matter much or go the way we want. Our turbulent and sometimes painful lives diminish our hope and raise doubts that there is a "plan" for us that will get us out of the mess we're in and lead us to God's good will and blessings for us. Hebrews (12:1-2), James (1:2-4), 1 and 2 Peter (1:3-11), Revelation and many other Bible texts shine bright lights on this hope and promises of God, however. It's natural then, to hear Jeremiah 29:11 this way—in the context of this common, perhaps universal, experience of longing and hoping. If we read the next verse or two, the encouragement grows: "Then you will call on me and come and pray to me, and I will listen to you. You will seek me and find me when you seek me with all your heart" (29:12-13). So what's not to like or use about this verse?

Nothing—as a summary of our heartfelt trust in God's love and provision for us. But if we want to use the Bible to hear from God, perhaps we should not interrupt so quickly. Reading a little more begins to paint a different picture: "'I will be found by you,' declares the Lord, 'and will bring you back from captivity. I will gather you from all the nations and places where I have banished you,' declares the Lord, 'and will bring you back to the place from which I carried you into exile.' Because you have said, 'The Lord has raised up prophets for us in Babylon,' . . ." (29:14-15). Babylon? Carried into exile? Banished? How many of us have ever been exiled to Babylon? Hmm. And if we begin reading at verse 10—before our oft-cited verse—the situation begins to clarify itself: "For thus says the Lord: 'Only when Babylon's seventy years are completed will I visit you, and I will fulfill to you my promise and bring you back to this place. For surely I know the plans I have for you . . .'"

The people were expecting God to do it now—or at least very soon. That's what some of their religious leaders were telling them—within two years, one of them said. Now that's hope I can believe in. But in sovereign defiance of what some were saying, God says it's not for 70 years that he will execute his plans for them. And—did you notice—those plans were for the people as a whole (in this case, Judah)—"you" is plural and refers to the nation and people. If we move back a little further in the immediate context (zoom out a little), we see that Jeremiah had sent a letter to the leaders and Jewish people living in exile in Babylon and told them that the Lord said to go ahead and build houses, get married, have kids, and build their lives there in Babylon. Even to pray for the city where they were living, since their future rested within the future of Babylon—"'*cause I'm not going to rescue you for 70 years.*" And if we read a little more, we learn that this was a response to the spiritual leaders who were telling them that God had plans that they'd really like, that he was going to overthrow their enemies and make things right again (thus, the imagined sentiments of the people at the beginning of this section).

Chapter 6

"Not quite the plan I had hoped for," you might think if you were a Jew living exiled in Babylon at the time. God did have a plan, a plan for his people, a plan to bring the exiles home, but not for a while and not specific for each of them, unless of course we deduce that God's plan for them was to live and probably die in Babylon. The hope was still there, the future was still there, but not exactly the way we tend to quote this verse regarding our individual hopes and dreams for our earth-bound futures. God may very well have a specific plan for each of us for the journeys of our lives, but is it possible we're missing some of his divine message, if we use this verse to expect God to "make it right" now, in a relatively short period of time—maybe a year or two?

If we zoom out more and put this text into the book-level picture as a whole, we begin to see some world-level themes come into focus (not just my personal comfort or discomfort): the amazing story of the prophet Jeremiah, his difficult life and messages to the kingdom of Judah, his great longing and faithfulness in spite of the specifics of his trouble-filled journey, the tense prediction and violent fulfillment of the carrying off of Judah into Babylonian captivity, and the healing promise of the restoration of Jerusalem and the bringing back of God's remnant at the appropriate time. Jeremiah struggled with and for his people; he's often called "the weeping prophet":

> My joy is gone, grief is upon me, my heart is sick. Hark, the cry of my poor people from far and wide in the land: "Is the Lord not in Zion? Is her King not in her?" . . . . "The harvest is past, the summer is ended, and we are not saved." For the hurt of my poor people I am hurt, I mourn, and dismay has taken hold of me. Is there no balm in Gilead? Is there no physician there? Why then has the health of my poor people not been restored? O that my head were a spring of water, and my eyes a fountain of tears, so that I might weep day and night for the slain of my poor people! (8:18-9:1).

Our text—Jeremiah 29:11—is a small piece of this. The hope and the future are big. The struggles and the heartaches are deep and wide. And to those hearing these words of Jeremiah in 29:11, the message had as much to do with "no" and "wait," as to how God would swoop down and save the day so they could go home. The prophets they were listening to were wrong: their rescue and immediate relief were not God's plans. Perhaps that's a message we could use in our day as well: can we trust in God for the long term and the big picture, even in the darkest of days?

As much as we need encouragement with the day to day struggles—life is often tough—we also need to be reminded that God is a big God and his plans cover the church, the world, and all of history. Of course, God has good plans for us as individuals. We need his love every day, or I wouldn't want to get out of bed. So please don't misunderstand me. But I wonder if when we use Jeremiah 29:11, we're really wanting or expecting to wait 70 years or so, or if we're thinking and asking about something different—something legitimate, but different. And I wonder if we forget to zoom out and hear the message of Jeremiah—a message of great plans and great hope and a bright future, not only for us, but for God's people then and now and everywhere. I wonder if we're strengthened to hold on, like Jeremiah, through many tears and many troubles. (After all, there *is* a "balm in Gilead.") The difference is the difference between "me and now" (or "soon") and "us and God"—God's divine, big picture plans. I wonder if some of the things that happened to the people in this book happened to us, if we'd be singing "I know the plans I have for you . . ." Or, at least, I suspect we'd quote them with a different perspective. These verses certainly should speak to us; they should speak to us from God's inspired book of Jeremiah.

Since we don't use a book from the Old Testament as part of our example texts in the second part of our study (we use Philemon and Mark) and as a way of transitioning into Part 2, I'd like to take a little more extended look at our next classic inkblot. We can't take the time to study the book in depth, but we'll anticipate some of the principles of good Bible reading that I'll delineate later. For now, I'd like to explore some of the key themes of the Old Testament book of Ecclesiastes, as we seek to hear Ecclesiastes 3:1-8 ("For everything there is a season . . .") within its book-level focus, as an antidote to the common, dis-integrated use of this classic inkblot.

Ecclesiastes 3:1-8:
"For everything there is a season..."

For everything there is a season,
    and a time for every matter under heaven:
    a time to be born, and a time to die;
    a time to plant, and a time to pluck up what is planted;
    a time to kill, and a time to heal;
    a time to break down, and time to build up;
    a time to weep, and a time to laugh;
    a time to mourn, and a time to dance;
    a time to throw away stones, and a time to gather stones together;
    a time to embrace, and a time to refrain from embracing;
    a time to seek, and a time to lose;
    a time to keep, and a time to throw away;
    a time to tear, and a time to sew;
    a time to keep silence, and a time to speak;
    a time to love, and a time to hate;
    a time for war, and a time for peace (Ecclesiastes 3:1-8).

Many songs ("Turn! Turn! Turn!" by the Byrds, for example), artistic expressions, and mementos of all sorts have been crafted from these verses. The tremendous beauty and eloquence of the passage immediately show why it has become a classic, and why it invites us to "punch it out" and use it as an isolated text (even here, you got more than usual). We employ these verses in connection with some of the most important moments of our lives—like weddings and funerals—to frame the event, to honor the moment, and to affirm the deep value we place on the people and places of our lives. We thus use the passage as a sort of monument to life and to meaning—rarely quoting the whole thing—but using a few of the examples to stand for the whole (= a synecdoche, in rhetorical terms). An invitation to a high school graduation my daughter recently received illustrates the point. Underneath a picture of a butterfly, it said, "For everything there is a season, a time to laugh, a time to mourn, and a

Chapter 6

time to dance. My time has come. I am finally done with High School!"

"For everything there is a season . . ." "What does this mean to you?" someone might ask in a small group or class discussion. And there certainly will be various shades of meaning when the passage is interpreted in the contexts of our differing experiences. On the other hand, even when taken out of its book-level context and seen as an independent piece, a relatively consistent understanding tends to come through, which is not necessarily surprising. This can happen either because the meaning is obvious and everyone sees it alike or because—like some inkblots—the passage by itself assumes a recognizable shape and allows our shared experiences to create a similar interpretive picture (like the head of a fox). To many people, some inkblots look the same. But this passage is not an inkblot; it's part of a bigger picture. It's more like a piece of a mosaic or a puzzle.

So what happens when we put the isolated passage back into the assembled picture of the book as a whole? This is our question. Not what does it mean to me or to you, but what did the writer mean in the context of this book? Good Bible reading asks how a passage fits into the picture created by the book as a whole, and—like a put-together puzzle—when seen within the rest of the book, one can point to the passage in question and the world of the book controls the meaning (rather than just what we already know and think). Taken apart, it's an inkblot—which many people sometimes interpret similarly. Put together, something different happens.

How Does It Fit?

As we'll talk about more in chapters to come, the first thing we need to do to understand a Bible verse is to read the entire book from which the verse or set of verses is taken. This may sound like it's asking a lot—perhaps too much—for every verse, but it's really not. Most Bible books are relatively short (especially by some of today's popular standards); and once you've begun to read and envision the picture and message(s) of entire books, you'll always have the big-picture framework to fall back on and control how you're understanding the individual verses. This is Rule for reading #1: read the whole thing. Rule #2 is to see the individual verse(s) as part of the put-together whole (like looking at the picture on the box or at a piece of a puzzle once it's put together). This is where The Question comes into play and guides our thinking. How do these verses contribute to the picture and purposes of the book? (More on this later.)

Were I to offer a typical analysis of Ecclesiastes 3:1-8, I might start by underscoring the fundamental insight of the words as an artistic expression of an important fact of life: that life goes on and certain things are inevitable (like death and taxes, but also graduations and weddings); and, beyond that, that there is an appropriate time and place for everything. In fact, immediately following this passage, the author—Solomon—provides an interpretive clarification: "I have seen the business that God has given to everyone to be busy with. He has made everything suitable for its time; moreover he has put a sense of past and future into their minds . . ." (3:10-11). Indeed, there is an appropriate time and place for most everything. This is a valuable insight. I might then take you through the examples given, noting that each is an illustration of the topic sentence that there is a season and a time for everything, providing contemporary parallels or explanations to amplify the idea. We might then seek to apply these thoughts to various moments in our lives or focus on a particular event to underscore the value of that moment and the moments as a whole. A whole sermon or book could thus be written on the wonder of life, how we should capture and celebrate it, and the wisdom of knowing when to do what. (Just think how many embarrassing moments could be avoided if we always knew when to do what. I'm for that.)

These are legitimate topics. There is certainly nothing wrong with the idea that life has a recognizable ebb and flow and that important events punctuate the movement of our lives. There's nothing wrong with affirming the highs and lows of life; with celebrating the real and inherent meaningfulness of the things we experience, the people we know and love; the thresholds we cross and the milestones we achieve in our journeys. There is a time . . . It's real . . .

Chapter 6

It's meaningful . . . It's now. And "this is mine," as the young lady wanted us to know. There's nothing bad about that . . . *except that affirming the inherent value and meaningfulness of life is the opposite of what the writer of Ecclesiastes does throughout most of the book.* Like a repetitious refrain in an over-sung chorus, Solomon explicitly says otherwise: "All is vanity and a chasing after the wind." Had I quoted just a little more of the writer's explanation of our passage, you might have caught a clue that there's more to this than meets the eye: ". . . moreover he has put a sense of past and future into their minds, yet they cannot find out what God has done from the beginning to the end" (3:11). Why would someone want to know what God has done and is doing? We need to read more, and as soon as we do, it becomes obvious that there's a bigger issue at the heart of Solomon's discourse.

The real question is what did Solomon want his audience to take away from this passage and this book. A general understanding that there is a right time and place for everything (even if some things in the list are obviously negative and destructive)? A recognition and affirmation of the big moments that come as part of the ongoing cycles of life? Or the speed with which time flies by, as a memorable moment in *Fiddler on the Roof* resonates: "Sunrise, sunset. Swiftly fly the years. One season following another. Laden with happiness and tears"? Is this the primary meaning of this often quoted passage, or has removing these words from their context given them a new twist—a life and focus different from God's original, inspired meaning? Bluntly, have we effectively tuned out God's first conversation with us with our own second or third level preoccupations? To use our puzzle analogy, we must always seek to answer The Question: how do these verses fit and function in the book of Ecclesiastes? I'll anticipate the answer: they fit snugly as part of a graphic, honest, heartfelt, gut-wrenching, instructive, and powerful exhortation about how not to lose life while trying to find it.

Parties and Puppies

When it comes to reading a passage of scripture in context, it's often good to look at the beginning and the end of the book you're reading (more on this later). Typically, the beginning will highlight important things the writer wants to get across to the readers. In other words, it introduces key ideas. The ending or conclusion sums things up and brings home the movement and messages of the book. Of course, there's variety in how different writers accomplish these tasks, but the beginning and end are good places to start when you're trying to get some focus on the book-level meaning—that is, after you've read the whole book to start with, of course. When you do this with Ecclesiastes, it doesn't take long to see that the picture on the box is not of Times Square on New Year's eve, of sandy summer fun on a playful white beach, of hot chocolate by the fireplace on a snowy winter night, or cute puppies.

Ecclesiastes starts like this:

> The words of the Teacher, the son of David, king in Jerusalem. Vanity of vanities, says the Teacher, vanity of vanities! All is vanity. What do people gain from all the toil at which they toil under the sun? A generation goes, and a generation comes, but the earth remains forever. The sun rises and the sun goes down, and hurries to the place where it rises. The wind blows to the south, and goes around to the north; round and round goes the wind, and on its circuits the wind returns. All streams run to the sea, but the sea is not full; to the place where the streams flow, there they continue to flow. All things are wearisome; more than one can express; the eye is not satisfied with seeing, or the ear filled with hearing. What has been is what will be, and what had been done is what will be done; there is nothing new under the sun (1:1-9).

Almost immediately, we hear echoes of our passage—that for everything, there is a season—and yet, almost immediately, just by adding a little of the book-level context, we begin to see it in a different light.

The sentiment is not happy—at least most of the time and from a particular perspective—and herein lies the wisdom of the book. From the dominant perspective of the language of Ecclesiastes, the fact that there is a time for everything is not a *celebration* of the cyclical ebb and flow of life, but a *lament* of it.

The very first words reveal much of the perspective of the writer: "Vanity of vanities . . . All is vanity." The word "vanity" means meaningless, as the New International Version translated it, and much of the book clamors deeply and loudly against the meaningless of the events, efforts, and cycles of life—cycles within which we're apparently stuck. No matter what we do, nothing is really new. And nothing fulfills. Nothing makes life worth living. A few excerpts underscore the point:

> I, the Teacher, when king over Israel in Jerusalem, applied my mind to seek and to search out by wisdom all that is done under heaven; it is an unhappy business that God has given to human beings to be busy with. I saw all the deeds that are done under the sun; and see, all is vanity and a chasing after wind (1:12-14).

> Then I considered all that my hands had done and the toil I had spent in doing it, and again, all was vanity and a chasing after the wind, and there was nothing to be gained under the sun (2:11).

> What do mortals get from all the toil and strain with which they toil under the sun? For all their days are full of pain, and their work is a vexation; even at night their minds do not rest. This is vanity (2:22-23).

> And I thought the dead, who have already died, more fortunate than the living, who are still alive; but better than both is the one who has not yet been, and has not seen the evil deeds that are done under the sun (4:2-3).

(Now that'll brighten up a graduation party!)

This also is a grievous ill: just as they came, so shall they go; and what gain do they have from toiling for the wind? Besides, all their days they eat in darkness, in much vexation and sickness and resentment (5:16-17).

Dead flies make the perfumer's ointment give off a foul odor ... (10:1).

... as does much of the language of Ecclesiastes. Ecclesiastes 2:17 powerfully encapsulates the author's feelings: "So I hated life, because what is done under the sun was grievous to me; for all is vanity and a chasing after the wind."

The dominant perspective of the book of Ecclesiastes is not a cheerful or enchanting lyric on the highlights of life, but, on the contrary, a dark and depressive literary struggle with the meaning of life—whether anything has meaning. A deeply anxious, weary, and despairing spirit oozes from its pages. These are the sentiments of a man trapped in the exhausting pursuit of something that always eluded him, and now, looking back on it all, he despairs at "the facts of life" his journey uncovered.[3] For most of the book, "the Teacher" writes from that perspective. But he does not stop there. That is not the whole story or the message of Ecclesiastes. It is not just a lament. But it is the way things look from one side of the fence.

Life 101: Dust in the Wind

Ecclesiastes (compare *ekklesia*—church) is the Greek translation of the Hebrew word *Qohelet*, meaning gathering or gatherer and is obviously where we got the title of the book. It's the word used in the opening verses to introduce the writer, usually translated as "preacher" or "teacher." Why does the writer of Ecclesiastes refer to himself as "the Teacher" or "the Preacher"—and in the very first verse? This is a piece of the literary context and should affect how we hear and apply the text. In other words, whatever we get out of the book of Ecclesiastes, the writer saw it as "teaching." So what does he want to teach us? If the only purpose were to show how much life sucks, I doubt we'd take many of that professor's courses. On the other hand, if someone who spent most of his life in search of meaning and fulfillment in all the things that enchantingly call out for our time and energy with exciting but illusory promises of fulfillment, someone who had the means (being one of the richest and most powerful men who ever lived) to deny himself no pleasure . . .; if he decided to communicate to us what he'd learned, something irreversibly unpleasant and destructive, something we'd rather not have to learn on our own the hard way, something potentially life-changing and life-giving, would it be worth hearing? I think I'd sign up for that class.

After disturbingly and grippingly introducing the idea that everything is meaningless in the opening of the book, the author then goes on to explain how he knows that. As king, Solomon says, I tried everything. I tried education and wisdom. I tried sex and more sex. I tried food, alcohol, art, great agricultural and architectural projects, toys, nature, entertainment, power, money, reputation and fame . . . You name it, I did it. "Whatever my eyes desired I did not keep from them; I kept my heart from no pleasure . . ." (Read that last sentence again; it's highly significant.) So what happened? Nothing worked. "I searched . . . until I might see what was good for mortals to do under heaven during the few days of their life" (2:3). But nothing worked to break the interminable cycles of life and death on planet earth—or "under the sun," as the author puts it. It's as if—to use a modern analogy—we're all swirling down a great big, cosmic toilet bowl that's hung and automatically keeps on flushing. "Then I considered all that my hands had done and the toil I had spent in doing it, and again, all was vanity and a chasing after wind, and there was nothing to be gained under the sun" (2:1-11).

Pretty depressing, huh? And yet we put the words of Ecclesiastes 3 on invitations to weddings and graduations. Hmm. Nothing especially wrong with using "For everything there is a season . . . a time to mourn, and a time to dance" on those occasions . . ., unless

... there's some more meaningful message God intended for us from these scriptures that we never really get around to because we've cut them out. As we talked about in previous chapters, there's nothing wrong with second and third level conversations with God, unless we never hear what he was saying in the first place or unless the lack of context prompts us to distort something God was trying to say. In other words, unless it causes us to miss God's point.

Without going into a deep analysis of the whole book, it's fairly obvious that the writer was looking for an escape from the unsatisfying experiences of life. Drinking deeply of the most alluring activities, his spirit was crushed nonetheless and his heart emptied by the results. What's more, he learned that there's nothing more, nothing new, and he couldn't find a way to free himself from the crushing effects—a means to make it new, so to speak. He thus concludes that his experiences are all a part of ongoing, unbreakable cycles—the circles of life, for *Lion King* fans—but with an eye on the distressing reality that they all end too soon and in the same place.

These dark sentiments of Ecclesiastes are similar to those of the song "Turning"[4] in the musical adaptation of Victor Hugo's novel *Les Misérables*, where the women of Paris bemoan the endless cycles of poverty, survival, war, and death; rhythmically and repetitiously averring that nothing ever changes. The difference between "Turning" from *Les Mis* and the "churning" of Ecclesiastes is the difference between a filthy rich king's and dirt poor commoners' perceptions of the same thing: the cycles are unbreakable and the end is miserable.

The author of Ecclesiastes longs for escape from bondage to the empty rhythms and routines, with their punctuating physical, psychological, and emotional milestones. Though they appear enticing and important at the onset or from a distance (and thus suggest that if a little is good, a lot must be great), they always disappoint. So Solomon looks for some sort of secret door into something new: something real, better, more-fulfilling; something that can transcend the never-ending, locked and chained cycles of life; something that "I can find if I just look long and hard enough. It must be here. It must be. All I have to do is find it." So he tries everything, as we've seen: money, women, and song, as the old saying goes. After years of trying to escape and discover the secret to a meaningful and fulfilling life, he learns—compounding depression upon depression—that none of those things provides a doorway to something different. God has apparently shut and barricaded the door. All these things exist and disappoint *within* the captive cycle, and, in fact, more wasn't better. "Freedom" and license did not bring meaning and happiness. On the contrary, they brought despair—an utter sense of worthlessness and hopelessness. Same ol' story: like a broken record, the pattern repeats itself—from dust to dust (Ecclesiastes 3:19-20; Genesis 3:19).

Divine Barbed Wire

Scattering throughout the book of Ecclesiastes is the idea that some sort of impenetrable boundary exists between us and God (and apparently between us and some of the things we want). Everywhere Solomon looked he found he could only go so far, as if there were an invisible and impenetrable fence between daily reality and our pursuit of something better, and the results left him unfulfilled. I'm sure you've experienced a similar feeling when something you thought was worth your time and effort turned out to be disappointing in the end. It's like giving everything to climb the corporate ladder of success, as our pastor is fond of saying, only to find when you get to the top that you put the ladder on the wrong building. We all run into brick walls and suffer the reverberating disappointment. Solomon ran into lots of them.

Ecclesiastes says there's a stone wall between us and God, and—here's the challenging part—God is the mason.[5] Apparently, he built the fence and locked the gate. Hmm. In other words, there's a fundamental, radical boundary or difference between us and God (even for a powerful king). Attempts to dissolve or blur that difference are a downhill slope to an unfulfilled life. "Just as you do not know how the breath comes to the bones in the mother's womb, so you do not know the work of God, who makes everything" (11:5). I might want to be like God (compare the temptation of Adam and

Eve); at least I might like to ask him a question or two (like Job) about why some things are the way they are. I might want to know what God is doing and why. I would like to be able to climb up a celestial ladder and stick my head into heaven and look around a bit.[6] But that doesn't change the reality that I can't. Only God is God. "Never be rash with your mouth, nor let your heart be quick to utter a word before God, for God is in heaven, and you upon earth; therefore let your words be few" (5:2). From our passage, "He has made everything suitable for its time . . ., yet they cannot find out what God has done from the beginning to the end" (3:11).

The book of Ecclesiastes thus expresses the human desire to understand and even change basic principles of life on planet earth, for they seem to get in the way of finding fulfillment—at least if you pursue it through experience and accomplishment and pride, as Solomon did. In other words, we put the ladder on the wrong building. Solomon came to recognize and accept this: "In the day of prosperity be joyful, and in the day of adversity consider; God has made the one as well as the other, so that mortals may not find out anything that will come after them" (7:14). After "all this time" (remember the song by Sting?) that the Teacher gave to finding a way out of the broken and terminal cycles of life, he concludes that the wall is too high and there is no key. So perhaps we *are* just dust in the wind.

Well . . . not so fast. Unlike other discussions (songs and literature) of the potential meaningless of life, however—and this is a huge "however"—Solomon does not conclude that finding a key to the barricade between us and God is the only approach. In fact, *that's the main point of Ecclesiastes*—the approach matters. When you read the whole book, a new possibility begins to reveal itself in the language. Real life starts, according to Ecclesiastes, with an all-defining choice, a first and essential step: *humility before God as Creator and Lord*.

The Gift of Joy

There is a time and season for everything under the sun, Solomon says. We are aware of the passing of time. We can't break out of it or go beyond it to find fulfillment: as long as the desire to make ourselves happy through our experiences and accomplishments dictates our path, we will fail. On the other hand, a radically different possibility emerges when we approach the question of meaning and fulfillment in life from the perspective that God is God and we are his creation, his children. God is the one in control, and he wants us to be happy:

> I know that there is nothing better for them than to be happy and enjoy themselves as long as they live; moreover, it is God's gift that all should eat and drink and take pleasure in all their toil. I know that whatever God does endures forever, nothing can be added to it, nor anything taken from it; God has done this, **so that all should stand in awe before him** [my emphasis]. That which is, already has been; that which is to be, already is; and God seeks out what has gone by (3:12-15).

After trying it all, the writer of Ecclesiastes concludes that "everything is futile" and pointless. We're all trapped inside the cycles of brokenness, and the cycles are unbreakable: "For everything there is a season . . ., a time to be born, and a time to die . . ., a time to laugh, a time to mourn, a time to . . ." Wow, that's a different slant than when we hear these verses, isn't it? Solomon uses the list as part of a complex portrait of life as a series of unbreakable, captivating circles, with common experiences ("there's nothing new under the sun") punctuating the passing of time. But then he reaches an extraordinary conclusion—a conclusion that essentially wads up the paper he'd written and throws it into the proverbial trash can. There is only one thing above the cycle and one most important thing within the cycle that actually has the power to transform the stuff "under the sun" into something completely different: instead of seductions to despair, they become divinely blessed occasions for joy.

So now we look at the end of the book (remember, the beginning and the end are usually very helpful for getting the big picture): "The end of the matter, all has been heard. Fear God, and keep his commandments; for that is the whole duty of everyone. For God will bring every deed into judgment, including every secret thing, whether good or evil" (12:13). Whew! Now that says something! And the word "duty" isn't actually in the original Hebrew. It just says, ". . . for that is the all of humans" (literally: "of the man"). Or in other words, *"This is everything."* (Do you see how this connects back to our passage that outlines some of the fundamental times and seasons of human life?)

The book of Ecclesiastes uses the cycles of life as an artistic and graphic reminder that a search to escape or free ourselves from the inevitable decay and brokenness of life is futile. We are earth-bound. Attempts to escape are worse than futile. Attempts to escape (what we really are in the presence of God and one another) are the pathway to despair and worthlessness. They are, in the end, attempts to deny and be God. When one realizes that God is God, however, and gives him the rightful place in life, the picture changes (as if our puzzle box-top is more like a modern digital picture frame than a single snapshot). The events of life, thus freed of their illusory goal of ultimate and independent spiritual freedom and fulfillment become signposts to the only thing that stands above the cycle and can give us life and purpose: to honor God and do what he says. *This transforms every minute and every experience of life.* Check out the author's amplification of our target text:

> I have seen the business that God has given to everyone to be busy with. He has made everything suitable for its time; moreover he has put a sense of past and future into their minds . . . I know that there is nothing better for them than to be happy and enjoy themselves as long as they live; moreover, it is God's gift that all should eat and drink and take pleasure in all their toil (3:11-13).

And here's a verse just before our text:

> There is nothing better for mortals than to eat and drink, and find enjoyment in their toil. This also, I saw, is from the hand

of God; for apart from him who can eat or who can have enjoyment? For to the one who pleases him God gives wisdom and knowledge and joy . . . (2:24-25).

One more:

> This is what I have seen to be good: it is fitting to eat and drink and find enjoyment in all the toil with which one toils under the sun the few days of the life God gives us; for this is our lot. Likewise all to whom God gives wealth and possessions and whom he enables to enjoy them, and to accept their lot and find enjoyment in their toil—this is the gift of God. For they will scarcely brood over the days of their lives, because God keeps them occupied with the joy of their hearts (5:18-20).

How would you like to be occupied always with the joy of your heart? . . . instead of brooding over the days of our lives ("Like sands through the hourglass . . .")? These are the two primary perspectives of Ecclesiastes.

Summit View

The Picture on the Box

When Ecclesiastes 3:1-8 is read in light of the bigger-picture context of the book as a whole, how much more does it speak to the issues and struggles of life, and to our greatest needs (than when we isolate it as an inkblot)? We often excerpt the passage to celebrate the milestones or potentials of life—sometimes to highlight significant moments, sometimes as a good excuse for a party, and sometimes (probably a less legitimate use) to justify certain types of activities. Not necessarily illegitimate uses of the passage, but much less than the point of God's original dialogue. I believe the author intended our text, not as a monument to our moments, but as a reminder—or perhaps better, as a foghorn or fire-alarm—of where those moments get any real meaning. To summarize: Put God first (where he belongs) and enjoy the moments. For it is only by such faith in God that the moments are enjoyable. Otherwise, everything is vanity and a chasing after the wind—weddings and graduations included.

The biggest point of Ecclesiastes is, therefore, not an affirmation of the inherent meaning of life—a credit card to fulfillment, satisfaction guaranteed—but an affirmation of the meaning that *God gives to life*, with a graphic and depressingly poignant picture of where you end up otherwise—irreversibly indebted to time and passion. That may sound like a small difference, but it's really everything. Of course, the primacy of God can be assumed when we use the verses, but *if it's not, every deduction is wrong*. Using Ecclesiastes 3:1-8 without the God-point is like contemplating the seasons of the earth without knowing anything about the sun. It's like looking at a great big horizon moon with no sun. Without the sun, it's just a big, cold rock. *When used as a simple glorification of the stuff of earth, Ecclesiastes falls, ironically, into the very trap that Solomon wanted out of and wrote to keep us from falling into. Without the God-point, Ecclesiastes 3:1-8 is a subtle temptation to repeat Solomon's folly.* Without recognition of and reverence for the sovereignty of God, Ecclesiastes 3:1-8 *is* dust in the wind.

Chapter 6

Does it make sense why the author refers to himself as "The Teacher"? Could there be a more important lesson? It certainly makes the book appropriate for a baccalaureate address or a graduation speech. Perhaps it has something to say to young people at the threshold of adulthood and their pursuit of life (12:1-8: "Remember your creator in the days of your youth . . . ."). "Take it from me," the Teacher says, "someone in a position to guide you . . ." And thus, the book becomes an inspired message to all of us about how to have real life, and about the enslaving addictions and consequences of trying to find it on our own. "It was a colossal mistake, a wasting of precious moments and a deleting of heart-warming memories before they happened. It was a chasing after the wind." Like an ex-con going back to the street to keep what happened to him from happening to some of the young men in his old gang, the Teacher hopes to light the path to a truly meaningful life. If you want to be empty (1:8: ". . . the eye is not satisfied with seeing, or the ear filled with hearing . . ."), then chase the wind. If you want to live and enjoy the best life has to offer, let God be God and receive his gifts with reverence and joy. That's what Ecclesiastes teaches us. Pursuing life outside of God is meaningless—it's like chasing the wind. Living life under God's sovereign and loving care turns each day into an opportunity to savor and celebrate the gifts he gives. Like the smell of cinnamon—or bacon and coffee—on a quiet, sun-lit morning, life simmers with wonder. Moments percolate with joy.

In a nutshell: You cannot find life by chasing it, no matter how far or fast you run. You can only receive it. And you can only receive it when you acknowledge its giver. You don't create it. It is not yours to define or control (we're all tempted to that). All you have to do is receive and celebrate. This is the big-picture—the summit-view—of Ecclesiastes. Viewed this way, graduation from high school is no longer just repetitious "pomp and circumstance," but a reminder and celebration of God's hand in shaping the unfolding life of a beautiful son or daughter, no matter how many times the band has to play through the song for all the graduates to make their way across the stage. *The cycles don't become boring or disapointing if they are received as a gift from the Father.* They are transformed. They are ignited. This is Ecclesiastes.

And now here's the punch line for Ecclesiastes 3:1-8 as an inkblot: without a clear emphasis on the message that our moments only have meaning as a gift from God, Ecclesiastes 3:1-8 loses much of what makes it inspired—much of what gives these verses the ability to create life. May I give you a lame analogy: it's sort of like visiting Lambeau Field in Green Bay, Wisconsin in July. It might be meaningful in its own right, but it's nothing like being there on a crisp, Sunday afternoon in late October. Football exists to be played and watched. The difference between game-day and a July 4th sightseeing tour is hard to quantify. Infinitely more is the difference between using Ecclesiastes 3:1-8 to justify our efforts to find life without reverently and joyfully receiving it as a gift from God. Setting it to music, pasting it on invitations, programs, or memorials is sort of like trying to get into the Super Bowl on your voter registration card. The card has a good purpose, but it won't get you into the game.

The Question

How does Ecclesiastes 3:1-8 fit into the big-, summit-access picture on the (puzzle) box of Ecclesiastes? How does it contribute to the picture and purpose of the book? This is the all-important question that helps us turn a potential inkblot into a message from God. Though of course there are other things and these are oversimplified, we've talked about three major themes in our brief look at the book: (1) life is meaningless, (2) life is a joyful gift, (3) God is the difference between the two. Our text wonderfully interacts with and extends each of these ideas.

Like pouring the foundation of a house, Ecclesiastes 3:1-8 helps to cement the idea that Ecclesiastes is about "the all" of man. It extends the view that there is nothing new "under the sun," that nothing gives life, and that everything is, therefore, pointless. Listing some of the most fundamental "times and seasons" reaches into our world memorably and concretely to help us connect with these ideas

Chapter 6

and thus adds depth and color to the author's picture of the unbreakable cycles of life. Trying to find fulfillment in the events and moments of our lives from an earth-bound perspective makes all such experiences momentary and ultimately pointless. Our passage amplifies this dominant theme by artistically outlining and underscoring some of the most significant times and experiences that constitute what it is to be human ("... a time to be born, and a time to die....").

This is not the only tone of Ecclesiastes, however, nor of these verses. Ecclesiastes 3:1-8 echoes and develops the second most prevalent theme: that God gives the stuff of life as a gift to those who receive it as such. Because "the whole of man" is to honor God and keep his commands (to do what he tells us), it's natural that those who live this way view life from this perspective. This way, every season and all times have the potential to become pitchers of meaning that God pours out on us as divine gifts of his sovereignty and grace. As readers who put God first, we identify with the specific items as recognizable moments that mark both a safe and exciting journey that comes from the God of the universe. Viewed this way, the times and the seasons become monuments to the real meaning God gives to the basic stuff of life.

Our passage thus fits within both perspectives: the contrasting hues of these very different approaches to life boldly color the meaning of the text. Viewing God as the center and rightful source of direction in life is the hinge or passageway between these mindsets. Ecclesiastes 3:1-8 does indeed give us the basis to celebrate the great moments of life—as we often use it—while accepting the inevitable pain as existing under the overall lordship and blessings of God. On the other hand—and this is the point we often lose when we take these verses out of the book—it also highlights the fact that life is a series of unbreakable cycles that can crush us and squeeze out every ounce of meaning and fulfillment. Just as these two perspectives (life sucks; life satisfies) punctuate the book, so Ecclesiastes 3:1-8 functions to affirm the fundamental relevance of these things to us as humans (they are at the core of what we are—"the all of man"). They boldly highlight what's at stake. These are not simple excuses to celebrate the big moments of life, regardless. They fall between the two biggest options presented to us as free creatures: for whom will I live—me or God.

Isn't it interesting that we take the implication of one of the main points—that life is something to celebrate and enjoy—and apply it without the other main point—that only trust in God gives us that ability? How ironic and sad that as an inkblot, Ecclesiastes 3:1-8 sets us up to fall headlong into the life-consuming trap Solomon fell many years ago. Is it any wonder that so many times when the party is over, we wake up hung-over and empty?

Chapter 6

The Zoom-Out Challenge

There are many other classic Bible verses that we could explore, like Philippians 4:8: "I can do all things through Christ who strengthens me," Romans 8:28: ". . . all things work together for good to them that love God," or Psalm 118:24: "This is the day that the Lord has made; let us rejoice and be glad in it." In many cases, these verses have become known to us, not in the context and power of God's first conversations with his people, but as detached statements and therefore aspiring inkblots.

The parables of Jesus are another good example. Because they exist as complete, miniature stories, almost all the parables of Jesus lend themselves to being isolated from their original book-level contexts, which, in some cases, might be perfectly legitimate. On the other hand, they all also have book-level settings that help us to see how Jesus used them and how the writers of the Gospels shape their inspired messages. For example, the story or Parable of the Prodigal Son in Luke 15 is a moving picture of the Father's great love for his children who have wandered—or, in this case, run—off. Jesus tells two other similar parables just prior to this one: the Parables of the Lost Sheep and the Lost Coin, indicating that this theme of God's undying love is more than just a one-story thought. Zooming out will no doubt reveal God-shaped meaning and purposes, if we take the time to read these in the context of Luke's Gospel. Same with the other parables. (We'll look more closely at this potential with the Parable of the Sower in our exploration of Mark's Gospel.)

Actually, every verse from the Bible and all sets of verses can be seen as potential inkblots—they don't have to be "classics"—since they can be read as independent units of thought that evoke ideas, memories, and feelings. The positive side of this scary reality is that this consistent potential suggests a consistent or common way of dealing with and preventing such disintegrated use. (The word "disintegrated" implies the solution, doesn't it?) If all verses can become inkblots by the way we read and use them, then we can envision a common way to solve the problem. In other words, if disintegration causes the problem, integration fixes it. As a conclusion to the first part of our study and transition to the second half where we focus in detail on how to treat the illness of inkblotitis, I'd like to suggest *a simple way to deal with every potential inkblot.* It's what we should do with every verse: *zoom out.*

I call this simple method of dealing with verse-level Bible reading—seeing and understanding verses as disconnected units of thought—"The Zoom-Out Challenge." The Zoom-Out Challenge is the simply-put way to go about answering The (all important) Question (How does this verse or set of verses fit/function in its book-level context?). And it works with every verse in every book of the Bible (though, of course, the results vary dependent on the genre and other factors). The Zoom-Out Challenge means that you need to *zoom out* as many times (levels or "clicks") as it takes to force yourself to deal with the question of how the verse or set of verses contributes to the book as a whole. Sometimes that's one click or level; sometimes it's several.

Matthew 5:5: "Blessed are the meek..."

I suspect you've heard the saying "Blessed are the meek, for they shall inherit the earth," which is actually Matthew 5:5 from the King James Version. We hear this verse thrown around in movies and conversations of various sorts (I'm seeing images of a burnt-out earth after a nuclear holocaust). But what's it mean? Of course, with just these few words, folks conjure up different mental images—which is what inkblots are made for—often with emphasis on what it means to be meek or to inherit the earth.

Suppose I'm extremely interested in eschatology (the end times); does this verse tell me something about what kind of people will be around the longest? (See how a particular interest or mental/emotional state can function as a sort of hyper-drive to launch me into my subject of interest—at light speed, no less? . . . which actually takes me light years from the intended meaning—to overplay the space-travel metaphor?) And what does it really mean? What if as Bible-readers we assume the statement means something good, and

Chapter 6

so we strive to be meek, 'cause we want to be blessed and perhaps "inherit the earth"? What if—to offer a silly illustration of the negative potential of a Bible inkblot—someone puts a lot of value on this particular saying (as an independent teaching) and dedicates his or her life to the pursuit of meekness? Nothing wrong with striving to be meek. That's a good thing, as Jesus said. But is that the message? What if, on the other hand, someone already is meek? Then I suppose he or she is done and can simply await the expected inheritance (whatever that will be).

Without trying at the moment to decipher exactly what this saying means, think with me about what happens when we zoom out. If we zoom out one level/click, we see that the saying is part of a series of "Blessed are . . ." statements, commonly referred to as the "beatitudes"—a group of statements by Jesus about what it means to be blessed in God's kingdom. Immediately, this gives us a wider and more challenging perspective. Now there's not just one thing to value or aspire to (meekness), but a whole group (Matthew 5:1-11) of somewhat related and surprising characteristics ("Blessed are the poor in spirit," ". . . those who mourn," ". . . those who hunger and thirst for righteousness," and so on). Of course, the picture of what it means to be or become blessed in God's kingdom becomes much more complex and much more profound (when we look at the whole group).

Click. Zooming out one more level takes us to the most famous and probably the most difficult-to-live-up-to sermon of all time—the "Sermon on the Mount" (Matthew 5:1-7:29). Reading the sermon as a whole reveals powerful themes about what it means to live in true righteousness before God within the coming kingdom of God (as opposed to what some might think and teach). Coming at the beginning of the sermon, it's not hard to see the importance of the beatitudes as an introduction, and as foundational for the nature of kingdom-life and true righteousness, set forth in the Sermon on the Mount.

If we zoom out one more time, we begin to observe how the book of Matthew as a whole is put together with several major speeches of Jesus, intermixed with narrative and dialogue material (this is where we have to read and explore the book as a whole, which is our focus in the next half of our study). The Sermon on the Mount builds on and fleshes out the concepts of its introduction—the beatitudes—and sets the stage for the unfolding of these ideas in the teachings and ministry of Jesus. It also gives us our first detailed glimpse into the content of Jesus' preaching, which Matthew has only summarized for us to this point (4:17, 23). How captivating is that! Jesus is healing, teaching, and preaching around the countryside of Galilee. The people are amazed and excited. And here Matthew slows down and zooms in on the nature and content of Jesus' message: "Repent for the kingdom of God is near." The beatitudes thus fit into the flow of Jesus' ministry and teaching about the coming of God's kingdom in the Sermon on the Mount. You can see it in the structure (shape) of the passages: "Blessed are the . . ., for theirs is the kingdom of heaven" (5:10). We won't pursue the book-level picture of Matthew's portrait of Jesus as "the Messiah, the son of David, the son of Abraham" (1:1) now. What I want you to see here is that with just a few clicks of our zoom-out button, we've begun to see how "Blessed are the meek, for they will inherit the earth" fits into Matthew's book about Jesus, and we're immediately given more comprehensive and profound ideas and direction. Instead of an isolated and vague prophecy about the end of the earth, Matthew 5:5 fits snuggly and purposefully into the word of God revealed to us in Matthew's book.

Romans 8:28: ". . . all things work together for good"

Let's look at one more example. This one is a common, "classic" inkblot. Romans 8:28 says, "We know that all things work together for good for those who love God, who are called according to his purpose." I've heard this verse quoted, clutched and proclaimed, stumbled over, and "explained" all my life—what it means, what it doesn't mean. And the reason is obvious. Taken as translated and at this zoomed-in, verse level, Romans 8:28 seems to offer an amazing promise to everyone who loves God—that all things work together (or work out) for good. Because it's so reassuring to think that everything that happens (to me/us) is ultimately God's doing and will be for my good (even if it seems bad), we don't have to debate long on whether we'd like to have this as part of our theology. Sold! In fact, it's used so often at this verse-level (and even smaller) focus that I think Romans 8:28 has become a staple or status quo Christian inkblot. It's quoted, shortened (I accidentally read that as "snorted" when proofreading this!), tossed around and held up as an independent piece of scripture, which—as you know—functions for most people as an inkblot.

This is a good example of a Bible inkblot that has a common interpretive theme (as some Rorschach inkblots do) that blurs itself across Christian circles. It appears to be or at least reinforces something we really like about "what the Bible says": "You can feel good about everything that happens because—even though you may not be able to see it—everything that happens to those who love God [but are you sure you *love* God?] is good or at least produces a good result." . . . which tends to become a sort of "God is behind everything that happens" and produces a sadly ironic "It's all good" theology in the face of some of the most horrible manifestations of sin and brokenness our planet has to offer, even labeling them as "God's will." The very fact that Paul has to point out that God will work in all things or situations for good for those who love God suggests the need for the same kind of transforming work that was manifest supremely in the cruel death of his own son (but I'm getting ahead of myself). Though you don't hear it expressed clearly or frequently, most of us struggle at some level with the idea that everything that happens on planet earth is God's doing and is good. But many accept it. It's in the Bible, right?

You see where this is going, don't you? And that's wonderful, because it shows that the ideas of inkblotitis and how to solve it are becoming a part of you. For starters, we don't hear the phrase ". . . called according to his purpose" frequently when this verse is cited. Nor—and this is the key point—do we have much idea what's going on in the immediate context, much less the book of Romans. *Click-Click. Zoom-Zoom.* What does it mean to love God and be called according to his purpose? That's really a huge idea in Paul's thinking. How does this verse relate to what Paul is talking about in the immediate context and to his purposes in the book as a whole? And what does he see as "good" in the context of this letter?

You know what to do. Zoom out. One click/level will provide some enlightening context.

Paul begins chapter 8 with "There is therefore no condemnation for those who are in Christ Jesus . . ." (8:1). "But you are not in the flesh; you are in the Spirit, since the Spirit of God dwells in you. . . ." (8:9). The flesh (life on planet earth) is not our essence or lord and, therefore, we can be victorious ("more than conquerors") over ". . . the sufferings of the present time." Can *anything* separate us from the love of Christ? "Will hardship, or distress, or persecution, or famine, or nakedness or peril, or sword?" (8:35). "For your sake we are being killed all day long; we are accounted as sheep to be slaughtered" (8:36). *It's not all good. In Christ, it's all redeemed and transformed.* Paul's solution is not to minimize the severity of the problem (evil, sin, suffering), but to maximize the superiority of the solution ("the power of God for salvation"): "He who did not withhold his own Son, but gave him up for all of us, will he not with him also give us everything else?" (8:32). The mushy middle gets us nowhere and pollutes our witness. (See what inkblots do to us?)

Zoom out again and we find Paul presenting profound (and controversial) ideas about Jews and Gentiles, about sin and the grace of God, about faith and forgiveness. If you've ever read Romans, you know that the presentation is at times complex and confusing, full of deep theological arguments, while offering some amazingly simple, life-changing conclusions: Paul is teaching us about "the power of God for salvation to everyone who has faith" (1:16). The impact of coming to know and share in the grace and power of God's salvation in Christ as expressed in this book has changed many lives and destinies; nevertheless, reading and understanding the book of Romans can certainly be difficult. I don't want to gloss over that. But did you notice that I went back to chapter 1 for the quotation about the power of God for salvation? What is Romans about? What did I do? I zoomed out again. And this is what we have to do. *You will never*

Chapter 6

know for sure that what you are getting from Romans 8:28 or any other verse in Romans or any other verse in the Bible is what God says until you hear/read the book and see those verses as part of the divine picture of that book of God.

This is the solution to any Bible inkblot: zoom out (pardon the mixed metaphor), and this is the subject of the second half of our study. We want to "rediscover" the books of God together: zooming in and out is a key component of that discovery. For now, let's conclude with The Zoom-Out Challenge.

The Zoom-Out Challenge means that you zoom out—not just once (unless the book is very short, like Philemon or Jude) until you reach the book-level itself. (Zooming out to the Bible-level comes later; more on this below.) Of course, we have to come back to the specific verse we're reading and want to understand. If we don't understand and apply the verses, we'd never get anything or anywhere. But it's the larger perspective that gives us the overall direction, purpose, and control over what we're reading. And I'm not talking about fuzzy, over-generalized concepts; I'm talking about the biggest and most important points. We all want "The Purpose Driven Life," but how do we know what that purpose is unless we see a bigger picture? It's the difference between hammering a nail and looking at or even designing a beautiful house. We still have to hammer the nails, but not just anywhere and everywhere (which is often how we handle the Bible). The Zoom-Out Challenge—the preferred treatment for the serious illness of inkblotitis—challenges us to see/understand each verse of scripture in the light of its own book, which should be the normal and natural (= healthy) way of reading the Bible.

To state it a little more formally: The Zoom-Out Challenge (ZOC) means that you must zoom out from the verse you are reading/using until you get to the point of the primary reason(s) the book was written. How do you understand a verse in context? ZOC it! (Now that doesn't mean you have to stop and start after every verse; it just means you have to get the zoomed-out perspective into your mind/memory.) This is really just another perspective on The Question (How does the verse fit?). The Question implies that a verse or set of verses fits in some way. We have to zoom out (to use our internet/map analogy) to look at the whole picture in order to see *how* it fits. *Answer The Question with The Zoom-Out Challenge.* To know that you understand a verse properly, you must zoom out until you reach the level of the picture and purpose of the book as a whole. This will give you the perspective you need to understand how the verses fit properly (as you zoom back in). How else will we know where the writer zooms in and out, and thereby, how God wants to shape our vision of the revelation of himself? And, of course, the best way to do that is *to read the whole book, preferably several times,* which is Rule #1 of the "Ten Rules for Good Bible Reading" to come.

What about the Bible as a whole? Don't all the books fit and work together? Of course. And at some point, we want to zoom-out to the Bible-library-as-a-whole level, but that comes later, once we have a book-level perspective; otherwise, we fall back into the random access, disintegration-method. In some respects, we want the biggest, most informed perspective we can have. So we could just say, "Zoom out until you can't zoom anymore." Ultimately, that will take us to God, and isn't that where we want to be? God's perspective. Of course, we want to come back to our specific verse or question, but just imagine the change of perspective we'll have after we've been to the summit ("I've been to the mountaintop . . ."). And that is the point of understanding what the Bible is and reading it in line with that reality. When we replace versing (the disintegration of the Bible) with zooming (rediscovering the Bible as the books of God), we'll be on our way to the top and begin to heal from the debilitating effects of inkblotitis.

Chapter 6

Conclusion

In conclusion, almost any Bible verse can become an inkblot—a personal canvas onto which we project our preexisting notions—if we remove it from its book-level focus. Even something as well-known and as basic as John 3:16 ("For God so loved the world . . .") may have yet undiscovered secrets or levels of meaning. Or, to put it more negatively, *could we be missing something important with Christianity's most widely cited verse?* I'll leave you with that question for now, and we'll come back to it at the end of our study. I trust we have seen enough to accept the point that context matters and that the contexts of the books of God matter immensely.

Inkblotitis is the disintegration of the Bible. Reading the books of God—from beginning to end—is the reintegration of the Bible. This is our topic in the second half of our journey, where we move from looking at the illness—how we read the Bible to *miss* God's point—to the treatment: how we read to listen and be changed by the presence of God's Holy Spirit—to *get* God's point. This is where we go now. "See, I am doing a new thing!" (Isaiah 43:19). Just kidding—couldn't resist one last, ridiculous example of a lifted passage (I recently saw this snippet as the title of a newsletter article). But I do believe the Lord can and will do a new thing in each of us who learns to listen carefully and patiently to the books of God. I invite you to continue the journey with me. Treasure stores of God's grace await us in his word.

(In other words, enter God's library and check out his books. Though it's just beginning construction at the time of the publishing of this book, we're hoping to have a website where we can do this together on an ongoing basis in online (virtual) small groups. Check us out at www.LibraryofGod.com.)

Chapter 6: Classic Inkblots

Chapter Resources

Schaeffer, Francis. *True Spirituality*. Wheaton, IL: Tyndale House, 1971.

Notes

1. From the CD *By Your Side*, © 1999 Hillsong Music Australia; "You Said" © 1998 Reuben Morgan. I offer the following citations from the song as part of an academic/critical review of its use of scripture.
2. Compare also, among others, Matthew 18:19; 21:22; John 14:13-14; 15:7, 16; 16:23-24.
3. Here is a good example of where our knowledge of history outside of a particular book can be enlightening. Even though the results of the Teacher's pursuit of meaning in every form of physical and emotional pleasure can be used by the book of Ecclesiastes to instruct us about the real meaning and purposes of life, Solomon's quest can be and is seen from a different perspective in other scriptures. 1 Kings 1:1-13 describes how his ambitions took him far afield of the instructions and heart of God about how to live and rule as king. Having "loved many foreign women"—Solomon had 700 wives and 300 concubines, to be exact—the Bible says that he allowed these women to lead him away from God: "For when Solomon was old, his wives turned away his heart after other gods; and his heart was not true to the Lord his God" (1 Kings 11:4).
4. "Turning" was written by Alain Boublil as part of Claude-Michel Schönberg's musical adaptation of Hugo's novel.
5. Other books of the Bible contain additional teaching about the nature of "the wall" as part of the effects of sin, symbolized somewhat by Adam and Eve's being kicked out of the Garden of Eden. The barrier was not God's intention in the first place.
6. I'm reminded of Francis Schaeffer's observations about the Christian view that we have died to ourselves and been raised with Christ. He speaks of what it would be like if a person could visit heaven, be in the presence of God, and then come back to earth. "Would anything ever have looked the same to him again?" In light of what he had seen in

Chapter 6

God's realm, all earth-stuff, including the sorts of things Solomon (and the rest of us) look to, to find fulfillment would look and be different:

"What would the praise of the world be worth when one had stood in the presence of God? The wealth of the world, what would it look like beside the treasures of heaven? Man longs for power. But what is earthly power after one has seen the reality of heaven and the power of God? All things would look different. Surely . . . this is involved in the statement that we are to live by faith now, as though we had already died, and already been raised from the dead" (*True Spirituality*, 41-43).

Appendix 1

Questions from Genesis

(These are the questions from my young friend who was attempting to read through the Bible for the first time and the responses I gave at the time. I don't pretend that the answers are perfect. I provide them here, with only slight alterations, merely as a first step toward thoughtful consideration in light of the context of Genesis. Thorough answers would require careful consideration of the historical and literary context of Genesis.)

As I told you on the phone . . ., these are all good and difficult questions. Genesis is a very old document—some of its sections may go way back to times before Abraham—from a very different time and culture. The Hebrew is sometimes curt and difficult to translate, but I'll do my best to answer your questions (as much as I know) without going into great depth.

Also, Genesis (the name means "beginning," as you probably know) was never intended to be a "scientific" document according to modern "scientific" perspectives and standards. It is a spiritual/theological and literary history.

1: Genesis 6:4 "In those days, and even afterward, giants lived on the earth, for whenever the sons of God had intercourse with human women, they gave birth to children who became the heroes mentioned in legends of old."

Okay . . . Now this just gets me. Who are the Giants and how come they get to be referred to as the Sons of God? I thought that was reserved for two instances #1—Jesus #2—man as a whole. Who are the heroes? Are they like Hercules? Is this a parallel to other ancient beliefs? Why does this sound like something I would read in the

Appendix 1

legends of Gilgamesh? Goliath was a Giant, right? Was he a "Son of God"?

These are great questions. It is very difficult to say who these "giants" were. They are called the "Nephilim" in 6:4 (Hebrew: "The Nephilim were on the earth in those days . . ."). There are several places in the Bible that suggest the existence of giants ("great big people") in earth's history (Goliath, e.g., also the sons of Anak/the Anakim [cf. Numbers 13:33, Deuteronomy 1:28, 2:10, 9:2, Joshua 14:15; 15:13-14; Judges 1:20]).

You are astute to draw potential comparisons with Gilgamesh and/or other ancient documents. As I was telling you on the phone, the authors of the Bible sometimes used sources, and they were not afraid to take the contemporary writings/stories and relate the content to a different picture of God and morality. I suspect much of the first few chapters of Genesis relate to these kinds of "stories"—some would call them "myths"—of the day. The important point is what the author of Genesis is trying to say with the story to communicate to people who might know the story (like an allusion to a known movie or play) or in interaction/relation to it.

I doubt anyone really knows who is being called "the sons of God" vs. "the daughters of men" ("daughters of Adam") here. There are several views (which I'll list if you want them). It is interesting to me that Adam is called a "son of God" in Luke 3:37. Since Adam was made first, directly by God, and Eve came from Adam—in a sense—the meaning may simply be "guys and dolls." But here's what I think is most important: the context clearly indicates that something bad/evil is happening—this is part of the literary description of the populating and spiraling down the spiritual toilet bowl of earth (Adam/Eve . . . Cain . . . the sons of God . . . everyone/the flood, tower of Babel [from Genesis 3 – 11]). The sons of God (let's take it to mean ancient, strong men of God) looked at/saw the daughters of Adam (let's take it to mean "hot babes who didn't give a flip about God") and they "married [= took sexually] any of them they chose." That's the important point. A pattern has been established in the text at this point between being "from" or "of God" vs. "of Adam/

men"). The point is that earth's biggest/finest followed in the footsteps of Adam and Eve and pursued "whatever they wanted" instead of how God would direct their lives. The result was the filling of the earth with violence and complete corruption to the point that it made God sad that he had made us.

2: Genesis 19:30-36 "Afterward Lot left Zoar because he was afraid of the people there, and he went to live in a cave in the mountains with his two daughters. One day the older daughter said to her sister, 'There isn't a man anywhere in this entire area for us to marry, and our father will soon be too old to have children. Come, let's get him drunk with wine, and then we will sleep with him. That way we will preserve our family line through our father.' So that night they got him drunk, and the older daughter went in and slept with her father. He was unaware of her lying down or getting up again. The next morning the older daughter said, 'I slept with our father last night. Let's get him drunk again, and you go sleep with him. That way our family line will be preserved.' So that night they got him drunk again, and the younger daughter went in and slept with him. As before, he was unaware of her lying down or getting up. So both of Lot's daughters became pregnant by their father."

Why were Lots Daughters not punished for getting him drunk and raping him?

Does every bad thing anyone does have immediately observable consequences? Perhaps a better answer . . .
Remember, this is not only God's story, but it's Israel's story. It's written with wonderful techniques of ancient Hebrew narrative, some of which we still use today in modern literature and arts. The last lines of the episode (19:36-38) give the punch line, with powerful artistry: the sons that were born (Moab and Ben-Ammi) were the fathers of other nations who created tremendous problems for the children of Israel (Abraham and Jacob's descendants—Jacob's name was changed to "Israel"): the Moabites and the Ammonites. (Perhaps you remember the issue about Moab from *Sweet Dreams* [a musical I

Appendix 1

wrote] and the book of Ruth.) These were peoples who pursued polytheism—other gods and practices that went against the teachings of the Bible (like child-sacrifice, for example). The consequences of the sins of the daughters of Lot haunted God's people for years to come. There is much more of a community understanding of people and life than we have today. Instead of saying, here's the consequence/punishment for their sin, the author uses the understanding of the audience to say in implicit but powerful fashion: "sin messes things up more than just for those involved."

3: What happened to all the fish during the flood of Noah's Ark? They are never mentioned. But it does say that EVERY living thing that was not on the boat was destroyed.

"Every living thing" may simply be too specific a translation. Look at 6:20, 7:21-23. Seems to me to just assume that the fish weren't included: "Every living thing that moved on the earth perished—birds, livestock, wild animals, all the creatures that swarm over the earth, and all mankind. Everything on dry land that had the breath of life in its nostrils died. Every living thing on the face of the earth was wiped out . . . ." (Contrast the mention of "the fish of the sea" in 9:2.) The word "earth" often just means "land," as they didn't have quite the same concept of earth as a planet in the universe as we do today. I certainly don't know for sure, but it seems to me to assume the fish weren't included.

I think it's interesting that many cultures across the earth have some sort of ancient story of a flood that killed off all humanity—not just the Bible.

4: Genesis 9:8-16 - I am not going to type this one out but basically God is admitting that he made a mistake. He is saying that he will never send a flood to destroy all living things again and gave them rainbow and all that . . . God made a mistake?

Why is it a mistake for God to give humans—who will in the future, just like in the past, not deserve it—a promise that he won't destroy the world with a flood like that again? The rainbow becomes a beautiful promise of grace rather than justice (an archer's bow of destruction). How is a promise of grace rather than judgment a mistake? I don't see the idea of "mistake" here, only that God is a living personality who interacts with people in a dynamic, creative, unfolding existence.

5: Genesis 9:5-6 "And murder is forbidden. Animals that kill people must die, and any person who murders must be killed. Yes, you must execute anyone who murders another person, for to kill a person is to kill a living being made in God's image."

Okay . . . But look at this . . .
Genesis 4:15 (after God finds out that Cain killed his brother, Abel, and Cain is scared that he will be killed by anyone who finds out that he is a murderer) "The Lord replied, 'They will not kill you for I will give seven times your punishment to anyone who does.'"

It also says later about someone who would have 7 times 77 the punishment of the one they murder [I'd have to look at the specific verse here]. Can God please make up his mind?

Interesting observation. The principle is that people are so valuable because they are made in God's image that anyone who violates that by taking a life should sacrifice his own. Cain's reaction shows that the principle had been disseminated to some extent. I think the point is made to help humans continue to understand the value of life. The fact that "exceptions" are made in the case of Cain (which technically happened before Gen. 9) and others is another example of grace over justice. Though admittedly "contradictory," I believe both are a necessary part of reality. In fact, they are in some cases flip sides of the same coin. God is always portrayed throughout the Bible as a living, dynamic personality—not a contradictory, capricious one, but a being that lives and engages with us. On the other hand, it might be instructive to ask the question—sort of as you have done—why was Cain spared at this point in history and in the

Appendix 1

context of Genesis (remember we're seeing the initial downfall of humanity and the spreading of evil/sin).

6: Okay, I was trying to ignore that EVERYONE in the book of Genesis lives to be about 900 years old . . . but this REALLY bothered me.

Genesis: 6:3 "Then the Lord said, 'My spirit will put up with humans for such a long time, for they are only moral flesh. In the future they will live no more than 120 years.'"

Then AFTER that Noah lives to be 950—Shem died at age 600—Arphaxad lived 438 years—Shelah lived 433 years—Eber lived 464 years . . . and so on and so on down Noah's family tree for as far as I read.

    This is an admittedly difficult verse. Some people think that it's not intended to refer to the length of humans' lives, but to a period of time that God would wait/be patient with humans before the flood, implying that Noah may have been around 480 when he was called on to build the ark and 600 (Genesis 7:11) when the flood came. Compare 1 Peter 3:20-21: ". . . when God waited patiently in the days of Noah while the ark was being built. In it only a few people, eight in all, were saved through water, and this symbolizes baptism that now saves you . . ." So some believe the verse is saying that God would wait for 120 years before the flood.
    If it is referring to the length of life, then it's intended—as many things are in scripture—as a general spiritual principle/truth, not an absolute or immediate dictum (compare the statement that Adam and Eve would surely die if they ate the forbidden fruit. They may have "died" in a spiritual sense immediately, but their physical death came years later). From that angle, it would seem to me to be noticeable more for its general accuracy than inaccuracy. Notice how after the flood (chapter 11), the life spans decrease so that by the end of the book of Genesis, Joseph lives to be 110.

As I mentioned on the phone, there are some non-biblical ancient documents with lists of the "ancient kings" with very long lifespans like those here. Though the Bible doesn't comment on it, Noah's flood may have been a part of radical changes in the nature/history of earth, such that all life changed drastically (perhaps contributing to the extinction of the dinosaurs). Just conjecture, though.

Extra Stuff

I really hope you guys will keep reading. If you want to go from the beginning, I would recommend that you read all of Genesis, then the first 20 chapters of Exodus ("exodus" being about how Israel got out of Egypt). Then just skim through the rest of Exodus, Leviticus, and Numbers (these are how-to-do-Jewish-sacrificial-religion books [kind of like a "How to be a good Catholic" guide might be today for a non-Catholic, but obviously more ritualistic]). Then read Deuteronomy 1 and 30-34. Deuteronomy means "2nd law," and in a sense is a retelling of the first 4 books in condensed and summary fashion. The end of Deuteronomy tells of the death of Moses.

These first 5 books are called the "Pentateuch" (which means 5 books) and is the "Law of Moses." The Bible then continues with the history of Israel in its relationship to God. Here's an outline of the meaning/purpose of the Old Testament books:

Law (Genesis – Deuteronomy)
History (Joshua – Esther)
Poetic Literature (Job – Song of Solomon)
Prophetic Literature (Isaiah – end of Old Testament)

The New Testament has this general outline:

Gospels (the life of Jesus: Matthew, Mark, Luke, John)
History (of the early church: Acts)
Letters (to the first churches)
Revelation (book of Revelation)

Appendix 1

If I were you guys, I think I might skip over to the New Testament Gospels next (maybe starting with John) and then read the other parts. I hope you will continue to ask questions, and I'll try to keep my answers relatively brief and to the point.